TROJANS ESSENTIAL

Everything You Need to Know to Be a Real Fan!

Steven Travers

TRIUMPH
BOOKS

Library of Congress Cataloging-in-Publication Data
Travers, Steven.
  Trojans essential : everything you need to know to be a real fan! / by Steven Travers ; foreword by Terry Marks.
    p. cm.
  ISBN-13: 978-1-57243-925-2
  1. Southern California Trojans (Football team)—History. 2. University of Southern California—Football. 3. Football players—California, Southern. I. Title.
  GV958.U5857T728 2008
  796.332'630979494—dc22   2008005824

This book is available in quantity at special discounts for your group or organization. For further information, contact:

Triumph Books
542 South Dearborn Street
Suite 750
Chicago, Illinois 60605
(312) 939-3330   Fax (312) 663-3557

Printed in U.S.A.
ISBN: 978-1-57243-925-2
Design by Patricia Frey
Editorial production by Prologue Publishing Services, LLC
All photos courtesy of AP/Wide World Photos except where otherwise indicated.

To my sweet daughter, Elizabeth Travers
To my parents, Don and Inge Travers
And to my Lord Jesus Christ
Thank you.

"There are two kinds of people: Those who are Trojans and those who wish they were!"

Contents

Foreword vii

Acknowledgments xi

Introduction: "You're a Bruin for
   Four Years, but a Trojan for Life!" xiii

USC Replaces Notre Dame as the
   Greatest Football Tradition in History 1

Trojan Excellence in Broadcasting,
   the Law, at War, in Outer Space,
   Social Justice, Academics, and Hollywood 7

How Good has USC Gotten under Pete Carroll? 12

USC in the Pros 20

USC's Numbers Don't Lie 24

The Tradition of Troy 30

USC and the All-Time Best Teams 37

A Football Coach Named "Gloomy Gus" 45

The Head Man 48

Gwynn Wilson and the Notre Dame Rivalry 52

The Duke 57

Johnny Baker and the Comeback at South Bend 62

The Thundering Herd 67

Nave-to-Krueger 72

1939: Jones's Last National Champions 77

The Giffer: Everybody's All-American 82

Mr. Trojan 87

The "Little White-Haired Man" 92

Fertig-to-Sherman 97

Mike Garrett: USC's First Heisman Winner 100

Juice 105

The City Game: "It's Not a Matter of
    Life or Death. It's More Important than That" 109

Woody vs. McKay 114

Turning the Crimson Tide 119

The Greatest College Football Team Ever Assembled 124

It Wasn't a Football Game. It Was a Sighting! 130

Alabama Redux 134

Anthony Munoz Goes Hollywood 138

"Young Juice" 141

All Right Now 144

The Promised Land 147

Re-Pete 151

Three-Pete 156

The Four Horsemen of Southern California 162

2005: Quest for History 167

The Ring of Fire and Those Most
    Worthy of All Foes, the Texas Longhorns 175

Carroll, USC, and the Future 180

All-Time USC Football Team 185

Answers to Trivia Questions 187

Bibliography 192

Appendix: University of Southern California
    Football Letterwinners 198

Foreword

I was born and raised in Rochester, New York, and I love the University of Southern California.

I didn't always love USC. At various times in my life, I have hated it, resented it, envied it, and, on rare occasions, admitted to admiring it. More often than not, I think I experienced these feelings concurrently. But love it? Never! You see, not only did I spend the first 19 years of my life 3,000 miles east of University Park, I did so as a rabid fan of Notre Dame football. This was pretty typical of people of my ilk at the time. As the youngest of five in a distinctly Irish Catholic family, I spent the first 12 years of my academic life "studying" in Catholic schools. I must say, Catholic education was a bit different in the '70s than it is today. One of the great rites of passage in my all-male high school was an annual football game that pitted the Italian seniors against the Irish seniors in a no-pads, full-contact, tackle-football game with the resident priests serving as officials. Somehow, I don't think my son, who is now a 9th grader in Catholic school, will ever be afforded the opportunity to participate in a similar faculty-sanctioned event.

But I digress. Like most Catholic families at that time, we had our rituals. Long car rides were great opportunities to squeeze in a decade or two of the rosary. Fridays meant fish fries at the Fireman's Exempt, and of course Sunday mornings meant...the sweet strains of Lindsey Nelson bringing Notre Dame football highlights from Saturday's game into our home (Mass would be fit in around the ND highlights). Remember, this was back in the day of three local network affiliates and one PBS channel. We were lucky to see a live ND football broadcast three times in an entire year. I watched those highlights almost every Sunday morning—almost—but I'd hardly ever watch the day after the USC game. USC beat Notre Dame eight times in the 1970s. I just couldn't bear to watch the ND defense, which stopped everybody else, be completely run over by seven behemoths blocking for the latest thoroughbred tailback, over and over and over again.

Of course, it wasn't just Notre Dame that experienced this fate. Seemingly every New Year's Day some poor collection of hearty souls from the heartland of America would head west and witness the complete demolition of their beloved state university football team at the hands of these same Trojans. After the event, the 'SC faithful headed home for a celebratory backyard barbecue, while their guests from the Big Ten went home to confront Minsk-like climatological conditions for the ensuing three months.

Inevitably it would be early evening on most New Year's Days when hatred and resentment gave way to envy and, ultimately, admiration. USC always seemed to win, especially when it mattered most. I'm sure it wasn't the case, but it almost seemed like they didn't even have to try as hard. They had better players, more striking uniforms, prettier cheerleaders, and the coolest mascot in all of sport—every honest ND fan will admit to mascot-envy of 'SC. Most of all, they had...Southern California.

We've all heard about the city of Pasadena's uncanny knack for ordering up chamber of commerce weather every January 1. To a teenager watching on TV from Rochester, the idea that snow was something to be admired from a distance while sitting on a beach eventually became too much to take. But that wasn't all.

I was a member of Red Sox Nation before there was a Red Sox Nation, and I recall the impact of learning that the great Fred Lynn, 1975 AL Rookie of the Year and MVP, was a Trojan. The Red Sox also had a free-spirited, left-handed pitcher at the time named Bill Lee, who was also one of Rod Dedeaux's protégés. Lee wasn't just entertaining, he was one of the top left-handers in the American League, at one point winning 17 games in three consecutive years. It was around this time that the USC baseball machine began minting one major league all-star after another. Steve Kemp, Rich Daur, Steve Busby, Roy Smalley, on and on it went. At first it didn't seem possible, but eventually it became clear that USC's baseball team was actually more successful than its football team!

That was all it took to hook me. I had become a convert! (How to tell my father?!) Around the age of 18 I determined that my goal in life would be to play baseball at the University of Southern California.

After one year at a junior college, I finally made my way west to USC. I had never set foot on the campus until the day I arrived to enroll and move into my university-owned apartment. The area did not look as I imagined it would. On my second night in L.A., I became lost while walking near campus at nightfall. A friend later suggested to me that I should endeavor to avoid this.

I could not see the beach, nor could I see any mountains. (Though I recall the pleasant surprise one mid-October afternoon when the winds lifted the smog from the basin to reveal that in fact there were mountains very nearby.)

But none of it mattered. I was in L.A. and I was a Trojan. I remember putting on my baseball uniform for the first time and staring into the mirror in the old clubhouse at Dedeaux Field. It was surreal. This was the same uniform worn by Fred Lynn, Tom Seaver, Bill Lee, etc. No matter that on their worst days they each did more to bring glory to that uniform than I did on my best, I was now forever connected in a small way to the greatest baseball tradition in college history. It almost seemed impossible.

But to me, that's what makes USC so incredibly special. Anything is possible. Yes, part of it is the psyche of California in general and L.A. in particular. But if California is the land of opportunity within the land of opportunity, USC is its epicenter. Unfortunately there are too many regions of our country that seem to be hostage to the past. Places where dreaming really big dreams is seen as squandering time. When I arrived at 'SC, I was struck by the sheer optimism of the place. People didn't dream, they made plans! A sense of the ability to achieve anything abounded. There was no looking back among the students I interacted with. 'SC was the place where the optimism of youth met the sense of boundless opportunity that was so endemic to the geography. The combination made it the most exhilarating place I had ever experienced.

It is no exaggeration to say that I discovered a sense of self-confidence while at USC that has served me my entire life. Perhaps it was just the natural process of maturation. Maybe I would have grown as much elsewhere...but I doubt it.

I met the love of my life while we were both undergrads at 'SC. We have been married for 24 years and have three beautiful children who bring us joy every day. I met my best friends while at USC, including this book's author. What more could one ask from a college experience? Now, I spend hours on end following 'SC's athletic successes with my son, feeling pride but, more important, still feeling connected in some small way.

So now you know why I love USC. I think my son does, too. If perfect weather combined with success in baseball and football are as influential to him as they were to me some 30 years ago, I don't like the odds of another conversion in our family.

— Terry Marks, Coca-Cola/North American President

Acknowledgments

Thanks to Tom Bast, Jess Paumier, Amy Reagan, Kelley White, Linc Wonham, Jennifer Barrell, Adam Motin, Laine Morreau, Morgan Hrejsa, Mitch Rogatz, Scott Rowan, Don Gulbrandsen, and all the great folks at Triumph Books and Random House Publishing for having faith in me. Thanks also to Craig Wiley and my agent, Peter Miller of PMA Literary and Film Agency in New York City. I want to thank Pete Carroll, Tim Tessalone, the USC bookstore, USC Collections in Orange County, Professor Dan Durbin, and the USC Annenberg School of Communications. Thank you to Lloyd Robinson of Suite A Management in Beverly Hills, California; to Jim Starr and Trojan great Anthony Davis. Thank you to John Robinson. Thanks to Charles "Tree" Young, Manfred Moore, Sam "Bam" Cunningham, John Papadakis, Dave Brown, Rod McNeill, Willie Brown, Craig Fertig, Dennis Slutak, and Terry Marks. Thanks also to the Amateur Athletic Foundation of Los Angeles.

Thank you: Mrs. Patricia Goux, Tom Kelly, the USC Alumni Association, the NorCal Trojan Club, Bruce Seltzer, Jim Perry, and Red Smith.

Of course, my thanks as always go out to my daughter, Elizabeth Travers; my parents, Don and Inge Travers; and to my Lord and savior, Jesus Christ, who has shed his grace on thee, and to whom all glory is due!

Introduction: "You're a Bruin for Four Years, but a Trojan for Life!"

Ken Norton, an All-American linebacker at UCLA and an All-Pro with the Dallas Cowboys and San Francisco 49ers, decided after a few years of retirement that he wanted to enter the coaching profession. He approached then Bruins coach Karl Dorrell about working on his staff. Dorrell told him, "No!"

Just to prove he was serious, Norton volunteered for one season at Hamilton High School in Los Angeles before approaching Dorrell a second time. Again, Dorrell showed no love to the Bruins legend, possibly because he did not want a charismatic black assistant coach stealing his thunder. Who knows? What we do know is that when USC coach Pete Carroll (who was the defensive coordinator of the 49ers when Norton played for them) heard about Norton's availability, he hired him immediately. As Norton said:

"It's true what they say. You're a Bruin for four years, but a Trojan for life!"

The day Norton's quote appeared in the *Los Angeles Times*, I visited my friend Jim Saia at Heritage Hall. Saia had been an assistant basketball coach under Steve Lavin at UCLA. Now he was at USC, where he was the interim head coach in the 2004–2005 season.

"You know something?" said Saia, who also experienced life at both of Los Angeles's major colleges. "Norton's right."

There is something very special about being a Trojan. It is not just the fact that the University of Southern California has the greatest football, baseball, track, swimming, Olympic, and overall athletic tradition in all of collegiate sports. It is not just that it is "Hollywood's school," or that Trojans have for well over 100 years shaped the course of Los Angeles, the state of California, America, indeed, the world, and—when one considers that USC graduate Neil Armstrong was the first man to set foot on the moon—the universe. It's more than that.

So, yes, we love our football at Southern California, but take it from a Trojan who knows how lucky he is to be a Trojan: there is much more to USC than national championships and Heisman Trophies, because you, indeed, are "a Trojan for life!" Delores Homisak, the counselor who gave me the opportunity to enter USC, believed I had what it takes. This book is my way of saying, "Thank you, I hope I made you proud."

USC Replaces Notre Dame as the Greatest Football Tradition in History

Notre Dame started the 1990s riding high, but it fell off somewhat, its reputation shaken by revelations in Don Yaeger's book, Under the Tarnished Dome. Other traditional powers that had fallen were on the rise: Texas, Michigan, Ohio State, and Oklahoma, among others. USC just observed it all in spectator mode.

By 2000, Notre Dame was still the "College Football Program of the 20th Century." USC may only have hoped they were still third. By season's end, after Oklahoma completed its return to prominence with an unbeaten national championship season, the Sooners could lay claim to USC's old poll position. Troy was lucky to still be in the top five, derided as "Yesterday U.," its glory days relegated to old clippings and grainy pre-video footage. They were like aging rock stars who were unknown by the young girls who preferred Korn and Eminem.

Pete Carroll's University of Southern California Trojans returned to dominance behind Heisman Trophy–winning quarterback Carson Palmer in 2002, won the national championship in 2003, completed the most perfect season in collegiate football history in 2004, and followed that up with an almost more perfect one in 2005. They took a shot at four "titles": 1) greatest college football dynasty of all time (2002–2006); 2) greatest historical college football tradition of all time; 3) greatest college football player ever (Matt Leinart); and 4) greatest collegiate athletic department of all time. Lofty titles, to be sure. Controversial and worthy of argument? You bet. Justifiable hype? You got that right, too.

Certainly the 1993–1997 Nebraska Cornhuskers, the Notre Dame Fighting Irish of the late 1940s, and Bud Wilkinson's Oklahoma Sooners

In the 2000s, Reggie Bush and his Trojan teammates just may have soared past Notre Dame to become the greatest program in college football history.

of the mid-1950s could make a claim for the best short-term dynasty. Leinart's position as the preeminent collegiate player ever may have been upended by the deeds of his own teammate, Reggie Bush.

But USC seemed at the very least to have "tied" Notre Dame as the greatest all-time tradition, and the record of their overall athletic department had long before established itself as the preeminent one in the land. Only cross-town rival UCLA is really close.

Had USC beaten Texas in the 2006 Rose Bowl, they would have entered the '06 season one 12-game regular season away from Oklahoma's all-time modern record of 47 straight wins, set in the 1950s. They were ranked number one a record 33 straight weeks in the Associated Press poll from 2003 to 2006, with a chance to extend that the next season.

There have been many "perfect" teams; that is, teams that went undefeated and untied en route to a consensus national championship. USC itself has enjoyed their fair share of these kinds of wire-to-wire perfect seasons. But the stars were never aligned for any team quite like the 2004 and 2005 Trojans. First of all, they were the sixth and (nearly) seventh teams to be ranked number one in the nation from the preseason polls through the bowl games. The 1972 Trojans, considered by many to be the greatest team of all time, accomplished the feat as well.

The 2004–2005 Trojans boasted the '04 Heisman Trophy winner and '05 finalist, three-time All-American senior quarterback Leinart. Leinart returned for his senior year, amid the talk that he was the greatest college football player in history. While that lofty moniker can be debated, nobody could deny he was the most hyped Big Man on Campus, whoever came across the pike.

His teammate, two-time All-American running back Bush, was a New York finalist for the award in 2004 and won in 2005. Had running back LenDale White returned for *his* senior year, he would have been favored in 2006. USC came within 19 seconds and nine yards of becoming the first team in history to win three consecutive national championships. They reached a national-longest 34-game winning streak, tied for second among modern major college teams. They annihilated Oklahoma 55–19 in the 2005 BCS Orange Bowl, a game that was previewed as the greatest game in college football history. No less an expert than Lee Corso said the Trojans' performance against the Sooners was the best he has ever seen. Period.

Possibly, Nebraska's thrashing of Florida in the national championship game of January 1996 was as impressive. Possibly. The 1944–1945 Army Cadets featured a similar winning streak and two Heisman winners, Doc Blanchard and Glenn Davis. There are other teams that compare, but nobody has done it quite the way Carroll's team has done it. A few came close. The 1983 Nebraska Cornhuskers featured an undefeated regular season that included winners of the Heisman and Outland Trophies. They lost to Miami in the Orange Bowl. The 2003 Oklahoma Sooners looked to be on a

TRIVIA

Why are other schools' claims to national championships not as strong as USC's?

Answers to the trivia questions are on pages 187–191.

similar path, but their Heisman winner, Jason White, faltered in the Big 12 championship game as well as the Orange Bowl.

In light of USC's recent dominance, it is worth considering their place in history. Not just the current Trojans, but USC's football program going back to the beginning of the 20th century. It is time to take the mantel of "greatest program in the history of college football" away from the Notre Dame Fighting Irish and either lay it squarely with the deserving new champions from USC or, at the very least, consider that the landscape of the collegiate game has changed to the point where each succeeding season, every USC–Notre Dame game at the Coliseum or South Bend has the potential of determining not just that season's national champion, but sways the pendulum of all-time supremacy from year-to-year.

The Trojans of the 2000s bid to be the greatest dynasty ever assembled. Leinart returned for his senior year, having turned down a for-sure number-one draft selection in 2005. The team may or may not have been "better" than they were in 2004, or even when they won the first of Carroll's national championships in 2003. Other

TOP 25

All-Time College Football Traditions

1. USC Trojans
2. Notre Dame Fighting Irish
3. Alabama Crimson Tide
4. Oklahoma Sooners
5. Ohio State Buckeyes
6. Miami Hurricanes
7. Penn State Nittany Lions
8. Nebraska Cornhuskers
9. Texas Longhorns
10. Michigan Wolverines
11. Florida State Seminoles
12. Tennessee Volunteers
13. Louisiana State Tigers
14. Auburn Tigers
15. Florida Gators
16. Michigan State Spartans
17. Georgia Bulldogs
18. UCLA Bruins
19. Arkansas Razorbacks
20. Washington Huskies
21. California Golden Bears
22. Pittsburgh Panthers
23. Minnesota Golden Gophers
24. Stanford Indians/ Cardinal
25. Brigham Young Cougars

TOP 30

Greatest Singe-Season College Football Teams

1. 1972 Southern California Trojans
2. 1995 Nebraska Cornhuskers
3. 2004 Southern California Trojans
4. 2005 Texas Longhorns
5. 1947 Notre Dame Fighting Irish
6. 1971 Nebraska Cornhuskers
7. 2001 Miami Hurricanes
8. 1945 Army Cadets
9. 1979 Alabama Crimson Tide
10. 1956 Oklahoma Sooners
11. 1999 Florida State Seminoles
12. 1989 Miami Hurricanes
13. 1986 Penn State Nittany Lions
14. 1968 Ohio State Buckeyes
15. 1969 Texas Longhorns
16. 1988 Notre Dame Fighting Irish
17. 1932 Southern California Trojans
18. 1975 Oklahoma Sooners
19. 1921 California Golden Bears
20. 1973 Notre Dame Fighting Irish
21. 1948 Michigan Wolverines
22. 1928 Southern California Trojans
23. 1991 Washington Huskies
24. 1985 Oklahoma Sooners
25. 1976 Pittsburgh Panthers
26. 1962 Southern California Trojans
27. 1987 Miami Hurricanes
28. 1966 Notre Dame Fighting Irish
29. 1992 Alabama Crimson Tide
30. 1924 Notre Dame Fighting Irish

teams have had more dominating defenses, run the table by wider margins of victory, and had fewer close calls (the Trojans had their share). But considering their offensive prowess, their winning streak, the pressure of going for history, the accumulation of their awards, records, and honors, and finally the sheer hype attached to them in Hollywood fashion—all of it totally lived up to—no team from Nebraska, Notre Dame, Oklahoma, Alabama, Miami, or even from

USC's storied past could legitimately have called themselves better than the 2005 Trojans...with the exception of the 2005 Texas Longhorns.

Leinart walked away from his career with more honors than any player ever: two national championships, the Heisman, the Johnny Unitas Award, the Walter Camp Award, the *Sporting News* Sportsman of the Year, and the Davey O'Brien Award.

Bush and Leinart were both drafted among the top 10 picks of the 2006 NFL Draft. Eleven USC players were selected overall, although USC did not match the college records for most players drafted (USC, 15 in 1953) or most players drafted in the first round (originally set by USC with five in 1968).

How great has USC been under Carroll? Great enough to have back-to-back 11–2 seasons and enormous victories in the Rose Bowl (including victory over one-loss Michigan on January 1, 2007); two top five finishes and in 2007 the *USA Today* number-two ranking; the 2007 Heisman preseason frontrunner (quarterback John David Booty), All-Americans, and first-round draft picks (Dwayne Jarrett, Lawrence Jackson, and Cedrick Ellis); the moniker "potentially the greatest college football team of all time" (2007); and the first-ever team to win 11 games six years in a row (2002 through 2007); great enough to say that, despite doing all that, they were *disappointing* in 2007! Great enough to say that the 2007 Trojans, at 11–2 the winners of their sixth straight, were the winners of their sixth straight Pacific-10 title and fifth BCS bowl win in six tries, generally considered to be the best team in the nation, despite being omitted by the computers' strength of schedule component from the BCS title game, was *the worst USC team Pete Carroll coached* since his first season!

Trojan Excellence in Broadcasting, the Law, at War, in Outer Space, Social Justice, Academics, and Hollywood

The University of Southern California has long been used for many scenes of campus life. The 1967 classic *The Graduate* was supposed to feature Dustin Hoffman pursuing Katharine Ross up at Cal-Berkeley. In truth, it was shot at USC. Ironically, *The Hunchback of Notre Dame* was filmed not at Notre Dame (either the Paris or South Bend version), but at USC. The Academy Awards have been held at various locations throughout Los Angeles, often at the Shrine Auditorium, located across the street from USC. On a clear day, the Hollywood sign can be seen from the 'SC campus.

Famous showbiz Trojans include ex-Trojan football player John "Duke" Wayne; *Star Wars* director George Lucas; actor-director Ron Howard; former *Three's Company* star John Ritter; *The Breakfast Club* co-star Ally Sheedy; *Boyz n the Hood* director John Singleton; former All-American Aaron Rosenberg, producer of countless 1960s and '70s television shows; ex-*Magnum P.I.* star Tom Selleck, who played baseball, basketball, and volleyball at 'SC; *That Girl!* star Marlo Thomas; producer David L. Wolper; *Forrest Gump* director Robert Zemeckis; *Dirty Harry* and *Magnum Force* screenwriter John Milius; musicians Herb Alpert and Lionel Hampton; and opera star Marilyn Horne.

The USC connection is a golden one. My previous book, *One Night, Two Teams: Alabama vs. USC and the Game that Changed a Nation*, is being made into a major motion picture by virtue of this connection. Trojan legend Anthony Davis told his friend, Jim Starr (USC '79) that he wanted to produce it. Starr then told his agent, Lloyd Robinson (USC '64) of Suite A Management in Beverly Hills to make it happen. Lloyd happened to be *my* agent, too. Lloyd then honchoed a deal with top producer Kerry McCluggage (USC '74). At one point we took a meeting at the William Morris Agency in Beverly Hills with Lon Rosen, Magic Johnson's agent. There were eight people in the room. Every one of them was a Trojan!

TRIVIA

What USC professor has earned the Nobel Prize?

Answers to the trivia questions are on pages 187–191.

Many Trojan sports heroes have made their mark in broadcasting. They include Hall of Fame pitcher Tom Seaver, a former *Baseball Game of the Week* partner of Vin Scully as well as the voice of the Yankees and Mets; Hall of Fame running back Frank Gifford of *Monday Night Football* fame; Trojans and Rams quarterback, Rhodes Scholar, attorney, and national college football announcer Pat Haden; Hall-of-Famer-turned-sideline-analyst (and 2006 Pennsylvania Republican gubernatorial candidate) Lynn Swann; Olympic gold medallist John Naber, a national swimming broadcaster; ex–big leaguer Ron Fairly, who became an Angels and Giants broadcaster; quarterback and Fox Sports football analyst Craig Fertig.

Legendary sportswriters from USC include Mal Florence of the *Los Angeles Times*. USC national media figures include Kathleen Sullivan and Sam Donaldson of ABC News. Leading politicians, jurists, and statesmen are former Secretary of State Warren Christopher; ex-Congressman and current Chairman of the Securities and Exchange Commission Christopher Cox; former California Assembly Speaker Jesse "Big Daddy" Unruh, whose name graces USC's political science school; Congressman and former California Attorney General Dan Lungren; U.S. Congressman Dana Rohrabacher; All-American John Ferraro, a longtime Los Angeles city councilman; and California Supreme Court Chief Justice Malcolm M. Lucas.

In the 1960s NASA created what came to be known as "the Bubble," a device that tested the manufactured atmosphere of space.

Because of this, many well-known astronauts of the Mercury, Gemini, and Apollo space programs earned advanced degrees at USC. The most famed of these American heroes is Neil Armstrong, the first man on the moon.

Other distinguished alumni include architect Frank Gehry; Persian Gulf War commander General Norman Schwarzkopf; syndicated columnist Art Buchwald; as well as top-ranking executives, including Coca-Cola/North American president Terry Marks, Public Storage founder Wayne Hughes, and Peter Cooper of Guy Carpenter & Company.

Just like the Trojans of Homer's *The Iliad* and *The Odyssey*, the modern-day version fights harder and has more moral fiber and better character than the competition, in this case, representatives of other colleges. USC has always been a traditional school that has extolled the patriotic values of God and country. Countless Trojans have fought with valor, and many have died for our freedom on the fields of our nation's battles.

From its earliest days, USC has been a place of equal opportunity. The first black professionals in medicine, architecture, and other fields were trained at USC prior to World War I. Women have prepared for meaningful careers at USC since its earliest days in the 19th century. The ridiculous moniker "University of Spoiled Children" was given to a great university that was opening its doors to all when those hypocritically deriding it were still part of cloistered all-white boys' clubs.

USC was once falsely described by its jealous detractors as a "football school," despite the fact that the ranks of judges, lawyers, doctors, dentists, and other professions in greater Los Angeles have long been been dominated by Southern California men and women.

TRIVIA

Where is *General Hospital* of soap opera fame?

Answers to the trivia questions are on pages 187–191.

Products of the USC School of Cinematic Arts now dominate Hollywood. One of the ways they have achieved this is by instituting a producer's division into their curriculum. Instead of simply educating writers, directors, and actors in the art of film (but not the business of it), USC has created a real-world model for Hollywood success. Directors, writers, and actors network and connect with fellow Trojan producers and agents. The result is that USC alumni at every level of the business now dominate the film industry.

The music school and the drama school have reaped natural ancillary benefits of a great film school. Former Ambassador to the Court of St. James Walter Annenberg donated $120 million for the establishment for a world-class communications program, which has produced graduates skilled in advertising, public relations, political campaigns, and Hollywood publicity, just to name a few areas of expertise.

Undergraduate applications doubled over the last few years, as the school led a citywide revival following the 1992 riots and a large 1994 earthquake. Bold political leadership under Mayor Richard Riordan helped decrease crime and clean up the streets. Enlightened corporate and auto industry responsibility resulted in a major decrease in L.A. Basin air pollution from the 1970s and '80s to the 2000s.

USC has made a fabulous, bold outreach to its community. Located in one of Los Angeles's oldest (once one of its best) neighborhoods, the university never ignored its responsibilities as that South-Central neighborhood deteriorated. It has been the driving force behind gentrification projects that have created new housing and shopping in the area. Faculty housing has invested USC professors in the neighborhood many of them now live in. New schools and day care centers have been built and run by USC. Excellent outreach programs have provided deserving African American, Latino, and other minority students from L.A.'s inner city a chance to matriculate at a

DID YOU KNOW . . . That Trojan football reached an 82 percent graduation rate, an all-time high, and more than 20 percentage points higher than the average Division I college football program? In 2001, 14 members of the team had 3.0 G.P.A.'s. USC ranks in the top 10 in the number of NCAA postgraduate scholarship recipients (49 as of 2004) and has had 26 first-team Academic All-Americans. Three Trojans have earned Rhodes Scholarships.

school that otherwise would only be a so-close-and-yet-so-far dream. Freshmen in local high schools enter a program in which, if they maintain high grades in academic coursework, they are given full scholarships to USC.

First the building of Staples Center in downtown L.A., a short distance from campus, and now the erection of Galen Center, 'SC's shining new basketball arena, has created a new corridor of upscale businesses, restaurants, night life, and condominiums that, in years past, seemed impossible.

USC has one of the highest tuitions, is among the richest colleges in the nation in terms of private endowments, and among the top three in athletic financial donations. It is a university that has managed to seamlessly combine social responsibility with American capitalistic principles, in a manner not unlike the way Olympic President Peter Ueberroth was able to make the 1984 L.A. Games the most successful before or since.

USC athletes are universally recognized for their approachable, media-savvy demeanors. They are considered unusually articulate and intelligent by local and national sports journalists. Sportstalk host Jim Rome has repeatedly expressed amazement at how outstanding interviews with USC athletes on his program are.

How Good has USC Gotten under Pete Carroll?

Frankly, things started to get out of hand with Pete Carroll and USC. Number-one NFL draft picks, first-round draft picks? Aside from Carson Palmer, there was Matt Leinart and Reggie Bush. Let's go back to Palmer and the 2002 Trojans. Then consider LenDale White. Beyond that: Keith Rivers, John David Booty—these are just the obvious possibilities. Let's go back to Palmer and the 2002 Trojans. Palmer won the Heisman and was the NFL's number-one draft choice. He is currently starring for the Cincinnati Bengals after signing a multimillion dollar bonus. The 2002 Trojans finished 11–2, were co–Pacific-10 champs, and won the Orange Bowl. They finished fourth in the nation, but the pundits were in agreement that by season's end, they were the best team in the country, even though Ohio State defeated Miami in the BCS title game. Had there been a playoff, 'SC probably would have won.

In 2003 USC won the national championship following a victory over Michigan in the Rose Bowl. Considering that they had a spectacular wide receiver, Mike Williams, a comparison of the 2003 and 2004 teams may very well favor the '03 squad. The '05 team, however, was (almost) better than anybody—ever!

How good has 'SC been under Carroll? Consider that the All-American Williams had his NCAA eligibility taken away prior to 2004. Had he played, he would have been in New York instead of Bush, and he may well have won the Heisman. Bush just took his place, and the beat went on. Speaking of first-round picks, Williams was the top selection of the Detroit Vikings, despite being out of the limelight for one year. Future drafts promise to be 'SC highlight films. Every year. But wait, there's *still more*.

Pete Carroll has orchestrated a Trojan renaissance since he arrived to take over the head coaching reins in late 2000.

The 2005 Trojans were thought to be the finest team in history right up to the point when Vince Young broke their hearts in the Longhorns' 41–38 win at the Rose Bowl, a game considered the best ever played. With this in mind, consider that had Williams played out his entire career, or been redshirted, he would have been a senior in 2005. Consider that the best defensive rookie in the National Football Conference, Lofa Tatupu, led the Seattle Seahawks to the Super Bowl. Had he not come out early, he would have been there to help slow up Young!

Coach of the Year? In 2003 it was Carroll. The only reason he does not win it every year is because they like to spread those kinds of things around. Give it to him every second year. This guy has gone through Troy's old nemeses, UCLA and Notre Dame, like Patton's army charging through the Low Countries. Between 2002 and 2005, he presided over a re-Pete national title, three Heisman winners (very possibly four if White had played his senior year in 2006), one NFL number-one draft pick (it easily could have been three going on

TOP 35

Greatest College Football Teams by Chronological Order

1902 Michigan Wolverines
1913 Washington Huskies
1922 California Golden Bears
1924 Notre Dame Fighting Irish
1928 Southern California Trojans
1930 Alabama Crimson Tide
1932 Southern California Trojans
1936 Minnesota Golden Gophers
1945 Army Cadets
1947 Notre Dame Fighting Irish
1948 Michigan Wolverines
1956 Oklahoma Sooners
1962 Southern California Trojans
1966 Notre Dame Fighting Irish
1968 Ohio State Buckeyes
1969 Texas Longhorns

1971 Nebraska Cornhuskers
1972 Southern California Trojans
1973 Notre Dame Fighting Irish
1975 Oklahoma Sooners
1976 Pittsburgh Panthers
1979 Alabama Crimson Tide
1985 Oklahoma Sooners
1986 Penn State Nittany Lions
1987 Miami Hurricanes
1988 Notre Dame Fighting Irish
1989 Miami Hurricanes
1991 Washington Huskies
1992 Alabama Crimson Tide
1995 Nebraska Cornhuskers
1996 Florida Gators
1999 Florida State Seminoles
2001 Miami Hurricanes
2004 Southern California Trojans
2005 Texas Longhorns

four if Leinart had gone out in '05; if a question regarding Bush's parents had not overshadowed the '06 draft; and if White had stayed in '06), seven first rounders, 25 NFL draftees, 19 All-American first-teamers, two Orange Bowl wins, one Rose Bowl victory, five bowl appearances, four BCS appearances, four AP top-four finishes, four Pac-10 championships, four straight national-best recruiting classes, a wire-to-wire number-one perfect season (and one nine-yard Vince Young run with 19 seconds left from making it two straight), a 34-game winning streak, a number-one poll ranking for a record 33 weeks running, and four straight undefeated Novembers.

Take your pick on the following records (up until the 33–31 loss at Oregon State on October 28, 2006): 43–2 (2003–2005), 54–4 (2002–2005, 93.1 percent), 51–2 (since October 2002), 54–10 (2001–2005, 84.4 percent), or 60–10 (overall); and 38 straight regular season wins. Add to that 35 straight Coliseum victories (until 2007), 27 consecutive conference wins (until 2006), 22 straight versus AP Top 25 teams (until 2007), and 63 straight games scoring 20-points or more (until 2006).

Those are the facts. After that comes the speculation, the predictions, the hype. Has any coach ever done more in his first five-plus years? Probably not.

Had USC defeated Texas in the 2005 Rose Bowl, they would have carried a 35-game winning streak into the 2006 season. That would have fueled speculation that they could tie Oklahoma's all-time record 47-game winning streak of the 1950s by beating UCLA in the last regular season game, and breaking the mark with their 48th straight victory in the January 8, 2007, BCS national championship game at the Fiesta Bowl in Glendale, Arizona! As it was, the Oregon State loss would have ended the streak at 41.

Victory over Texas also would have extended their AP record for number-one rankings to 34 (second is Miami with 20 from 2001 to 2002, while USC from 1972 to 1973 is fourth with 17). Had they accomplished this, they very likely would have had the imprimatur to enter the 2006 season ranked first instead of Ohio State. If LenDale White had come back, this possibility would have increased exponentially. Their six-game winning streak to open the season likely would have extended the AP number-one streak to 43 consecutive weeks.

Wait, there's more. The Oregon State defeat was Pete Carroll's 11th loss against 60 wins. Of those 11 losses, only one was by more than a touchdown (27–16 when Notre Dame scored late at South Bend in 2001). Beyond that, Carroll's first Trojan team lost 10–6 against Kansas State, 24–22 at Oregon, 21–16 versus Stanford (the last home loss), 27–24 at Washington, and 10–6 against Utah in the Las Vegas Bowl.

His 2002 team lost 27–20 at Kansas State and 30–27 (after a missed extra point and missed chip-shot field goal in overtime) at Washington State.

His 2003 national champions were beaten 34–31 (again after missing an easy kick in triple overtime) at California. His 2004 national champions—maybe the finest college team of all time—lost to nobody. His 2005 team was thought to be greater, the best collegiate team ever assembled, until losing on Young's last-minute touchdown, 41–38, in the BCS national championship Rose Bowl that has been described as the best, most exciting game ever played by college teams. The 33–31 loss at Oregon State came only when a two-point conversion try with seconds remaining was batted down.

Consider further that USC lost to UCLA by four points in 2006 and was driving deep in Bruin territory in the last minute; was beaten by one against Stanford in a game in which their kicker missed an extra point (2007); and was driving for the tying score against Oregon before back-up quarterback Mark Sanchez's pass was intercepted (2007).

Therefore, with a little bit of luck, a few breaks, some lucky bounces perhaps, Pete Carroll and USC could have been *89–1 with*

IF ONLY . . . Rodney Peete had not injured his shoulder before the 1988 USC–Notre Dame game, USC may have won the national title that year, too. The unbeaten, second-ranked Trojans were only down by three at the half against the unbeaten, first-ranked Irish at the Coliseum. A healthy Peete might have engineered victory and won the Heisman, giving 'SC 12 national titles (to Notre Dame's 11), eight Heismans (to Notre Dame's seven), and propelled the program to glory under Larry Smith that they finally attained under Pete Carroll.

TOP 11

Greatest Single-Season College Football Teams of Each Decade

1900s: 1902 Michigan Wolverines

1910s: 1913 Washington Huskies

1920s: 1928 Southern California Trojans

1930s: 1932 Southern California Trojans

1940s: 1947 Notre Dame Fighting Irish

1950s: 1956 Oklahoma Sooners

1960s: 1968 Ohio State Buckeyes

1970s: 1972 Southern California Trojans

1980s: 1989 Miami Hurricanes

1990s: 1995 Nebraska Cornhuskers

2000s: 2004 Southern California Trojans

seven straight national championships between 2001 and 2007! Of course, Carroll's November record requires no conjecture of lucky breaks or bounces. He has simply *never lost in November.*

Had they won those five less-than-a-TD losses in 2001, they would have been ranked ahead of Nebraska after the Cornhuskers lost the Big 12 title game, chosen to play Miami in that year's BCS championship game.

The 2002 Carson Palmer juggernaut was generally thought to be the best in the nation by the end of the season anyway. They would have been favored over an injury-depleted Miami team, or the Ohio State Buckeyes, who won the BCS Fiesta Bowl, despite little in the way of an offense.

The 2003 team of course won the national championship, as did the unbeaten 2004 Trojans. The loss to Vince Young and Texas was razor-thin, as were all four defeats in the 2006 through 2007 seasons. In 2007 experts agreed USC should have gone to the BCS title game, was the nation's best team at season's end, and, had there been a playoff, just like in 2002 USC would have been favored to win it. Pete Carroll has raised the bar so high at USC that no prospect for success is out of the realm of possibility.

That said, greatness—whether it be empires or sports teams—must beware of arrogance and *hubris*. In 1979 USC entered the season as the consensus number one. Experts were saying *that* team could contend for the title "greatest college football team ever." They were the defending co-national champions and heralded that season's Heisman Trophy winner, Charles White, and Lombardi Award winner, Brad Budde, along with other stalwarts like Anthony Munoz. Not quite midway into the season, they took on Stanford at the Coliseum. At halftime the Trojans led 21–0 en route to another stomping. In the second half the Cardinal scored three touchdowns, 'SC's offense stalled, and that 21–21 tie (before the advent of over-time) was just enough to deny them the national title along with the "greatest ever" label.

In 1980 the best prep quarterback available was Escondido, California's Sean Salisbury. USC legend Sam Cunningham told his alma mater about his brother, Randall, in Santa Barbara, and asked if he would start. He was told Randall would be offered a ride but the job was Salisbury's. Randall went to UNLV and then made millions with the NFL's Eagles. Salisbury was a bust. USC lost coach John Robinson to the Rams, went on probation, and took 20 years to recover fully.

Troy thought they were back when, in 1987 to 1989 under Larry Smith, they went to three consecutive Rose Bowls, were 10–0 going into the '88 Notre Dame game, featured Junior Seau, and recruited the all-time prep passing leader, Todd Marinovich. By 1990, Marinovich was a problem child, and in '91 they lost to Memphis State.

These are just some of many examples that USC avoided in winning two and nearly three national championships in a row, yet they remain enduring cautionary tales in the endless quest for more. After all, sportstalk host Jim Rome has proposed that he sees "no reason why Carroll and USC can't win five or 10, just like John Wooden did." USC lives in the pressure-cooker of ultimate expecta-tions in that most pressurized of atmospheres, Los Angeles. Still, Carroll has insisted that he and his team "embrace" it.

It doesn't take much to derail a team when they are riding in the clouds. Bad recruiting, drugs (Marinovich), coaches leaving for the NFL (John McKay and John Robinson did; some say Carroll considers his pro work undone), NCAA violations (their first-half 1980s teams), or just a slip against great competition can be enough to derail a team and separate the great from the legendary.

Unlike in the NFL, a single loss (or tie) can upset the apple cart. USC is the hottest ticket in America's hottest town, the toast of Hollywood, the biggest thing in a media hothouse that doesn't have a pro football franchise and whose NBA team experienced a period of inconsistency. They set the all-time USC attendance record in 2003, continued to break that in 2004, and sold out every home game in the 2005 through 2007 seasons. For 20-year-old student-athletes in such a crazed atmosphere, staying balanced is a major challenge, but they overcame it and, under Carroll, appear capable of continuing their focus.

It's fun to talk about, and at 'SC, a school that went through a long (13 or 20 years, depending on your standards) down period, it is especially fun. Their fans were made giddy and have stayed that way.

USC in the Pros

Entering the 2004 season, USC had more players on NFL rosters than any other college in 17 of the previous 29 years. In 2005 42 Trojans were on 19 rosters, the most of all programs. Sixteen USC rookies were on pro rosters at the beginning of 2006 training camp. By 2007, Southern Cal had 41 players on NFL rosters.

Through the 2007 draft, 430 USC football players have been drafted, the largest number of any college. Many others have made NFL rosters as free agents. Twenty-eight were drafted by the old AFL, and numerous others drafted by the All-American Football Conference. USC has produced the most overall pro football players.

The Trojans have had three of the most highly drafted classes in history. The 1953 class produced the most of any college, with 15 draftees, while both the 1975 and 1977 drafts produced 14 each. Entering 2007, USC had the most first-round selections (67 to Ohio State's 65, followed by Notre Dame, 58; Miami, 57; and Texas, 41). USC had the most players selected in the first round since 1990 (12) and had the most first-round selections in the 1980s (16). The university's five first-round picks in 1968 were an NFL-college record. No school has had more number one overall selections than USC (Ron Yary '68, O.J. Simpson '69, Ricky Bell '77, Keyshawn Johnson '96, and Carson Palmer '03). USC is the only school to have the first pick in two straight drafts (Yary and Simpson, 1968–1969).

USC has had the most players play in Super Bowls. Trojans (94 overall through the 2007 Super Bowl) have appeared in all but two of them, with two earning MVP honors (Lynn Swann in 1976, Marcus Allen in 1984). The 1977 Super Bowl between Oakland and

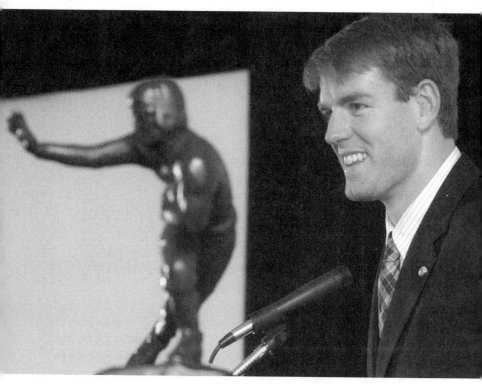

Carson Palmer poses with the Heisman Trophy after winning the award at The Yale Club in New York in December 2002.

Minnesota featured nine ex-Trojans. Two hundred one Trojans have been selected for the Pro Bowl, also the record (through the 2006 season). In January of 1999 *ESPN The Magazine* stated, "One of the best ways to win a Super Bowl is to have [a USC player on the team]." USC has had players on the most winning Super Bowl teams (44). In the 2008 Super Bowl the Trojans could not lose, since the New England Patriots featured Matt Cassel, Oscar Lua, Tom Malone, and Junior Seau; the New York Giants saw the emergence of star receiver Steve Smith.

USC is tied with Notre Dame for most players in the Pro Football Hall of Fame (11), including Allen, Swann, Simpson, Red Badgro, Frank Gifford, Ronnie Lott, Ron Mix, Anthony Munoz, Willie Wood, Ron Yary, and Bruce Matthews. Three ex-USC assistant coaches have been inducted at Canton: Al Davis, Joe Gibbs, and Mel Hein. Munoz

TOP 10

Greatest College Football Teams by Decade

1910s: Washington Huskies

1920s: Notre Dame Fighting Irish

1930s: Southern California Trojans

1940s: Notre Dame Fighting Irish

1950s: Oklahoma Sooners

1960s: Southern California Trojans

1970s: Southern California Trojans

1980s: Miami Hurricanes

1990s: Nebraska Cornhuskers

2000s: Southern California Trojans

and Lott were picked for the NFL's All-Century Team in 2000. *The Sporting News* chose four USC players among the 100 Greatest Pro Football Players: Munoz (17th), Lott (23rd), Simpson (26th), and Allen (72nd). Munoz was chosen as one of the "NFL's top 10 players of the 20th century" by *SPORT* magazine. The Dick Butkus Football Network also named Munoz and Lott to its NFL All-Century first team.

In 1999 the *San Diego Union-Tribune* examined all the Pro Bowl selections and determined that at 162, USC led Notre Dame (135) and Ohio State (122) in producing the most players selected. They also led in producing the most running backs and safeties. Entering the 2004 season, USC's total number had increased to 193.

A 1999 *SPORT* article determined that in the 1990s, arguably the weakest decade in 'SC football history, the Trojans had the most Pro Bowl selections (14). "The most measurable sign of a player's success—and thus his pedigree—comes in the form of the NFL's highest honor: the Pro Bowl," the article read. "It's not enough to make it to the league, you've gotta make it *in* the league."

"USC is a football factory," said Keyshawn Johnson. "Every kid in L.A. grows up wanting to play there, and the coaches know how to translate that into elite athletes."

A 1994 *College Sports* study rated USC first among running backs, offensive linemen, and defensive backs, and third among linebackers, using a rating system of top sources to determine combined college and pro success. A 1985 *Sports Illustrated* poll of NFL player personnel directors ranked USC first in preparing college players for the NFL, particularly at the running back, offensive line, and tight end positions.

Former Trojan players, coaches, and assistants who have become head coaches in the NFL include Seattle's Mike Holmgren, Tennessee's Jeff Fisher, Miami's Dave Wannstedt, Detroit's Steve Mariucci, Jacksonville's Jack Del Rio, Oakland's Norv Turner, the Rams' John Robinson, Tampa Bay's John McKay, Detroit's Wayne Fontes, and the New York Giants' Jim Fassel. Other assistant coaches and head coaches of note include R.C. Slocum, Ted Tollner, Bob Toledo, Bruce Snyder, Ed Orgeron, Ken O'Brien, Ricky Hunley, Paul Hackett, Norm Chow, Jerry Attaway, and Raiders' head coach Lane Kiffin.

IF ONLY . . . Quarterback Todd Marinovich had not turned out to be a bust! Craig Fertig's nephew set the national passing yardage records at San Juan Capistrano High School and was perhaps the most heralded prep football player of all time. He led USC to the 1990 Rose Bowl victory, but drugs and a bad attitude destroyed his life, career, and the program. The Marinovich fallout took a decade to recover from, costing Larry Smith his job and putting USC into a historical hole that took Pete Carroll to dig out of. Had Todd been half the player advertised, the winless streaks to Notre Dame (13) and UCLA (eight) may have been replaced by a national title...or two.

USC's Numbers Don't Lie

Entering the 2008 season, USC's all-time won-loss record stood at 754–302–54 (.704), the best in Pacific-10 Conference history (going back to the days of the Pacific Coast Conference). They had a conference-best 397–157–29 record against Pac-10 foes. USC was 25–6 versus Arizona, 15–9 against Arizona State, 60–30–5 against Cal, 36–16–2 versus Oregon, 58–9–4 versus Oregon State, 58–25–3 versus Stanford, 42–28–7 against UCLA, 48–26–4 against Washington, and 55–8–4 versus Washington State. USC has had the most All–Pac-10 selections.

USC was 65–27–2 versus the Big 10 Conference, which includes 11–2 versus Illinois, 4–0 versus Indiana, 7–2 versus Iowa, 6–4 versus Michigan, 4–4 versus Michigan State, 4–1–1 versus Minnesota, 5–0 versus Northwestern, 11–9–1 versus Ohio State, 4–4 versus Penn State, 3–1 versus Purdue, and 6–0 versus Wisconsin.

They were 32–42–5 versus Notre Dame, 3–0–1 versus Nebraska, 6–2–1 versus Oklahoma, 4–1 versus Texas, 3–0 versus Texas A&M, 2–5 versus Alabama, 3–0 versus Georgia, and 4–0 versus Tennessee.

USC was 397–123–27 at the Los Angeles Coliseum, and 30–18 in all games played at the Rose Bowl. With the Rose Bowl game on the line for one or both USC and UCLA, the Trojans are 22–12–2 and 15–5 since 1976. When both teams are playing for it, they are 17–6–1 (11 of the past 12).

Their bowl percentage, based on a 30–16 record, was the best in the country. USC won nine straight bowl games when they played in them between 1923 and 1945. They have appeared in the most Rose Bowls (32), with the most wins and the best percentage (23–9). It is the most victories by any college in a single bowl. Since the BCS era began in 1998, they are the most successful team in BCS bowl games and have appeared in the most consecutive BCS games (six, 5–1 record).

There have been various polling services and statistical calculations that have ranked USC number one in the nation at the end of 16 seasons, but the school only recognizes 11 of them as legitimate national championships (1928, 1931–1932, 1939, 1962, 1972, 1974, 1978, 2003–2004). Howard Jones won four national championships between 1928 and 1939. Knute Rockne of Notre Dame won three national championships in his tenure from 1918 until his untimely death in a 1930 plane crash.

In the 1963 Rose Bowl number-one USC beat number-two Wisconsin 42–37. In the 1969 Rose Bowl number-one Ohio State defeated number-two USC 27–16. In 1981 number-one USC beat number-two Oklahoma 28–24 in Los Angeles. In 1988 number-one Notre Dame upended second-ranked Troy 27–10 at the Coliseum. In the 2005 BCS Orange Bowl top-ranked 'SC devoured number-two Oklahoma 55–19, and in the 2006 BCS Rose Bowl number-one USC lost to number two Texas 41–38.

When ranked number one against Notre Dame, USC has never lost to the Irish (1962, 1967, 1972, 2004, 2005). USC tied Nebraska in 2005 for fifth place among the most-frequently ranked teams in the Associated Press polling, going back to its inception in 1936, which of course does not count the fact that they would have been ranked in the top 20 in the vast majority of AP polls conducted since World War I, had there been one.

Through 2007, USC has been ranked number one 89 times, tying them with Notre Dame for the most of any college football program in history. Oklahoma and Ohio State are tied for second with 86. Should they be ranked number one again, they will pass the Irish.

In 2005 USC (33 from 2003 to 2005) passed Miami (20 from 2001 to 2002) for most consecutive weeks ranked number one in the AP

TRIVIA

When did Traveler, a magnificent white horse, make his first sideline appearance as USC's mascot?

Answers to the trivia questions are on pages 187–191.

TOP 20

Greatest College Football Dynasties

1. Southern California under John McKay and John Robinson (1960s–1980s)
2. Alabama under Bear Bryant (1960s–1980s)
3. Miami (1980s–2000s)
4. Ohio State under Woody Hayes (1950s–1970s)
5. Oklahoma under Bud Wilkinson (1950s)
6. Nebraska under Bob Devaney and Tom Osborne (1970s–1990s)
7. Penn State under Joe Paterno (1960s–1990s)
8. Oklahoma under Chuck Fairbanks and Barry Switzer (1970s–1980s)
9. Notre Dame under Knute Rockne (1920s)
10. Notre Dame under Frank Leahy (1940s)
11. Southern California's "Thundering Herd" under Howard Jones (1920–1930s)
12. Notre Dame under Ara Parseghian (1960s–1970s)
13. Florida State under Bobby Bowden (1990s)
14. Texas under Darrell Royal (1960s–1970s)
15. Michigan under Bo Schembechler (1960s–1980s)
16. California's "Wonder Teams" under Andy Smith (1918–1922)
17. Army under Red Blaik (mid-1940s)
18. Minnesota under Bernie Bierman (1930s, early '40s)
19. Stanford under Pop Warner (1920s)
20. Michigan's "point-a-minute" teams under Fritz Carlisle (1900s)

NEXT: Southern California under Pete Carroll (2000s)

poll. Notre Dame (19 from 1988 to 1989) is third, with another USC team (17 from 1972 to 1973) in fourth place.

The 2005 USC team was almost the third team ever to be ranked number one in the AP preseason poll and hold it until after the bowls. The others are Florida State (1999) and USC (2004). Four other teams: Notre Dame (1943), Army (1945), Nebraska (1971), and

USC (1972) were not ranked number one in the preseason, but were ranked first in each regular season poll and the final post-bowl poll.

Prior to USC's two-time national championship run of 2003 and 2004, the only repeat AP winners were Minnesota (1940 and 1941), Army (1944 and 1945), Notre Dame (1946 and 1947), Oklahoma (1955 and 1956), Alabama (1964, though Alabama lost its bowl game after the polls closed, and 1965), Nebraska (1970 and 1971), Oklahoma (1974, though Oklahoma was on NCAA probation, and 1975), Alabama (1978 and 1979), and Nebraska (1994 and 1995).

Back-to-back champions prior to the AP polling also included California (1920, 1921, and 1922), Alabama (1925 and 1926), USC (1931 and 1932), and Minnesota (1934 and 1935). Other Pacific-10 Conference teams that can claim national championships include California (four: 1920, 1921, 1922, 1937), Stanford (three: 1905, one under Pop Warner in 1926, one under Clark Shaugnessy, 1940, plus one Heisman), Washington (three: 1909, 1913 under Gil Dobie; 1991), UCLA (1954, one Heisman), Washington State (one, 1915), and Oregon (one, 1916).

Beyond the leaders, (USC, Notre Dame, Alabama), other traditional football powers with national championships include Oklahoma (seven: 1950, 1955, 1956, 1974, 1975, 1985, 2000, with four Heismans), Michigan (four: 1923, 1933, 1948, 1997, with two Heismans), Ohio State (five: 1942, 1954, 1961, 1968, 2002, with seven Heismans), Miami (five: 1984, 1987, 1989, 1991, 2001, with two Heismans), Nebraska (five: 1970, 1971, 1994, 1995, 1997, with three Heismans), Penn State (two: 1982, 1986, with one Heisman, although the Nittany Lions could easily have won three more: 1968, 1969, 1994), Texas (three: 1963, 1969, 2005, with two Heismans), LSU (three: 1958, 2003, 2007, one Heisman), Florida State (two: 1993, 1999, two Heismans), Florida (two: 1996, 2006, with three Heismans), Tennessee (two: 1950, 1998, no Heismans), and Auburn (one: 1957, two Heismans).

USC ranks in the top 10 among all-time college football victories, but this is a skewed statistic since Michigan, the leader, was a major college program for decades before USC shed its rugby image after World War I.

USC is also in the top 10 in all-time winning percentage, surpassing the impressive .700 mark (.704). This is an amazing statistic, since USC has traditionally played the strongest conference, non-conference, and intersectional schedule in the nation since the 1920s. USC has subjected itself on a yearly basis to death matches with Notre Dame and UCLA, and a host of national powers in the Rose Bowl and other bowls.

When trying to determine the greatest program ever, another factor in USC's favor is the fact that they have the most bowl wins and the best bowl winning percentage. They have achieved this playing in that most competitive of historical games, the "Granddaddy of 'em all," the Rose Bowl. They have also competed in

Matt Leinart's last-second plunge to score the winning touchdown against Notre Dame in the epic 2005 game may have signaled the passing of the torch for the greatest tradition in college football.

most of the best bowls, including two Orange Bowls, the Fiesta Bowl, and the Cotton Bowl. Each of their national championships has come with victories in the Rose Bowl, except for one Orange Bowl win and one year in which they did not play in a bowl game. There are numerous other teams that lay claim to national titles despite having lost bowl games. Seven of Notre Dame's national championship runs came in seasons in which they did not play in a bowl. Obviously, had they played in bowl games, they may well have lost

TRIVIA

In the Pete Carroll era, how many national-best recruiting classes has USC had?

Answers to the trivia questions are on pages 187–191.

some of those games. Their "bowl game" in those seasons was USC, who also could have won a few more had they not subjected themselves to the yearly game with the Irish (and vice versa).

Since USC has the most impressive bowl record, it stands to reason that, had there been a playoff system in place throughout all those years, they may have won more national championships than the 11 they have. They also probably would have had more undisputed titles instead of sharing a few with other teams of dubious merit. The Trojans have been accorded national championship status by varying polls, rankings, and formulations in five additional non-title seasons. It is not hard to conceive that, with a playoff format in place, they may have beaten LSU or Ohio State in 2007; either Miami or Ohio State in 2002; Alabama in 1979; Pittsburgh in 1976; Texas, Penn State, and Arkansas in 1969; and maybe a few others.

The Tradition of Troy

Entering the 2008 season, USC had 151 All-Americans, along with Notre Dame the most of any school in the nation. From 1962 to 1990, USC placed at least one player on the All-America first team. From 1972 to 1987, at least one was a consensus All-American. Twenty-nine offensive linemen made first-team All-American since 1964. Entering 2008, 112 USC players have made unanimous, consensus, and/or first-team All-American, and many of them were chosen in two and even three seasons.

USC, of course, has seven Heismans, which ties Notre Dame and Ohio State, and has been well documented, but several Trojans on the 2008 roster could make up the school's eighth and ninth Heisman winners before the decade is over. Offensive tackle Ron Yary won the Outland Trophy in 1967. Offensive guard Brad Budde won the Lombardi Award in 1979. Free safety Mark Carrier won the Jim Thorpe Award in 1989. Middle linebacker Chris Claiborne earned the Butkus Award in 1998. In 2007 tight end Fred Davis earned the Mackey Award. Twenty-eight Trojan players have been elected to the National Football Foundation's College Hall of Fame, in addition to two head coaches (Howard Jones and John McKay), three assistant coaches, and former athletic director Mike McGee.

Six USC players have won the Walter Camp Award, three the Maxwell Award, three the Johnny Unitas Golden Arm Award, and 17 the Glenn "Pop" Warner Award. Nine have won the Voit Trophy. Three coaches have been named American Football Coaches Association Coach of the Year (Carroll in 2003), two the Football Writers Association of America Coach of the Year, and eight the Pac-

10 Conference Coach of the Year. Fifteen Trojans have been named the Pacific-10 Conference Player of the Year (the most), and 12 the Morris Trophy. Twenty-six have won the Rose Bowl Player of the Game award (the most of any school). Eighteen (also the most) have been inducted into the Rose Bowl Hall of Fame.

O.J. Simpson was named the "50th greatest athlete of the 20th century" by ESPN. Simpson, Yary, and Lott were named as starters on the Walter Camp Football Foundation All-Century Team, with Brad Budde and Tim McDonald named as reserves. *Football News* ranked Simpson the 10th greatest player of the 20th century. Yary and Lott made the Scripps Howard News Service College Football All-Star Team of the Century. Swann, Yary, and Lott were first-team, and Tony Boselli second-team, on the Dick Butkus Football Network College Football All-Century Team. Reggie Bush was selected among the 25 greatest college football players in history by ESPN in 2007.

TOP 25

All-Time Greatest Collegiate Athletic Traditions

1. Southern California Trojans
2. UCLA Bruins
3. Texas Longhorns
4. Miami Hurricanes
5. Michigan Wolverines
6. Alabama Crimson Tide
7. Ohio State Buckeyes
8. Florida State Seminoles
9. Stanford Indians/Cardinal
10. Oklahoma Sooners
11. Louisiana State Tigers
12. Tennessee Volunteers
13. Notre Dame Fighting Irish
14. Penn State Nittany Lions
15. Arkansas Razorbacks
16. Florida Gators
17. Indiana Hoosiers
18. Georgia Bulldogs
19. Texas A&M Aggies
20. Oklahoma State Cowboys
21. Arizona State Sun Devils
22. Auburn Tigers
23. Duke Blue Devils
24. North Carolina Tar Heels
25. California Golden Bears

Collegefootballnews.com chose Simpson, Charles White, Marcus Allen, Ron Yary, Ronnie Lott, Lynn Swann, and Tony Boselli among its "150 greatest college football players."

Since joining the Pacific Coast Conference in 1922, USC has won the most conference titles and had the most all-conference selections. Entering 2007, USC has had the most players in postseason all-star bowls: the Hula Bowl (133), the East-West Shrine Game (103), the Senior Bowl (56), the College All-Star Game (72), the Japan Bowl (40), and the Coaches All-America Game (26).

They have also landed the most players on the prestigious *Playboy* preseason college All-America team. Since 1957, when the magazine first started selecting teams, 67 Trojan players, as well as three Coaches of the Year and one Scholar-Athlete, have been picked. Prior to 2005, the school with the next-most picks is Michigan (46), followed by Notre Dame (40, plus one Coach of the Year).

Eleven times, USC has played against that season's Heisman Trophy winner. They defeated Notre Dame's Paul Hornung (1956) and John Huarte (1964); UCLA's Gary Beban (1967); Ohio State's Archie Griffin (1974); and South Carolina's George Rogers (1980).

USC's media guide bills the Trojans as the true "America's team" because they had played on television 308 times going into the 2004 season. At one point, 111 straight games were televised. They were on a record six national telecasts in 1987. From 1972 to 1981, USC had the highest average viewer rating in America. Sports Inc. ranked five of the USC–Notre Dame telecasts among the 12 highest-rated games ever. The 2005 USC–Notre Dame game was the most-watched regular season college football game in 10 years; the 2005 Orange Bowl (versus Oklahoma) and 2006 Rose Bowl (versus Texas) the two most most hyped ever!

TRIVIA

What is the inspiration for USC's stirring battle cry, "Conquest"?

Answers to the trivia questions are on pages 187–191.

The Trojans have played in front of more than 100,000 fans in the Coliseum on six occasions, with the 104,953 for the 1947 game with Notre Dame holding the record. The biggest road crowd was 100,741 at the Rose Bowl for the 1988 Rodney Peete–Troy Aikman battle with UCLA. The biggest crowd ever was 120,000 at Soldier Field in Chicago for the 1927 Notre Dame game, with 112,912 watching the teams play at the same site in 1929. The biggest Rose Bowl game crowd was 106,869 for the 1973 national championship–clinching win over Ohio State.

On top of all this, USC has the greatest overall men's and women's collegiate athletic tradition in the nation. Its closest competition comes from UCLA. Entering the fall of 2007, USC had the most men's national championships (86). UCLA had won 70 NCAA titles (Stanford had won 58 prior to the 2007–2008 academic year). USC had won 106 combined men's and women's NCAA/national titles. UCLA made much of their "first to 100" accomplishment, and deserve kudos for in fact being the first school to earn 100 combined men's and women's *official* NCAA championships. Among other facts, it should be noted that USC's legitimate 11 national championship in football (16 total including all sources) are not official NCAA championships.

Among the top five college sports (football, basketball, baseball, track, and tennis) USC had won 11 in football, 12 in baseball, 16 in tennis, and 26 in track and field (the most of any sport, men's or women's). In addition, USC had earned 301 NCAA men's individual championships (second: Michigan, 246). UCLA had won 11 basketball titles entering the 2007–2008 school year, plus one in football and none in baseball.

From 1959 to 1985, USC won a national championship for 26 straight school years. They won five each in 1962–1963 and 1976–1977. In 2000 USC was named "Collegiate Athletic Program of the Century."

Thirty-one Trojans (prior to '04) have been named the Amateur Athletic Foundation Southern California Athlete of the Year.

While it may be a question of debate as to whether or not USC boasts the greatest football tradition in America, no debate exists when it comes to baseball. USC's 11 national championships under Rod Dedeaux, and a 12th under Mike Gillespie in 1998, are unprecedented. Texas is second with five. When Dedeaux retired after the 1986 season, his 1,332 wins were the most of any coach.

USC has had the most baseball Olympians and the second-most members of the USA National Team. USC baseball players have graced more *Sports Illustrated* covers than players from any other school.

USC has had the most All-American baseball players, the most players drafted (263 entering 2006), the most players drafted in the first round, the most professional players, and the most major league baseball players. They boast the most baseball Hall of Famers, the most All-Stars, and the most Cy Young Award winners (nine). In 2002 Barry Zito and Randy Johnson both won the Cy Young Award. Fred Lynn won the 1975 American League MVP award. Trojans have been Rookie of the Year three times, one has been the All-Star Game MVP (Lynn), and in 2001 Johnson was the World Series MVP.

In 1997 Johnson, Mark McGwire, and Jeff Cirillo were in the All-Star Game. In 2003, Jenkins, Aaron and Bret Boone, Zito, and Mark Prior were there.

In 2004 USC had 15 players in the big leagues, including the Boones, Cirillo, Morgan Ensberg, Geoff Jenkins, Johnson, Bobby Kielty, Jacque Jones, Jason Lane, Eric Munson, and Zito. Mark McGwire set the all-time big league record for homers in a single season (since broken) with 70 in 1998.

While only one Trojan (Tom Seaver) is in the Baseball Hall of Fame in Cooperstown, New York, it is a safe bet that Johnson will make it. Mark McGwire's status is now questionable. Arizona State has Reggie Jackson, and eventually Barry Bonds should be their second, although his status is now in question like McGwire's.

TRIVIA

What is considered the top film school in the world?

Answers to the trivia questions are on pages 187–191.

Despite not being known for basketball, a disproportionate number of Trojans from the 1940s and '50s are considered hoops pioneers. Such stalwarts as Bill Sharman and Alex Hannum played at USC before Hall of Fame induction in Springfield. Standout Trojans include Ken Flower, Mack Calvin, Paul Westphal, Gus Williams, Cliff Robinson, Harold Miner, and Sam Clancy. Six ex-Trojans became NBA coaches, including Hannum, the coach of the

All-Time College Baseball Programs

1. USC Trojans
2. Texas Longhorns
3. Cal State Fullerton Titans
4. Arizona State Sun Devils
5. Miami Hurricanes
6. Stanford Indians/Cardinal
7. Louisiana State Tigers
8. Florida State Seminoles
9. Oklahoma State Cowboys
10. Florida Gators
11. Mississippi State Bulldogs
12. Texas A&M Aggies
13. Arkansas Razorbacks
14. Arizona Wildcats
15. Georgia Bulldogs
16. Oklahoma Sooners
17. California Golden Bears
18. Oregon State Beavers
19. Fresno State Bulldogs
20. Michigan Wolverines

1967 Philadelphia 76ers, who posted a then NBA record of 68–13 and, led by Wilt Chamberlain, won the world championship. Sharman, a star on the great Boston Celtics teams of the 1950s, coached Chamberlain and the 1972 Lakers to a 69–13 mark, breaking the Sixers' record. They won a pro sports record 33 straight games and the NBA title. Paul Westphal later was a standout coach of the Phoenix Suns.

USC also boasts (along with UCLA) the most Olympians (340), the most Olympic gold medallists (104), and if they had been a country in 1976, they would have placed third in total medals at the Montreal Games. A Trojan has medaled in every modern Olympic Games (beginning at St. Louis in 1904), including the boycotted Moscow Games of 1980.

Just as no debate exists regarding USC's status as the greatest of all college baseball programs, none even remotely exists when it comes to their track program under legendary coach Dean Cromwell. For decades, the U.S. Olympic teams (many coached by Cromwell) were seemingly the Trojans clothed in red, white, and blue.

USC's swimming and diving teams have won nine NCAA titles, the women's tennis team has won seven. Academically, USC ranks in the top 10 of all collegiate programs in the production of NCAA post-graduate scholarships. Three Trojans have earned Rhodes Scholarships.

USC and the All-Time Best Teams

Ranking the greatest of anything is subjective and opinionated. It is meant to stir debate, controversy, and argument. It is not written in stone. When ranking all-time college football teams and traditions, extra credit goes to the more modern powers. Miami's success in the 1980s is more impressive than Cal's Wonder Teams after World War I. Oklahoma's early 2000s run, while only resulting in one national championship instead of three, is, in the modern context, almost as impressive as what they accomplished in the 1950s. The game has changed. Competition, money, television, scholarship limits, NCAA rules, recruiting violations, and parity all play a part in this evaluation. To the extent that the so-called "modern era" began, trace it to 1960, which is subjective, yes, but as good an embarkation point as any. It was in the 1960s when the players starting getting bigger, the equipment became up to speed, the coaching techniques improved, and the color of the player's skin became increasingly something other than white.

Based upon history, one is increasingly impressed with USC. Overall, Notre Dame's ranking as the greatest college football program of all time has to take a back seat to their biggest rivals from the West Coast. In light of USC's new status—the dynasty that Pete Carroll built on top of their previous tradition—it is time to officially acknowledge that it is the Trojans, and no longer the Fighting Irish, who have risen above all other historic college football programs.

In 2004 USC tied the Irish for the most national championships (11), and in 2005 tied them for the most Heisman Trophy winners (both with seven; Ohio State's Troy Smith became the Buckeyes' seventh in 2006). Notre Dame still holds the lead over the Trojans in their intersectional rivalry, and trace their glory days back to when Knute Rockne invented the forward pass in time to beat favored Army in 1913. However, while Charlie Weis *appeared* to have righted Notre Dame's listing ship until their atrocious 2007 campaign, they have struggled too much in the modern decades to hold the title any longer. Call the Men of Troy the New Centurions of the Millennium; the dynasty of all dynasties!

Notre Dame was the best college team under Rockne in the decade of the 1920s and under Frank Leahy in the 1940s. They had another major "era of Ara" (Parseghian) in the 1960s and '70s, and are listed among the top two-year dynasties (1946–1947), 5-year dynasties (1943–1947, 1973–1977), and have three dynasties that are included among the 10- to 15-year period. Furthermore, they are Notre Dame, and all that that stands for: "Win one for the Gipper," the Catholic Church, "Touchdown Jesus," Ronald Reagan, *Rudy*, "subway alumni," the Four Horsemen "outlined against a blue, gray October sky," "wake up the echoes," and so on.

Notre Dame's fans are the most intense and loyal. They are the team that played in Yankee Stadium, in Soldier Field, and at the Coliseum. Many of their historic games were against 'SC. The traditions of these two teams are the best and the oldest.

For decades, the number-two team was Southern California. This was not a coincidence. No rivalry in sports (or politics or war, probably) has done so much to elevate both sides as the USC–Notre Dame tradition. It put both schools on the national map. It pits, as 'SC assistant coach Marv Goux put it, "the best of the East versus the best of the West." It matches the Catholic school with its Midwestern values against the flash 'n' dazzle of Hollywood, and it has never failed to live up to expectations.

Beginning in the 1980s, however, 'SC dropped while Notre Dame stayed at or near the top throughout the Lou Holtz era. Other contenders emerged. Miami and Florida State ascended to the top. Nebraska left opponents in the dust. Programs like Alabama and Oklahoma had, like 'SC, faltered, but regained their footing. Tennessee, Georgia, LSU, and other teams, many in the South, rose in prominence. This was a direct result of integration, and its impact has been very positive, but a school like Southern California could no longer lay claim to black athletes that were spurned by the SEC or the Southwestern Conference.

USC began to win awards and recognition for its academic excellence, and it became an article of faith that this was the trade-off; great football teams and great students are not mutually compatible. Pete Carroll proved that theory wrong.

In 2000 a top 25 listing of the Greatest College Football Programs of All-Time would have shown USC to have slipped. However, in light of their national championships and continuing favored status, Troy is now ahead of Notre Dame and in the top spot.

Long dynasties are hard to come by in college football, but 'SC has a long history of doing just that. It is for this reason, combined with the glow of being Notre Dame's biggest rival, its great inter-city tradition with UCLA, and long histories with other powerhouse schools (Michigan and Notre Dame are among the short list of schools that go back as far and are still relevant) that Southern California is not just first all-time in football but first among all athletic programs (and first by a wide margin in baseball).

The Greatest College Football Team in history is generally considered to be John McKay's 1972 Trojans. Just ask Keith Jackson, who

DID YOU KNOW . . . That while USC was already considered the leading film and dental school and among the top business schools, MBA programs, law schools, and medical schools in America, under President Steven Sample it has become one of the top overall academic institutions in the nation? USC was named "College of the Year 2000" by the Time/Princeton Review College Guide, and America's "Hot School 2001" by the Newsweek/Kaplan College Guide. "More institutions might do well to emulate USC's enlightened self-interest," read the Time/Princeton Review. "For not only has the 'hood dramatically improved, but so has the University."

"Just as East Coast students go for New York and NYU, the West Coast is gravitating to USC in Los Angeles," wrote the Newsweek/Kaplan College Guide. "USC has morphed from a jock school to a serious contender for top students."

ought to know. In addition, 'SC claims the best single-season team in the 1920s (1928), 1930s (1932), and 2000s (2004). They are considered the best team of the decade of the 1930s, 1960s, 1970s, and now the 2000s.

Further proof of USC's ability to maintain a tradition is their consistency. The top dynasty period in history was the John McKay/John Robinson era, lasting from the early 1960s until the 1980s. The Howard Jones "Thundering Herd" teams of the 1920s and '30s also rank highly.

The best back-to-back teams ever? How about USC (2003–2004), Oklahoma (1955–1956), Nebraska (1994–1995), Notre Dame (1946–1947), Army (1944–1945), Nebraska (1970–1971), and Alabama (1978–1979)?

Among the best three-year periods ever, none is better than USC's run from 2003 through 2005, followed by their teams of 1972 through 1974. Oklahoma deserves mention from 1971 through 1973 or 1973 through 1975. Nebraska fans would scream and shout if their 1993 through 1995 or 1995 through 1997 teams are not mentioned. Miami from 1987 through 1989 deserves its place. Also, Minnesota from 1934 through 1936. Among five- to six-year periods, consider three of Troy's eras (1967 through 1972, the best of anybody, followed by 1974 through 1979 and 1928 through 1932).

The best 10- to 15-year period? USC from 1967 to 1979, but that is not all. Also ranked is the period 1962 to 1972 and 1928 to 1939. Among great long-term dynasties (20 to 25 years), nobody beats Southern California from 1962 to 1981, when they won five national championships and four Heisman Trophies. Alabama might argue that they won six national titles. Two of them are bogus (1964 and 1973 were bowl losses after the polls closed), they had no Heisman winners, and nowhere near as many All-Americans or first-round draft picks. Their complaints about losing the 1966 vote are no more legit than USC saying they should have won the '78 vote outright. USC is undisputedly a football factory. The empirical evidence cannot be argued against.

Aside from Bear Bryant's great run from 1961 to 1979, Alabama fans certainly have the *right* to argue against Trojan football hegemony, and they have plenty of ammunition. They were a national power as far back as the 1920s and '30s, when Don Hutson starred there. However, they slipped (as did USC during the same years) until the Bryant era. Bryant's dominant period parallels John McKay's (and John Robinson's) and is as impressive as any ever. However, the Tide was all white until 'SC's Sam "Bam" Cunningham showed them, in Bear's own (alleged) words, "what a football player looks like" in 1970. After USC's 42–21 victory at Birmingham, *L.A. Times* sports columnist Jim Murray welcomed 'Bama "back into the Union." If everything else was equal—legit titles, Heismans, All-American selections, draft picks—the fact that USC was integrated and Alabama was not for the first 10 years of the comparable Bryant-McKay period would be enough to give Southern Cal the nod.

The Crimson Tide experienced a down period after Bear departed, regained its place with the 1992 national title, but inexplicably fell from grace for another decade after that. Their 2002 embarrassment in hiring Mike Price only to fire him for cavorting with strippers was indicative of their malaise, but in 2005 Mike Shula looked like he was ready to lead them out of the wilderness. This was apparently a bluff.

Oklahoma's teams in the 1950s dominated as thoroughly as any in history, and Bud Wilkinson is to be commended for integrating the Sooners program, but that was a long time ago. They were not a major power prior to that decade. The Chuck Fairbanks/Barry Switzer teams of the 1970s and '80s were as impressive as any that have ever taken the field (albeit pockmarked by scandal and probation), but they became downright mediocre after Brian Bosworth's departure. Bob Stoops, however, brought them right back where they were before, and then some. However, in the 2000s Oklahoma has embarrassed themselves in the glaring spotlight of bowl games.

TOP 10 (OR NEAR)

Best Two-Year Periods

1. Southern California (2003–2004)
2. Nebraska (1994–1995)
3. Oklahoma (1955–1956)
4. Notre Dame (1946–1947)
5. Army (1944–1945)
6. Alabama (1978–1979)
7. Oklahoma (1974–1975)

Best Three-Year Periods

1. Southern California (2003–2005)
2. Nebraska (1993–1995)
3. Southern California (1972–1974)
4. Miami (1987–1989)
5. California (1920–1922)
6. Southern California (1930–1932)
7. Oklahoma (1954–1956)
8. Army (1944–1946)
9. Alabama (1964–1966)
10. Minnesota (1934–1936)
11. Oklahoma (1973–1975)

Best Five– to Six–Year Periods

1. Nebraska (1993–1997)
2. Southern California (1967–1972)
3. Notre Dame (1943–1947)
4. Miami (1987–1991)
5. Southern California (2002-2007)
6. Notre Dame (1973–1977)
7. Southern California (1974–1979)
8. Alabama (1961–1966)
9. Penn State (1982–1986)
10. Southern California (1928–1932)
11. Minnesota (1936–1941)
12. Oklahoma (1971–1975)

Best 10– to 15–Year Periods

1. Southern California (1967–1981)
2. Miami (1983–1991)
3. Southern California (1962-1972)
4. Oklahoma (1950s)
5. Notre Dame (1920s)
6. Notre Dame (1940s)
7. Nebraska (1990s)
8. Penn State (1982–1991)
9. Notre Dame (1966–1977)
10. Oklahoma (1974–1985)
11. Florida State (1990s)
12. Southern California (1928-1939)
13. Alabama (1964-1979)

Best 20- to 25-Year Periods

1. Southern California (1962–1981)
2. Miami (1983–2001)
3. Notre Dame (1964–1988)
4. Alabama (1961–1979)
5. Ohio State (1954–1975)

Close but No Cigar
(honorable mention, many of which appeard to be among the greatest ever until late-season upsets ended their glory)

1. 1913 Army
2. 1938 Duke
3. 1939 Tennessee
4. 1947–1949 California
5. 1954 UCLA
6. 1965–1966 Michigan State
7. 1968–1969 Southern California
8. 1969–1975 Ohio State
9. 1969–1978 Michigan
10. 1971–1973 Oklahoma
11. 1979 Southern California
12. 1983 Nebraska
13. 1979 Ohio State
14. 2003–2004 Oklahoma
15. 2005 Southern California

A Football Coach Named "Gloomy Gus"

After a Navy commission in 1918, Elmer Henderson was brought in to put the Trojans on the map with schools like California and Washington. He quickly earned the moniker "Gloomy Gus" because he regaled the writers with tales of his team's woes.

"Pomona will mop us up," he announced prior to Troy's 6–0 win.

"Did you ever see a rottener college outfit than that one of mine?" he asked rhetorically before taking on Poly High School.

"Nope, it isn't possible," Poly's coach said tongue in cheek.

When asked about his "star" player, Charles Dean, Henderson scoffed, "Stars? Why, I haven't a man on the team who could make a first-class high school 11. Someone told me when I came here that Charles Dean was a star. I never suffered such a surprise in my life when I beheld him in action. He's a joke. I'll have to start him Saturday because my squad is limited in size. He's a good fighter, that's all I can say about him."

Dean took affront to his coach's assessment of his abilities and was seen stomping off the practice field shortly thereafter. They eventually reconciled, and Dean led the team's win over Pomona.

DID YOU KNOW . . . That a Methodist, a Catholic, and a Jew founded the University of Southern California in 1880 as a private institution near downtown Los Angeles? It was a non-denominational university, but became identified with the Methodist Church. In its early years, its sports teams were known informally as the Methodists.

DID YOU KNOW . . . That Pasadena, eager to draw business and tourism, decided that football would be a big draw? In 1902, when Stanford journeyed from the north and Michigan from the Midwest to play each other. Michigan won going away, 49–0. Eventually, USC would play in and win so many Rose Bowls that a ticket to the game would be included in student season-ticket packets. Their 49 points versus Illinois in the 2008 game equaled Michigan's 1902 output for most points scored in a Rose Bowl game.

"It was our only chance," said Henderson. "Fight, that's what did it. I knew if I could instill the spirit of fight in my team, USC would be returned the victor."

The name "Gloomy Gus" was based on a popular cartoon character of the era. There was nothing gloomy about the Trojans' performance on the football field, however. Henderson coached from 1919 to 1924. His teams twice won 10 games in a season, won the first Rose Bowl played in the new stadium that stands to this day, and compiled an overall 45–7 record.

But Henderson's tenure was a harbinger of the future, and not just in terms of his negative assessment of his teams. He was hired to beat Cal. He failed in this endeavor (0–5). Despite the greatest winning percentage in USC history (.865), he was fired because of it.

After firing "Gloomy Gus," USC tried to hire Notre Dame's Knute Rockne. When Notre Dame beat Stanford, Rockne was in a jocular mood.

"I'll have to come out and coach USC to show them how to beat the California teams," he told the writers.

This statement was seen as an overture on Rockne's part to come west and take over at USC. In a move that was *not* USC's finest hour, school officials decided to fire Henderson and negotiate with Rockne. Records are sketchy, and the official mythology has it that Rockne never seriously considered the Southern Cal offer. His great loyalty to his alma mater is part of the legend.

It was during Henderson's tenure that the two great football stadiums that mark the L.A. landscape were built. The Los Angeles Memorial Coliseum was erected in 1923. It hosted the 1932 and 1984 Olympics, the 1967 and 1973 Super Bowls, the Trojans, Rams,

Raiders, UCLA, the Dodgers, one World Series, an All-Star game, Pro Bowls, L.A. City and CIF-Southern Section championships, North-South Shrine all-star high school games, international soccer matches, major music concerts, revivals, speeches (George Patton's 1945 homecoming), and would be depicted in numerous movies and TV shows. It would spawn the neighboring L.A. Memorial Sports Arena, the home of USC basketball for 45 years; the NBA's Clippers and the ABA's Stars; and the 1960 Democratic National Convention (nominating John Kennedy), just to name a few highlights.

The Rose Bowl almost was moved to Palo Alto instead of Pasadena. When Stanford Stadium was built in the early 1920s, there was talk of moving the New Year's Day game north, but when Pasadena succeeded in building a stadium in the Arroyo Seco for $272,000, the game was settled there. In 1922 USC entered into the Pacific Coast Conference and beat Penn State on New Year's Day, 1923, in the brand new Rose Bowl Stadium in Pasadena. At $5.50, tickets were priced beyond the ability of most students to purchase them. Penn State was late—caught in traffic. A crowd of 43,000 saw USC win 14–3 on a hot day. Penn State coach Hugo Bezdek challenged Gus Henderson to a fistfight afterward.

TRIVIA

When did USC's grid tradition begin?

Answers to the trivia questions are on pages 187–191.

"Hugo Bezdek is no gentleman," Henderson said.

It was the very first college football game ever broadcast in L.A., carried by KHJ.

The Head Man

"'SC wanted to get Knute Rockne," said Ambrose Schindler, the quarterback from 1936 to 1939, "and he said, 'No, but a young man who just beat me is Howard Jones.' He beat Notre Dame 7–6, and Rockne recommended Howard Jones to the University."

"Howard Jones was to USC what Pop Warner was to Stanford, what Knute Rockne was to Notre Dame," said Art Spander, an *Oakland Tribune* columnist. "They just took the program and pushed it to the next level. He made 'SC football what it later became. The tradition was started, the Thundering Herd, what people have always expected of USC started under him. Now they always expect them to be a great football team."

"He was the toughest taskmaster I ever knew," stated Nick Pappas, who played for the "Head Man" in the 1930s.

Players who hated his guts grew to love him because he made them great. He made athletes go above and beyond themselves.

"Jones was the kind of guy who would tell you to run through a wall—and you'd ask him, how high?" said Pappas.

Descriptions of Jones—"impeccable integrity," "honesty," "dignity"—remind one of the superlatives used to describe UCLA basketball coach John Wooden in a later era. His record included four national championships, five Rose Bowl games (without a loss), and eight PCC titles, with a record of 121–36–13 (.750, an average ironically lower than Henderson's).

"His team had more straight power than deception," recalled Nate Barragar, captain of the 1929 squad. "He always believed that if the men did their individual jobs, the play should go. There was nothing fancy. We'd actually tell the other team where we were going to run the ball—and then just ran it through that spot."

In 1928 USC stepped it up a notch, growing beyond the role of Notre Dame's West Coast rival. They firmly planted themselves at the apex of the football world. Up until that season, Cal's Wonder Teams were thought to be the best squads ever assembled, but a poem written after the USC-Stanford clash told the new story:

They whip the end, they buck the backs, the line begins to yield
And the "greatest team in history" backs slowly down the field
And finally comes the whistle as a seal to Stanford's fate
And the "greatest team in history" goes staggering through the gate.

The "greatest team in history" was a fan-favorite in Los Angeles long before the Dodgers, Angels, Lakers, or UCLA. Jones began to receive fan mail from the likes of Oliver Hardy of the Laurel and Hardy comedy team, Gary Cooper, Vilma Banky, Mary Pickford, Douglas Fairbanks Sr., Harold Lloyd, Norma Talmadge, Richard Dix, Hoot Gibson, Ronald Colman, Nancy Carroll, and Reginald Denny.

"Is the quarterback's value greater today than it used to be?" asked Hardy.

"Yes," was Jones's written reply, "because the introduction of the forward pass broadened the field for the employment of strategy."

Gary Cooper was interested in what constituted a penalty and why some were more severe than others.

Vilma Banky wanted to know who the best football player ever was. Jones's surprising answer was Tom Shevlin, Yale's captain in 1905, because he was "powerful physically" with "great mental characteristics."

Braven Dyer of the *L.A. Times* spared no hype in describing how the "battling sons of Troy scaled the heights of the Coliseum" to "[turn back] the Red Horde...in the most stunning upset ever recorded in these parts" after Troy beat Pop Warner and Stanford. He stated that it was the "most powerful team in Stanford history" at a time when they were one of the top programs in the nation.

DID YOU KNOW ... That USC's Dean Cromwell is considered by many to be the greatest track coach ever? In the entire history of college athletics, men's or women's, no coach and no program has ever been as dominant as track and field at the University of Southern California under Dean Cromwell. In 40 years at the helm, he produced champions in each Olympic Games from 1912 to 1948, and eventually he would become the American Olympic coach. His teams won 12 national championships in 19 years. His legacy helped launch the Trojans to seven more national titles after he left. The 26 national championships won by Southern California track is so far and above all other competition as to render a sense that there were, for all practical purposes, rules for the Trojans and then rules for the also-rans.

Ed R. Hughes called it Warner's "Waterloo" in the *San Francisco Chronicle*.

Warner called USC the "perfect 11," and many of the 'SC players said the game was their biggest thrill, which, considering the other events of that season alone, is quite a statement.

Still, the hurdle of Notre Dame stood in the Trojans' way. The Irish were down that year, at least compared to their usual standards. Furthermore, Rockne's son was ill in South Bend, Indiana, so the coach's mind was understandably troubled.

The Irish never had a chance. With the 27–14 victory came further analysis of the American football scene. Considering the earlier victories of Stanford and Oregon State over Eastern opponents, the question was no longer whether the best football was played in the West or the Midwest. It was definitely *not* played in the East. If Notre Dame was the epitome of Midwest football, then their loss to Southern Cal seemed to cede supremacy to the West, namely to the Trojans. Alabama was the kingpin of Southern football, and to be fair it was the lack of media coverage in that section of the country that cost the region its share of glamour more than any deficiencies on the field of play.

TRIVIA

Who was USC's first All-American football player?

Answers to the trivia questions are on pages 187–191.

"Southern California all but hugged the life
Bend Irish, and made it harder than ever for the
Great Divide to forget Los Angeles," intoned the L.A.
of the sea and the heart of the desert do not mak
not debilitated into softlings in the great open spa

Perhaps there had been some talk that warm w
able surroundings, and the glamour of the movie
players in L.A. "go Hollywood," but in reality Americ
the rugged nature of Western individualism, which
itself in the settlers who had forged a
nation against obstacles made by
man and nature. The more pertinent
question may have been whether
that "individualism" would lend itself
to a team game like football. It was
obvious by now that it did not

TRIVIA

How did U
nickname

Answers to the trivia ques

disrupt from it, and that good weather not only made
playing conditions but the best year-round training, as

The Rissman rating system awarded the 1928 natio
onship to the University of Southern California based on
record and 4–0–1 PCC mark, earning them the conferen

In t
ma
bec
ver
co

19
lie
th
se
St
N
g
s

h

Gwynn Wilson and the Notre Dame Rivalry

▬e beginning, at least, it was Notre Dame who put USC on the ▬ by scheduling them, but the rivalry very quickly evened out and ▬me something that elevated both programs, very evenly, to the ▬ highest perch of college football. They are still the two leading ▬tenders for that perch to this day.

The first game, in Los Angeles, drew 74,378 fans. The 1927 and ▬9 games were played at Soldier Field in Chicago, drawing unbe-▬able throngs of 120,000 and 112,000. This is the best evidence ▬t USC held their own as a rival right from the get-go. They were ▬n as the "best of the West," which no doubt annoyed Cal and ▬nford. The games drew interest above and beyond any possible ▬tre Dame opponent, thus effectuating the scheduling of the ▬mes at the biggest stadium in America. With the eventual expan-▬n of the Coliseum, L.A. crowds would top the 100,000 mark.

In 1925 Jones's team was 11–2. A Cal-Stanford dispute still had a ▬angover effect, with the Bears left conspicuously off the schedule. ▬anford gained a measure of revenge for the slights felt at ▬enderson's hands, beating Southern Cal 13–9 before 70,000 at the ▬oliseum. Washington State, who had been a Rose Bowl representa-▬ve a decade earlier, when football in the Pacific Northwest was, in ▬act, the best in the West, was more than happy to teach the Trojans ▬hat there were still plenty of good teams on the coast. Before a ▬altry crowd of 12,000, which may have contributed to the Trojans ▬aking the Cougars lightly, Washington State prevailed 17–12.

USC beat St. Mary's 12–0 to finish the 1925 campaign 11–2. The St. Mary's contest was not a cakewalk. When Stanford had threat-ened to cancel the 1925 game, USC canceled the 1924 game—one

week before the game. They invited little St. Mary's, a Catholic school in the Bay Area, to Los Angeles. The Gaels won 14–10. This began a fairly serious rivalry between USC and St. Mary's, who played off and on for two decades, both teams giving as well as they got. The 1925 Trojans featured the "Red Bluff Terror," Morton Kaer, and the school's first-ever All-American. Brice Taylor was a man ahead of his team. He was black, part Cherokee Indian, and had only one hand!

The story of how the USC–Notre Dame rivalry began is rife with the kind of storytelling myth that permeates its history. Jones had surveyed the landscape, nationally and locally. He saw that Notre Dame was the kingpin of college football, replacing the old champ, California.

And he knew, of course, that under Henderson the Trojans could not beat the Bears, and that both Cal and Stanford, while worthy opponents, were capable of classless acts of jealousy that he wanted his team to rise above. Jones understood that weather and demographics now favored USC over Northern California teams in the recruiting wars, but he wanted that higher profile.

He yearned for Southern California to achieve prestige over and beyond the other powers and wannabes of the 1920s, whether that was Illinois, Michigan, Army, Yale, or Alabama. The challenge in achieving that, as Jones saw it, would come by overcoming two huge obstacles. The first would be to get Notre Dame not just to schedule USC, but to schedule a series of games. The second would be to actually *beat* the Irish.

TRIVIA

Who is the largest private employer in the city of Los Angeles?

Answers to the trivia questions are on pages 187–191.

The nature of this way of thinking, which has always been a hallmark of USC's competitive nature, was embodied years later by USC coach and athletic director Jess Hill.

"There was a period when we were having trouble beating them, and people would ask me, 'Why do we schedule Notre Dame?'" he said. "I would answer, 'How are we going to beat one of the finest institutions in the country if you don't schedule them?'"

That the forward pass was, if not "invented," then popularized by Notre Dame end Knute Rockne and quarterback Gus Dorais in a 1913 upset of mighty Army? This put Notre Dame on the map. Over time their fortunes became intimately intertwined with that of the USC Trojans.

The beauty of the USC–Notre Dame rivalry is that there were periods when the shoe was on the other foot (such as has been the case for the last few years), and Notre Dame would answer the query exactly as Hill did.

Getting Notre Dame to agree to play his team was the task that Jones gave to USC student manager Gwynn Wilson in November 1925. Notre Dame was in freezing cold Lincoln, Nebraska, for a season-ending game with the Cornhuskers. Wilson and his young wife took the Sunset Limited to Lincoln to ask Rockne for the game.

Wilson could not get to the busy Rockne at the stadium or anywhere in Lincoln. Notre Dame's loss had Rockne in a less-than-jovial mood, anyway. He boarded the train Notre Dame was taking back to Chicago. With Rockne captive in the train and able to relax with the game now over, Wilson approached him, got the audience, and made his pitch.

Rockne was respectful and told Wilson the Trojans had gotten a great coach in Jones, but that the administration at Notre Dame was already giving him a hard time about putting the team on the road so much. Notre Dame Stadium was not yet built, and the audience demand to see them play required that they travel. Wilson may have gotten Rockne to agree had he painted a vivid picture of the enormous crowds that would see the teams play at the new Coliseum and at Soldier Field, but Wilson was unable to make the sale. He returned to his compartment, wondering how he would explain his failure to Jones.

Enter Mrs. Marion Wilson and Mrs. Bonnie Rockne. On a train filled with football players, football coaches, football writers, and football fans, they found in one another kindred spirits. Gwynn found his wife engaged in excited conversation with the coach's wife and was delighted at what they were talking about: shopping.

Yes, shopping, for it was shopping that started the USC–Notre Dame game. Mrs. Rockne liked to shop. She liked to travel. She liked to travel to warm weather places. She had just spent the day freezing her you-know-what off in a town that had no shopping! Mrs. Wilson, bless her, painted a colorful picture of Rodeo Drive, the emerging boutique boulevard of Beverly Hills where the nouveau riche and famous of Hollywood were buying all those fabulous fashions that she saw in the movie magazines. Mrs. Rockne had already gotten a taste of the Hollywood lifestyle when she had accompanied Rock to L.A. for a coaching clinic.

If Notre Dame would travel to Los Angeles and play the Trojans, Mrs. Wilson explained, Mrs. Rockne would have the chance to spend a few days in sunny California shopping on Rodeo Drive.

At some point, Rockne returned to see his wife. Her powers of persuasion were certainly better than Gwynn's. She talked Rockne into scheduling the game.

Wilson had achieved his goal after all. Of course, this story has been hyped in the traditional USC–Notre Dame manner. Rockne certainly recalled the promise of a game with Jones that the two had made after Iowa beat him in 1921. No doubt Rockne gave some further, serious thought to the gate receipts at the Coliseum and Soldier Field. He certainly thought about the recruiting value of playing such a national game. It would be a huge publicity boost. This was Jones's feeling, that the game would allow the Trojans to rise above all Western teams in the recruiting battles, compete with the Irish for other players across America, and use the PR value to boost the program and the school, with all the attendant financial value inherent therein. If indeed these were the hoped-for expectations of Rockne and Jones, their expectations came true in wildly successful fashion.

TRIVIA

USC has won 26 NCAA track titles. By comparison, how many national championships do other collegiate sports dynasties have?

Answers to the trivia questions are on pages 187–191.

"He told me that he couldn't meet USC because Notre Dame was traveling too much," Wilson once recalled. "I thought the whole thing was off, but as Rock and I talked, Marion was with Mrs. Rockne, Bonnie, in her compartment. Marion told Bonnie how nice Southern California was and how hospitable the people were.

"Well, when Rock went back to the compartment, Bonnie talked him into the game. But if it hadn't been for Mrs. Wilson talking to Mrs. Rockne, there wouldn't have been a series."

Despite the serendipitous nature of the Gwynn Wilson story, it was later revealed that Rockne wanted a game in a big cosmopolitan city on the West Coast in order to bookend their games in New York. He was also frustrated at anti-Catholic bigotry directed at Notre Dame in certain rural settings during a period of evangelical revival in the 1920s, and wanted to attract more urban Italian, Irish, and Polish Catholics. It has even been suggested that the game was a favor offered not by Rockne to Jones, but vice versa, since it was Rock who had recommended Jones to USC. Either way, to quote Hollywood actor Vince Vaughn, it's "worked out pretty well for everybody."

The Duke

Before he was an acting legend, John "Duke" Wayne was a USC student named Marion Morrison. He played football for Howard Jones. Wayne's teammate at USC was Ward Bond, who would go on to have a long film career.

Morrison met famed director John Ford, who made him a prop man and liked his rugged film presence enough to cast him in 1928's *Hangman's House*. Ford later made a football movie about the Naval Academy, *Salute*, and wanted USC players for it. Aside from *Salute*, extravagant Hollywood productions of the era often featured Trojan players in the roles of Roman Legionnaires, Napoleon's Grande Armée, or Biblical flocks. This was prior to the NCAA, and while there was grousing about "professionalism," there never were repercussions.

"It" girl Clara Bow invited USC football players to her parties. This was the kind of extracurricular activity that schools such as Iowa or Duke, where Jones had toiled previously, could not offer. Wild rumors about Clara and the Trojans abounded, but they were false.

The Duke spoke to the Trojans before the 1966 USC-Texas game. "The kids are all assembled in the locker room at 10:00 in the morning, and in walks Wayne," recalled Nick Pappas. "Damn, he was fantastic. He walks in with this white 20,000-gallon cowboy hat and black suit—he looked just beautiful."

USC won 10–6.

USC play-by-play announcer Mike Walden recalled the 1966 Texas game and Wayne's unique role in the events of that weekend.

"My first game in 1966 was on the road versus Texas," said Walden. "There'd be a press gathering in Austin, what they called 'smokers' down there, where everybody got together. Well, Wayne was down there making *War Wagon* in nearby Mexico, and he shows up with Bruce Cabot.

TRIVIA

In the three Olympics held in the 1960s, how many medals did the Trojans win?

Answers to the trivia questions are on pages 187–191.

"'I'm gonna have some whiskey,' Wayne says to the bartender, who pours it, and Wayne just looks at it, shoved it back, and said, '*I said WHISKEY!*'

"Texas had a quarterback they called 'Super Bill' Bradley who was supposed to be outstanding, but 'SC just controlled the ball and won 10–6. Afterwards, [assistant coach Marv] Goux came in and said wasn't it great, we didn't get anybody 'chipped off.' Well, Wayne and Cabot were somewhere, and someone got in an argument the next morning and their makeup artist was dead of a heart attack. It was confusing, I don't know for sure what all happened. Wayne and all of 'em were out drinking all night and came in at 7:00 in the morning, maybe it was too much for this guy, but this makeup artist died.

"'Well,' Cabot said, '*We* got somebody 'chipped off.'"

Wayne was a staunch Republican and made *The Green Berets.* Wayne's conservatism earned him plenty of critics, but even in 1969, when he won the Oscar for *True Grit*, Hollywood opened its hearts to him without reservation. Others found him to be a celluloid hero who had not served in wars while real war heroes like Ted Williams were thought to be "the real John Wayne."

Jeff Prugh, the *L.A. Times* beat writer for USC football in the 1960s and '70s, recalls a story from that 1966 weekend in Austin.

"Well, there was this one L.A. sportswriter whose name shall remain anonymous," said Prugh. "Everyone is gathered at the bar, and John Wayne's holding court. This old writer is off in the corner getting drunker and drunker. He's liberal, and Wayne's an outspoken conservative Republican. Finally, this old writer has had enough, and he approaches Wayne, interrupts him in mid-sentence with all Wayne's pals staring at him.

"'So,' the old drunk writer says, 'they tell me, uh...they call ya...*The Duke!*'

"'Yeah, what of it?' says Wayne.

"This writer just gathers himself," continued Prugh.

"'Waaal...Duke...You ain't [expletive deleted]!'

"Well, it was almost a full brawl right then and there, but his pals held Wayne back," said Prugh.

Craig Fertig was a star quarterback at USC and a graduate assistant in 1966.

"One time, the players wanted to go see *Easy Rider*," Fertig recalled. "Duke Wayne says, 'Don't let the kids see that crap!' So he arranged for 'em to see *War Wagon* instead.

"I'm low man on the totem pole in '66, so I gotta chaperone the team and do bed checks. Now McKay's hosting a party for Wayne."

(This contrasts with Nick Pappas's assertion that Wayne and McKay had not met prior to the morning of the next day's game, but considering that alcohol, old alums, and memories were involved, the discrepancy is a minor one.)

With alumni that include Hollywood legends like John Wayne, George Lucas, and Ron Howard, to leading American statesmen, to many of NASA's early astronauts, the University of Southern California has established itself as one of the great institutions in the world.

"I finally put the kids to bed, so I make it up to this party, see," continued Fertig. "I see John Wayne and introduce myself to him, and he's like, 'Oh, I saw you beat Notre Dame,' and he's just like my best friend.

"Well, he has Bruce Cabot with him, and this makeup artist, too. This makeup artist's mixing drinks—vodka one time, Bourbon, scotch, right? He's gettin' hammered.

"The next day, I'm assigned to Duke Wayne, 'cause he's gonna speak to the team. Wayne's mad as hell 'cause his make-up guy's not there.

"'Son of a bitch's never around when you need 'im,' he says. It turns out the man's died during the night, maybe 'cause he mixed drinks and it was too much for his heart. Anyway, I gotta get Duke ready, the job this dead makeup guy usually does."

Apparently, Wayne had not yet learned of the makeup artist's demise.

"'Whadda I wear?' asks Duke. I tell him, 'Everybody knows you as a cowboy, so dress like that.' Ten-gallon hat, cowboy boots, brass belt buckle; I got him lookin' good.

"We're scared shitless, Texas is number one in the country. So at the stadium he fires up our team. Then he's introduced to the crowd. He comes out and he's in this cart with my dad."

TRIVIA

How many consecutive national championships did USC's baseball team win at the height of their success?

Answers to the trivia questions are on pages 187–191.

Fertig's father, Chief Henry Fertig, was the longtime head of the Huntington Park, California, police department in L.A. County, and a tremendous USC booster.

"He's being driven around the stadium in this cart, and the whole time my dad's pouring whiskey into a cup and Duke's drinkin' out of it," continued Fertig. "Now, the Texas fans, they see the Duke, and he's wearin' this cowboy hat, and most of 'em don't know he's a USC football player. Duke's givin' 'em the hook 'em horns sign with his fingers, and the Longhorn fans are cheering.

"'Duke's a Texas fan,' they're sayin'.

"All the time, Duke's sayin' to my old man, '[Expletive deleted] the 'horns.'"

Jim Connor was a prep All-American baseball player being recruited by USC, Stanford, and other major colleges in 1977. He was leaning toward Stanford, where his brother played football, until his recruiting trip to USC.

"It was the weekend of the USC alumni and celebrity softball game," Connor recalled. "I've got Walter Matthau on one side of me and John Wayne on the other telling me I've gotta be a Trojan. Who could resist that?"

Connor led the 1979 Trojans in hitting (.333).

DID YOU KNOW . . . That *Collegiate Baseball* magazine chose USC baseball coach Rod Dedeaux as its College Baseball Coach of the 20th century, and the Trojans as College Baseball Program of the 20th century? USC also was named Collegiate Athletic Program of the 20th century.

Johnny Baker and the Comeback at South Bend

In 1931 all the previous highlights of USC football paled in comparison with the spectacular, dramatic events of that season. It is possible that the game played between 'SC and Notre Dame that year is, to this day, the most significant in school history.

Gus Shaver, Garrett Arbelbide, Johnny Baker, Erny Pinckert, Stan Williamson, Ernie Smith, and Robert Hall, all Trojan legends, made up that team's incredible roster. A first-year player, Aaron Rosenberg, would make All-American.

USC had won six straight games, five by shutout, but by November 21 the Monster lay in wait. The Siegfried Line. The Atlantic Wall. Hannibal staring at the Alps.

"Notre Dame is so good that [new coach] Hunk Anderson could lick any team he has played, Northwestern excepted, with his second string," USC scout Aubrey Devine told the reporters. "It is impossible to set a fool-proof defense for the Irish because they are such a versatile squad. Just when you think you have them stopped, they break out in another direction."

Notre Dame had beaten USC four out of the first five times they had met. Jones amped up his practice sessions and did it in secret. Notre Dame was indeed the "greatest American football team of the generation" under Rockne, but USC was right on its tail.

Jones bawled out Johnny Baker during a practice session in Tucson, causing Baker to come within a "whisker" of quitting the team right then and there and heading back to Los Angeles.

The Irish were riding a 26-game unbeaten streak with the imprimatur of invincibility. A crowd of 55,000 (a capacity audience, with 50,731 considered paid attendance) let USC know what they were in for from the moment they took the field. The Trojans were intimidated by the surroundings. The Irish had them off-balance early, and by the fourth quarter led 14–0.

"The score looked as big as the population of China," wrote *Los Angeles Times* sportswriter Braven Dyer. "In fact, it looked a darn sight larger than that, if possible, because of the consummate ease with which the Irish scored those touchdowns."

USC got it to the 1, where Gus Shaver bulled in. At that point, a tie seemed the best they could hope for, but when Baker missed the extra point, a 14–6 deficit in the fourth still looked insurmountable.

But USC held Notre Dame, got the ball back, went to the air, and when the Irish were called for pass interference (a brave call from an official in South Bend), they had a first-and-10 on the Irish 24. Shaver and Orv Mohler, fighting for every yard, pushed it to the 9. Mohler lateralled to Shaver, and he went around the left end to score. Baker made the conversion, and at 14–13 the crowd was silenced.

USC later had the ball on its own 27 with time left for one dramatic drive. Two plays failed, but Shaver made a daring pass after being forced to retreat from Notre Dame tacklers, spotting and hitting Ray Sparling with a diving grab for a first down at the Notre Dame 40 (Dwayne Jarrett, anyone?). This gave life to the Trojans and created a sense of foreboding in the Irish rooters, who by this time were counting on Baker's inconsistency if he lined up for a field goal.

Bob Hall caught a pass and got the ball down to the 18. A penalty moved it to the 13, and Sparling ran into the middle, putting the team into good field-goal position while the clock wound down. Some confusion reigned when Jones sent Homer Griffith into the fray with instructions to go for the kick, but Mohler waved him back.

"Cold sweat broke out on [Jones's] brow, and his assistant coach groaned in anguish," read one report.

DID YOU KNOW . . . That USC miler Lou Zamperini was a fighter pilot during World War II who was shot down and survived for weeks in the South Pacific before being rescued?

DID YOU KNOW... That USC has one of the most substantial foreign enrollments of any college in America? Because so many USC students hail from the Pacific Rim, the Middle East, Africa, and other locales, it proudly claims the largest non-white population in U.S. higher education. Countless foreign dignitaries—political figures, statesmen, business leaders—learned to love California and America at USC. In turn they have helped foster this nation's international friendships with its global partners.

(The "confusion" near the goal line in '31 was an eerie precursor to what happened in 2005 when Pete Carroll motioned to spike the ball before Matt Leinart snuck it in.)

But Mohler did call for a field goal. The team caught Notre Dame off guard and lined up for the kick, but it was Baker, he of the missed conversion who had come within a "whisker" of quitting in Tucson, who stood at the ready.

Baker was straight and true from 33 yards out. USC won 16–14 and celebrated as if it were Armistice Day in 1918.

"It has been seven years since any team has been able to manhandle the Irish as Southern California did," wrote Tom Thorpe of the *New York Evening Journal*.

Dyer seemingly lost much of his "journalistic integrity," morphing from colorful sentimentalist to wordy fan in his game story.

"Noah Webster's diction book does not contain enough adjectives to describe the way the Trojans refused to be licked," he wrote. "It did not seem humanly possible for them to win, but USC achieved the greatest athletic triumph in Southern California history.

"Yours truly has run out of paper, his typewriter has broken down completely, and it's getting late..."

In addition, the game was broadcast nationally by Ted Husing on radio. Millions of Americans could recall for years afterward being huddled around their radios, listening to the wild descriptions of this event.

"I was just a child growing up in California," recalled Donald E. Travers. "The Catholic family who lived below us had a radio, and they let me listen to the game. They were so wildly for Notre Dame, and so snide in putting down USC, as if God favored the Irish, that I just chose sides and rooted for 'SC. When 'SC came back to win, I hollered to spite those people and became a Trojan fan on the spot."

USC alumni actually crashed into the locker room to congratulate Baker—in the shower! Trojan fans danced with the naked, dripping Baker.

Jones was beside himself, disheveled, and totally beyond his normal reserved persona. He just went about shaking hands and declared that he was too "flabbergasted" to be eloquent.

"But I'll tell you that it was the greatest team in the world," he stated of his club.

"I never saw anything like it in my life," said future College Football Hall of Famer Ernie Smith. The team all wore bowlers, a style of the day, which were purchased for them in Chicago. Dressed in their best finery with the bowlers, the team was loaded into waiting cars upon arrival in Los Angeles, two per car, for a ride down Fifth Street to Main, then on to city hall.

"There seemed to be a half-million people lining the streets," said Smith. "When we left city hall and started down toward the school, ticker tape came flying out at us. We rode down Spring Street, I remember, and people had torn up telephone books, and they were throwing all this paper out of windows. It was a real thrill—it was unbelievable. For a football team to get this type of reception, I mean it was *really* something.

"It was the wildest sports demonstration that the city of Los Angeles ever had. Three hundred thousand? I don't know, there were at least 200,000 in the line to see the Trojans riding in their cars. Everyone got a helluva cheer."

The *Examiner* went on to say: "A reception never before equaled for athletic stars turned downtown Los Angeles into a half holiday as the triumphant Trojans rode through the city at the head of a three-mile parade beneath a barrage of confetti and flowers."

Mayor John C. Porter presided over a city hall welcome with 40,000 filling the area in front of the building, made famous in the

TRIVIA

USC has had an athlete in every modern Olympic Games. From 1912 to 1948, how many Trojan track stars won medals?

Answers to the trivia questions are on pages 187–191.

1950s TV police series, *Dragnet.* Bishop John J. Cantwell of the Roman Catholic diocese of L.A. and San Diego certainly seemed to favor the locals over Notre Dame despite the religious conflict.

A movie camera had captured the game, and it was replayed as a full-length feature in L.A. by MGM for a long while, with Dyer providing narration.

It played at Loew's State Theater, the top downtown movie house at the time. It began as the first of a double-bill, but was so popular it ran over and over, breaking all the house records at Loew's.

USC went on to play Tulane in the Rose Bowl. The Green Wave was a very tough challenge, very well coached, and the best team in their region at 11–0. Once the game began, Pinckert took charge, sweeping through Tulane to score from 28 and 23 yards out. USC led by 21–0. Tulane rallied, but it was too little, too late.

"Southern California had more power than any team I ever saw," said coach Bernie Bierman after the 21–12 defeat before 84,000.

"These players accomplished more throughout the season than any team I ever coached," stated Jones. USC was an undisputed national champion, and the new Knute Rockne Trophy was awarded to the "Head Man" and his team.

The Thundering Herd

Greatness also followed the Trojan players in the years after the 1931 season. Ernie Smith went from All-American to All-Pro and then the College Football Hall of Fame. Without his USC teammates, however, "I never would have achieved what I did," he said.

He and Aaron Rosenberg were the great off-tackle blocking combination that fueled the Thundering Herd. Smith also had the utmost respect for Jones.

"He was called the 'Head Man' and he was that in all respects," said Smith.

In 1932 a movie was made called *The Spirit of Notre Dame*. It was filmed at Loyola College in Los Angeles, and the football sequences were shot using Trojan and Loyola players (Smith among them).

In 1970 Smith was inducted into the College Football Hall of Fame along with the great Notre Dame coach Frank Leahy. His work with the Tournament of Roses Committee led to the foundation memorializing Howard Jones. Out of that grew sholarships for deserving USC students, leading to a number of football players going on to dental and law schools.

"There's a tendency to shove the greats of the past into the past," said Smith.

Nineteen thirty-two was the height of the Depression, and Los Angeles was hit as hard as most American cities. However, when it came to the world of sports, and especially college football, L.A. was "fat city." Dean Cromwell's magnificent track program was at full throttle, making the Olympic Games, held at the Coliseum, resemble a USC home meet of sorts. A Trojan had earned a gold medal in every Olympics since 1904 at St. Louis. The great Fred Kelly had taken gold

DID YOU KNOW . . . That a tradition at USC in Ernie Smith's day was the "haircut"? A player would take to the barber's chair. "Barber" Smith gave him the works: a shave, hot towel, but really a full body massage with extremely rough use of the hands, leaving black-and-blue marks on the poor guy. One day Smith gave the "haircut" and a teammate rose and pulled the towel off the "victim's" face.

It was Howard Jones, who had been duped into thinking he was getting a real haircut.

in the 110-meter high hurdles at Stockholm in 1912. Charles Paddock, the "fastest man alive," had competed in the famous *Chariots of Fire* Paris Games of 1924, where he came up empty after having earned gold in the 100 meters and four-by-100-meter relays of 1920. Frank Wykoff had earned gold in the 1928 four-by-100-meter relays, and Buster Crabbe had won a bronze in swimming.

The L.A. Games were a Trojan extravaganza, with 'SC trackmen taking five golds. The great Frank Wykoff took two of those, and Crabbe went for the gold and got one in the 400-meter freestyle swimming event.

Fresh off the glory of the Olympics, which by virtue of their being held at the Coliseum turned the campus into the Olympic Village, showing off the school, the city, and the greatness of its athletes as well, defending national champ USC and Los Angeles itself was flush with success as the 1932 football season got underway.

The participants and fans in L.A. simply had decided not to participate in the Depression. USC became not just a great football school, but a world-famous institution, in large part because it was showcased at the Games with Hollywood as its backdrop.

The 1931 team, number one and bathed in glory after beating the Irish and winning the Rose Bowl, were the epitome of college grid excellence. The 1932 team was even better, if that can be believed.

A new superstar, Aaron Rosenberg, emerged—an All-American defensive guard who powered one of the greatest defensive juggernauts of all time. Eight opponents were shut out (after six had gotten goose eggs in 1931). In 1938 Duke would be unbeaten, untied, and unscored upon in the regular season. So, too, would Tennessee the following year. Both those teams were beaten and scored on by USC in the Rose Bowl. In light of that, the '32 Trojans must rank as one of the truly great defensive teams ever.

"Aaron Rosenberg is still considered Troy's mightiest guard—on defense he stopped everything that came his way and charged viciously on offense," was one appraisal of the era.

Smith was described as "headline material," a "hammer-'em-down 200-pounder."

"I give credit to Rosenberg for playing a big part in the success of the team's defense against Notre Dame and Stanford in 1931 and 1932," Coach Jones said. Of the fullbacks he was assigned to tackle, he "cracked him and messed him up."

"The 1932 team was the strongest defensive team that USC ever had," stated former USC publicist Al Wesson. "There were only two touchdowns scored on us all season—and they were both by passes. No one could move, [much] less score on the ground against us. Smith was one of the greatest tackles we ever had. Rosenberg was a smart, fine athlete. You couldn't buy a yard against this team. I'd say without qualification that the offense of the 1931 team and the defense of the 1932 team were the best produced by Jones."

Captain Tay Brown was an All-American tackle. Left end Ray Sparling made huge plays in crucial situations. New recruits of equal strength, an indication of Jones's enormous recruiting ability, replaced the players from the 1931 champs who had graduated. There is little doubt that USC had gotten to the point where they enjoyed a huge advantage in attracting players to their school for reasons that went well over and beyond football. It was also obvious that the modest but steady success of UCLA was not preventing the great stars from wanting to be Trojans.

"If any of these players of prominence show signs of lagging," wrote one football magazine, "Jones will have somebody else in there in a hurry."

Jones knew that team competition was a very good thing that pushed everybody. "Players get one or two chances to make good, and if they fail it is a long time before they land on the first string again," the magazine continued. Shaver was thought to be the player most likely to be missed, and the backfield might "lack cohesion" early.

That in 1971 USC fielded the best basketball team in the school's history? Led by Paul Westphal, they only lost two games—both to national champion UCLA—and were number two in the nation.

A new superstar emerged in the USC backfield. Cotton Warburton quickly became a Trojan legend. He was only 140 pounds, but the sophomore from San Diego was a scatback, a term that applied to a number of great runners of the decade. Ted Williams, the great baseball star who also grew up in San Diego, had seen Warburton as a high schooler, would follow his career at USC, and later in his life counted Cotton as one of his all-time favorite athletes.

Warburton scored a touchdown in a 9–6 win over Washington and scored in the 13–0 defeat of Notre Dame. He scored twice in a 35–0 pasting of Pitt in the Rose Bowl.

"I was responsible for the one and only blemish on our undefeated, untied, and almost unscored on record," Warburton did admit. He slipped in the Cal game and let the Bears score. Against Stanford, Warburton knocked down multiple Stanford passes.

"The USC defensive power was absolutely astounding; their ability to out-dazzle Mr. [Pop] Warner's razzle-dazzle was uncanny," wrote Mark Kelly of the *Los Angeles Examiner*.

USC opened the year with five straight shutouts before Warburton slipped and Cal broke the string in 'SC's 27–7 victory. Cal was said to be desperate to win, or at least show, against the Trojans, so perplexed were they by their loss of football prestige over a decade against the team that they wanted to beat more than any. Stanford of course is their biggest rival, but USC is the top of the mountain. Perhaps they took some solace in that they ended USC's scoreless record, but the loss was hardly a "show." USC no longer even looked at the Bears as anything more important than the rest of the schedule. Oregon and Washington fell, and Notre Dame came into town.

Warburton returned a punt 39 yards to set up a touchdown pass, and USC recovered an Irish fumble to create another score. The game was not the dramatic extravaganza of 1931, but the Trojans faithful of 93,924 were happy to observe a good old-fashioned whuppin'.

The Pacific Coast Conference champions returned to Pasadena, where Pittsburgh came in hoping for some measure of respect after their 47–14 loss three years earlier. They should have stayed in the Steel City for the holidays.

East Coast independent Colgate was left home. The papers remarked that they were "unbeaten, untied, unscored on, and uninvited."

Sophomore quarterback Homer Griffith out of Fairfax High had mostly handed off to Warburton, but toward season's end he came into his own against Notre Dame and Pitt. He hit Ford Palmer for a 50-yard first-quarter touchdown in front of 78,874. Warburton starred on both sides of the ball. He scored twice late.

Pitt went home with their tails between their legs, 35–0. USC was the back-to-back national champion, and at that point, if a poll were taken to determine the greatest program of the century up to this season, it might very well have been a tie between USC and Notre Dame, with a slight edge to 'SC.

Four years later, Pitt returned to Pasadena to play Washington. Coach Jock Sutherland ordered the bus to stop on the hill overlooking the Arroyo Seco and announced, "There it is. There's the place two Pittsburgh teams were beaten by a total of 68 points."

DID YOU KNOW . . . That Minnesota pitcher Dave Winfield, a future Hall of Fame outfielder with San Diego and the Yankees, had struck out 15 Trojans and was leading 7–0 late in a 1973 College World Series game? USC rallied to win it 8–7 en route to a fourth straight NCAA title.

Nave-to-Krueger

Knute Rockne and Gus Dorais kind of invented the forward pass in 1913. One could throw the ball, of course, but in a football game it was not a very good idea. Even after they used the new technique to beat Army in 1913, the pass was a bit exotic. The traditional quarterback was not instituted yet. Various backs were used as all-purpose players who could run, maybe catch, sometimes throw.

The fat football, which was difficult to throw, was slimmed down, and in the 1930s the quarterback position began to evolve into its modern incarnation. Coaches like Howard Jones disdained the pass to some extent because they had huge blockers who could lead fast running backs. Why risk going to the air? As Woody Hayes would later say, "Three things can happen, and two of 'em are bad."

But the game was developing. The Trojans could not afford to be left behind. First Stanford's Vow Boys sapped all their previous arrogance away. Then in 1937 the Vic Bottari–led California team, which beat them 20–6 up at Strawberry Canyon rolled all the way to a 13–0 Rose Bowl win over Alabama and the national championship.

So in 1938 Jones would let his quarterback go to the air. By the end of the season, it would be a pass that earned USC not just a Rose Bowl win, but eternal glory for the passer and the receiver.

Doyle Nave became a national hero for winning the Rose Bowl game against Duke. He was named honorary Mayor of Gordo, Alabama. Women wrote love letters from many states. Sick children wanted autographs. An organization of deaf people tried to adopt him as hard of hearing even though he was not.

Nave's touchdown pass rivaled Johnny Baker's field goal. Years later, a magazine poll determined that the Rose Bowl game he won was the most thrilling of all holiday bowls—ever.

"I was nervous when I went in," Nave confessed. Oh, yes, he was not a starter. He had played all of 35 minutes in the regular season. He was a last-gasp hope against a team that stamped out all hope.

Grenville Lansdell, Mickey Anderson, and Ollie Day had tried their hand as USC's quarterback on January 2, 1939. Their opponents: the Duke Blue Devils. The 1938 record: unbeaten, untied, and *unscored on.* Unlike Colgate a few years earlier, the Blue Devils were not uninvited. The Associated Press had begun their poll in 1936. USC, at the top of college football's mountain, had not been ranked in the first two years of the poll. Bernie Bierman, now at Minnesota, had led the Golden Gophers to the pinnacle in 1936, followed by Jock Sutherland's Pitt Panthers in '37 (who won the AP version, Cal was number one in alternate rankings). In 1938 Duke looked to be a shoo-in. Number one.

DID YOU KNOW . . . That Southern Cal Chancellor Dr. Norman Topping was quarantined in a hospital with Rocky Mountain Spotted Fever, running a 105-degree temperature, during the 1939 USC-Duke Rose Bowl game?

"I was dying, they had given up on me," he recalled. "No visitors, not even my wife."

Barely aware of his surroundings, he had the presence of mind to request a radio.

"They said it was impossible," he said. "I insisted, demanding that they grant my last request." When Nave hit Krueger, "Something remarkable happened. A miracle. It did more for me than any medicine. My temperature immediately started going down."

Dr. Topping did indeed recover to collect on a $50 bet. Some would say his recovery was just thanks to good modern medicine. Dr. Topping and others think something else was at work.

When the Trojans upended them 7–3 on January 2, 1938, it knocked them off-kilter. Davey O'Brien and Texas Christian would win it, followed by Bob Neyland and Tennessee. USC was back in the hunt, finishing seventh on the strength of an 8–2 campaign. They would knock a Southern school out of a "sure" national title two years in a row. In so doing, they would return Howard Jones to the heights of glory.

Duke featured Eric "the Red" Tipton, a terrific punter who constantly kept opponents pinned deep in their own territory, from whence they never got out. In fact, so good was Tipton, he sometimes punted prior to fourth down because the Duke defense was more likely to make breaks deep in the other team's territory than they were to sustain long drives.

In the Rose Bowl, both teams held the other to zero until Tony Ruffa's 23-yard field goal made it 3–0 Duke in the fourth quarter. The previous quarterbacks were ineffective. Nave was known as a good passer, but lacked experience, knowledge of the first-team offense, and technical ball-handling ability. What he did not lack was heart.

Duke fumbled in their own territory, but USC's field goal for a tie missed on an official's close call. It gave them some hope, though.

When they got the ball back, they made it to the Duke 34 with two minutes remaining. At this point, Jones made a decision that was either a gamble or a calculated risk, depending on the perspective. He could have tried to stay conservative and play for a game-tying field goal. However, two things dissuaded the Head Man from this. First, he was the kind of coach who played to win, not to tie. He had played to ties in the past, with Cal and Stanford. In 1936 the 7–7 deadlock with UCLA was a moral defeat for Troy and a victory for the upstart Bruins.

Furthermore, USC's kicking game was not strong. The kick could miss. Unlike the 1931 Notre Dame game, a kick was not a winner. So, Doyle Nave's name was called.

"Jones gave me a few minutes to warm up," Nave stated, "and I was nervous, I'll tell you." The sound of 89,452 voices filled the air.

Because Nave was not first string, the receiver he was most comfortable with didn't start either. He schemed to pass one to "Antelope" Al Krueger, in the game to replace the ineffective first string and because he was Nave's partner.

"I completed the first pass and made 12 yards on a button hook," recalled Nave. He followed that up with a "27," a flair in which Krueger went down, pivoted, then broke to the outside. The catch went for a first down.

In 1988 announcer Tom Kelly narrated *Trojan Video Gold: 100 Years of USC Football 1888–1988*. Nave and Krueger were interviewed together. Nave claimed every ball was "right on the numbers" while Krueger rolled his eyes behind his back, indicating spectacular dives. In truth, the passes were not perfect, and Krueger indeed made excellent grabs, albeit not totally sprawled out. It was a moment of great humor and camaraderie.

"Was I havin' a good time?" Krueger asked rhetorically. "Why, of course. I was goin' to 'SC!'"

With the ball on the far left side of the field in those pre-hashmark days, Nave needed to devise a way to get Krueger some maneuver room. Nave worked a play toward the center of the field, but his pass was picked up on and Krueger dropped for a loss after snaring it.

On second-and-12, Nave told Krueger to go for the end zone; there was little time left for anything but heroics. On a "27 down-and-out" Krueger got away from Eric Tipton while Nave faded deep into the pocket. According to Nave, he unloaded the ball when

DID YOU KNOW . . . That two Trojan All-American pitchers faced adversity in different ways? Bruce Gardner, the 1960 College Player of the Year, injured himself and eventually committed suicide on the Dedeaux Field mound in 1974 (this was a taboo subject around Dedeaux). Bill Bordley was the star of the 1978 College World Series champs, at the time considered the best collegiate team ever. He became Chelsea Clinton's Secret Service protection after a rotator cuff injury curtailed his career.

DID YOU KNOW . . . That America's 41ˢᵗ President, George H.W. Bush, was captain of the Yale baseball team that lost the 1948 College World Series championship to USC?

Krueger was on the "seven or eight," which had to be an exaggeration. Nevertheless, the ball was thrown for the back of the end zone. With 40 seconds left, Krueger clutched the pigskin to his chest and "we went berserk," said Nave.

1939: Jones's Last National Champions

In 1939 USC suffered a scare in barely beating Washington 9–7 at home, setting up a huge showdown with UCLA before 103,303 fans. The Bruins had built themselves into a major football power by fully integrating their program. Even though the Trojans had starred Brice Taylor in the 1920s, they had not kept up with their crosstown rival's social progress. It cost them athletically. UCLA had the likes of Kenny Washington and future baseball great Jackie Robinson in the late 1930s. Largely through their heroics, UCLA had created parity with USC. In no prior year was this more apparent than in 1939. On December 9, Washington and Robinson led the Bruins into the Coliseum.

"I really was worried," stated Doyle Nave, now the starting quarterback (who also played safety). "I was trying to figure what I'd do if they tried a pass to Woody Strode, the big end [later the black gladiator who dies so Kirk Douglas can live in *Spartacus*]. He was the man I was assigned to cover. Woody stands about 6'5", you know, and I'm under 6'. I couldn't figure any way I could stop him from catching a high pass if they threw to him. Well, I was lucky. They didn't throw at him at all. I sure breathed a sigh of relief when it was over."

Indeed, so did the entire Trojan team. They were lucky to come out of it with a 0–0 tie. UCLA totally blundered the game by not going for a field goal with the ball on the USC 5 with 10 seconds left. Instead, quarterback Kenny Washington passed to Bob MacPherson in the end zone, but Bobby Robertson managed to knock it down. It cost UCLA a $120,000 invite to their first Rose Bowl. Coach Babe Horrell's Bruins had driven 76 yards, but play-caller Ned Matthews chose to try for six when three would do. With the ball just a few

TRIVIA

What was Jeff Cravath's career coaching record at USC?

Answers to the trivia questions are on pages 187–191.

yards from the goal line, USC's defense stiffened and held the Bruins to a fateful fourth-down situation.

In a strange twist of democracy gone too far, five UCLA players *voted* for a field-goal try, while five wanted the touchdown. Matthews opted for the latter course and came up snake eyes. The smart play not only would have been to try the kick on fourth, but to try it on third in case it missed, giving the team another crack at it.

Coach Horrell deferred the blame from Matthews, stating that he supported the decision. USC had also missed scoring chances of their own in a game that, while slow in terms of defensive dominance and lack of movement, built to a crescendo of pressure in front of the mammoth throng. In the first quarter, Grenny Lansdell, suffering from a hand injury that made it hard for him to grip the ball, fumbled at the Bruin goal. Lansdell fumbled again at UCLA's 22, and a Trojan drive that died at the UCLA 25 was their only other threat. After the game, he abjectly apologized to Coach Jones.

USC had their hands full boxing in Jackie Robinson, especially on UCLA's almost-successful final drive. The greatest criticism of Horrell came not from the decision not to kick, but his inexplicable choice not to get the ball into Robinson's or Washington's hands once inside the USC 5.

"It was one of the cleanest, yet most bitter struggles in Coliseum history," wrote Paul Zimmerman of the *Los Angeles Times*. After the game, in what has become tradition, players from both teams, acquainted with each other from high school, four years of rivalry, and sharing the same city, mingled in "the finest display of sportsmanship anyone could ask for," wrote Zimmerman.

USC was out-played by Robinson, Washington, and the Bruins. There was no haughtiness left, no returning to the days of yesteryear in which they looked down upon the public school from Westwood. They were lucky to be going to the Rose Bowl and they knew it.

UCLA felt no consolation, as they had in 1936 when they were still feeling their oats. They had blown it. Jones offered in his postgame commentary that the Notre Dame and Washington games had drained his team, but to a man credit was given to Kenny Washington. His "hip-wiggling" running style, which portended a revolutionary change in the running back position over the next decades, elicited praise from USC.

Jones made a point to console Lansdell over his fumbles. Grenny had given him all he had. Statements like "those Bruins are a fine bunch" and "give 'em credit" lent to the general feeling that Southern Cal welcomed a true conference rivalry on par with what Cal and Stanford had up north.

The two teams oddly were, and would finish, undefeated. USC was 8–0–2, while UCLA sported an unusual 6–0–4 record. Tennessee was invited to Pasadena in a true national championship game. The contests between integrated teams in front of mammoth Coliseum crowds in the 1930s also were visual testaments to social progress almost a decade before Robinson broke baseball's "color barrier" in Brooklyn.

Whereas the 1939 Rose Bowl game had engendered controversy over the selection of Duke over Texas Christian, with USC coming in as the underdog, the 1940 game promised to be the national battle America longed to see.

Bob Neyland, the Volunteers' coach, may not have been a legend at Jones's historic level, but in his neck of the woods you could not win that argument. The Vols, riding a 23-game winning streak, came in with the same credentials as Duke in 1939: unbeaten, untied, unscored on. Unlike the Duke game, which had been a donnybrook, the USC-Tennessee Rose Bowl affair was all Trojans from start to finish. They were bigger, stronger, and faster. Ambrose Schindler had a terrific day. Southern California prevailed, 14–0.

"We weren't stale or off-form," Neyland announced. "We were outclassed. We were badly beaten by a superior team, and my hat is off to Howard Jones."

DID YOU KNOW . . . That USC's All-American lineman of the 1940s, John Ferraro, was a classroom wunderkind who would put it to use as a city councilman and mayoral candidate in L.A?

Tennessee quarterback George Cafego had to be removed when he suffered an injury, but offered that he would not have made any difference "against those big guys anyway."

"I remember they [Tennessee] had two All-American guards, a guy named Sutheridge and a guy named Belinsky," recalled Carl Benson in *The History of USC Football* DVD. "These guys just said to me, 'You guys are something else.' I said, 'I can't even make the first ballclub, and we're coming right through ya.' And by God we did."

"I said, this is the Rose Bowl and I'll give these people something to think about," recalled Schindler. "It was the perfect play. I lobbed the ball out to Al Krueger and he turned and there it was. It was real neat."

A newspaper headline read: "Tennessee Unable to Cope With Might of Southern California Grid Machine."

"I believe it played the heaviest schedule and accomplished the most of any team I ever coached," Jones said (in archival footage that still exists) when he accepted the national title trophy from Professor Frank G. Dickinson, a respected analyst whose system was considered one of the arbiters of national championship status.

"The Trojans were the best team in the best section...and the nation's other top teams did not play as strong a schedule as USC," stated Professor Dickinson.

The win improved Jones's Rose Bowl record to 5–0. Their victory also restarted the talk of a decade earlier, when pundits were saying that the best football was played on the West Coast, particularly in the Golden State. Rose Bowl losses by Alabama (1938), Duke (1939), and Tennessee (1940) tarnished the Southern football reputation, especially considering that Duke and Tennessee had looked impregnable playing their regular schedules, only to be exposed by Southern Cal. The South still had its supporters, who pointed out that Texas at least was maintaining standards, what with TCU's and A&M's strong years in 1938 and 1939. But Alabama had been soundly beaten by California in 1938, the West's supporters pointed out.

TRIVIA

What is the Victory Bell?

Answers to the trivia questions are on pages 187–191.

"They raise them rugged out here," wrote Henry McLemore, which was an interesting side of the double argument: one that says Californians are indeed "raised rugged" and the other that says they have "gone Hollywood...soft," the warm sun creating a population of loafers who had never "walked a mile to school in the snow."

McLemore theorized that "nature" made for a tougher athlete who could "withstand earthquakes." He said it was the water that made for men who were bigger and even had to shave more often!

Jones was back on top, to be sure, but it was his final reach for greatness. California was the football capital of America in January of 1940, but a war would ensue and with it, innocence was lost.

The Giffer:
Everybody's All-American

Frank Gifford came to USC in 1949, and while in many ways he would come to be the glamorous face of the University of Southern California, in other ways he would indirectly be responsible for the firing of the man he admired, Jeff Cravath.

Gifford was a 6'1", 193-pound all-purpose halfback. He was born in Santa Monica, but had grown up in an "oil family" in Bakersfield, a dusty town about 80 miles north of L.A. Today, Interstate 5 winds over the mountain passes, known as the "grapevine," between the San Fernando Valley and Bakersfield. Descending from the higher altitudes, an entirely different world presents itself before the motorist; a seemingly endless stretch of highway along hundreds of miles of relatively barren farmland known as the San Joaquin Valley. Distant mountain ranges are visible: the coastals that shadow the spectacular coastline and strands of Ventura, Santa Barbara, San Luis Obispo, and Monterey to the west. The Sierras—the fabulous Yosemite and Mt. Whitney (the highest peak in the contiguous U.S.)—barely visible in the smoggy agricultural air to the east. But in the middle is the valley. It is hot in the summer with "toolie fog" in the winter. The towns have none of the Golden State panache: Bakersfield, Fresno, Stockton, and Sacramento are more like Iowa minus the harsh weather.

Oil is a fairly plentiful resource in Southern California. There are rigs off the coast, but a major spill near Santa Barbara sent environmentalists into apoplexy, shutting down operations ever since. Derricks still pump like Quixote-esque windmills in the Fox Hills of L.A., the surfer town of Huntington Beach, and of course, in Bakersfield.

Frank Gifford was one of USC's brightest stars in the early 1950s.

That Sam Barry was a great USC baseball and basketball coach, credited by his protégé, Tex Winter, with inventing the "triangle offense" that was a staple of Michael Jordan's championship teams in Chicago? When Barry joined the Navy, his *baseball* protégé, Rod Dedeaux, took over and, like Barry, called everybody "Tiger."

Gifford's family worked the rigs. It was hard work, and people who did it were not considered of the higher classes, even in a fairly "classless" place like Bakersfield. But Gifford was a "different breed of cat." He did not have good grades in school and had to go to Bakersfield Junior College before transferring to Southern California, but the man America came to know—the "golden boy" from California, the New York Giants' "man about town," the *Monday Night Football* icon, and husband of Kathie Lee Gifford—*that man* is erudite, articulate to a tee, the very picture of the All-American gentlemen. He remains a class act all the way.

When Frank Gifford would survey his life's achievements, however, trying to explain how he got so lucky and had so much, he would more often than not look back at his school and his first college coach when it came time to explain it all.

Gifford would earn All-America honors in 1951, induction into the College Football Hall of Fame in 1975, and the Pro Football Hall of Fame in 1977. He played on offense and defense. He was a triple-threat who could run, pass, and catch the ball. Make that a quadruple threat. His 22-yard field goal versus California in 1949 was, according to 'SC's football media guide, the Trojans' *first since 1935!*

A first-round draft choice, Gifford joined the New York Giants in 1952. He played for them in the greatest glory days of their franchise history (1952–1960, 1962–1964). At first, the grizzled vets put him down. Gifford may not be the most handsome athlete of all time, but he is probably in the top five. His big contract, dazzling visage, caramel rich voice, and Hollywood flair did not sit well, until he started carrying the ball and proved to be one of the toughest, hard-nosed football players of a particularly hard-nosed era.

After proving himself, he was idolized by his teammates and the fans. He was far more at ease with fame and the limelight than his baseball counterpart, the Oklahoma country boy Mickey Mantle. Gifford's experience at USC most likely was the best preparation he could have.

In the annals of American iconography, aside from Mt. Rushmore–level political figures, perhaps a few astronauts and war heroes, nothing equals the New York sports star. Marilyn Monroe discovered that when she married Joe DiMaggio.

"Joe," she gushed upon returning from Korea, "you never heard such cheering."

"Yes, I have," deadpanned the Yankee Clipper.

Gifford heard those cheers. In the Big Apple, there is Babe Ruth, Lou Gehrig, DiMaggio, Mantle, Tom Seaver, *maybe* Derek Jeter, Reggie Jackson, and a few more. Gifford is in this elite company. Gifford and Seaver, both Trojans. Giffer did advertisements. He was a Manhattan socialite. He appeared on TV and in movies. When *Monday Night Football* became a sensation, he was the star of the show. He aged as gracefully as a man can hope to.

Gifford's talents were obvious in 1949 and 1950, but when the Trojans failed to produce a winning record in his junior year, Cravath found himself on the hot seat. Once thought to be an innovator, Cravath now was thought to be a coach who had seen the game pass him by, all the while wasting the athletic genius of Gifford.

Cravath continued to have his supporters, especially among the student body. Rallies were held to support him, but they would be drowned by the drumbeat of criticism. Some years later, *Sports Illustrated* did a story on Gifford.

"A strong case could be made that Gifford was the most ill-used college player of all time," it read. "Cravath put Gifford on the defensive unit throughout most of his career, although he was probably the best all-around offensive player on the squad. He was its best runner and

TRIVIA

How many medals did Trojan athletes win at the London, Helsinki, and Melbourne Olympics?

Answers to the trivia questions are on pages 187–191.

passer, he punted and he place-kicked, and yet Cravath rarely gave him a chance to do these things. It wasn't until well into Gifford's pro career with the New York Giants that he was able to prove his full potential on offense. It might be argued that if Gifford had played before the free-substitution rule and under a coach who knew how to utilize the full measure of his ability, he would have to be named the finest player the West ever produced, maybe the best anywhere."

DID YOU KNOW . . . That Olympic gold medal diver Sammy Lee became USC's team doctor?

Mr. Trojan

Jess Hill grew up in Corona. Located on what is now the 91 freeway, about half an hour east from the Anaheim hills. It is a hot, small town with surrounding canyons, rock formations, and desert plateaus that looks as much like Arizona as California.

In 1926 Hill used his earnings from employment at the Corona Ice Co. and the Union Oil Station to attend the Rose Bowl between Alabama and Washington. Hill, a baseball fan, became a football aficionado, too. At Corona High School, he earned 10 varsity letters, was salutatorian and president of his senior class, earned a prize as the best extemporaneous speaker of Riverside County, and became a member of the California Scholarship Federation. He starred in basketball, football, baseball, and track at Riverside Junior College. His broad-jumping earned him notice from Dean Cromwell.

After his recruiting visit, he felt USC was "just too big for me."

Cromwell's assistant, Tommy Davis, persisted until Hill accepted a $300 scholarship and a part-time janitorial job. His original athletic ambitions were track and baseball. When he showed interest in football, Cromwell tried to dissuade him from going out for Howard Jones's team for fear of injury.

Hill told him that he planned to go into teaching and coaching, that this would probably mean coaching football, and that the experience of being a college player would make him more marketable as well as a better coach.

The prize-winning extemporaneous speaker and salutatorian of Riverside County made logical arguments. Cromwell had to let him do it. Thus did a protégé of Howard Jones emerge.

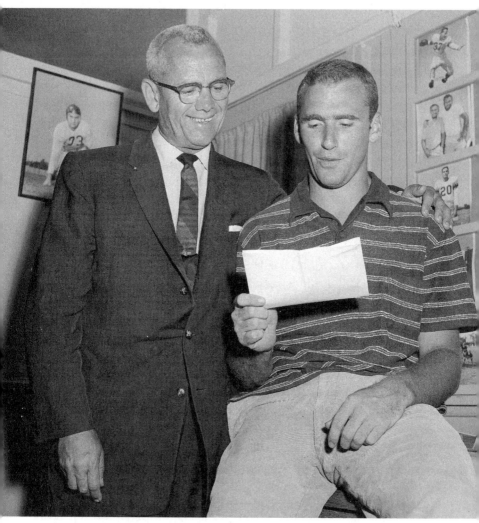

Star halfback Jon Arnett reads a statement at a Los Angeles press conference in August 1956 announcing he would stay at USC and turn down offers from nearly every team in the Canadian Football League because he thought his education came first. Standing beside Arnett is Coach Jess Hill.

"He was the fastest man I have ever seen on Bovard Field," stated Jones of the player he called "Hula Hula" Hill, because he swiveled his hips to evade tacklers. Hill starred on great Trojan football and track teams. He set the Intercollegiate Athletic Association record in the 1929 long jump at 25'7⅞".

Hill subbed for Jim Musick and starred in a rout of Washington, but the equipment manager had forgotten his shirt. Wearing Cliff Thiede's No. 32 instead (a number retired after O.J. Simpson won the Heisman but before his wife was murdered), Hill remained anonymous to radio listeners in L.A. who instead heard what a great game *Thiede* had.

The announcer went so far as to state that Thiede was the "greatest open field runner we've seen," and in what may rate entrance into the Hyperbole Hall of Shame, "maybe better than Red Grange."

Playing on teams with great depth, Hill shared playing time, but Jones knew how to use him. When he carried, he averaged 8.2 yards. Hill played in that 76–0 first game against UCLA in 1929.

"We had tradition and we had heritage behind us, and they didn't," he said.

Hill was still a fine baseball player who signed with the vaunted New York Yankees after graduation in 1930. In his first game with the Hollywood Stars, a Pacific Coast League team that had an arrangement with the Yankees, he homered against the L.A. Angels at the old Wrigley Field, a classic minor league park on Avalon.

As he rose through the Yankees' organization, he found himself playing alongside Babe Ruth, but by the time he made it to the major leagues in 1935, the Babe had moved on to the Boston Braves.

Hill was known for his base running with New York, but eye problems forced a trade to the Washington Senators. He hit .305 for the legendary Cornelius "Connie Mack" McGillicuddy and the Philadelphia A's in 1936, but when he dropped to a still-respectable .272 in 1937, Mack dealt him back to the Pacific Coast League. After playing for the Oakland Oaks, he decided to retire and pursue coaching.

His first stop was coaching baseball and football at his alma mater, Corona High, followed by a stint coaching track and football at Long Beach City College. In 1942 Hill joined the Navy, where he became associated with USC athletic director Bill Hunter.

TRIVIA

Who were the "twin holy terrors" of USC and how did they earn that moniker?

Answers to the trivia questions are on pages 187–191.

DID YOU KNOW . . . That in 1956 integrated Southern California played segregated Texas at Austin, and that 'SC's black running back, C.R. Roberts, gained 251 yards in *12 minutes of the first half* of the 44–20 victory? Texas players who had spat on him shook his hand, but the fans remained vicious. Coach Jess Hill moved the team to a new lodging the night before when Roberts was not allowed to stay at the planned hotel.

After the war, his connection with Hunter led to his taking over the USC frosh football team and a spot on Cromwell's track staff. Cromwell retired in 1949. Hill took over without missing a beat: two national titles and immediate recognition as the "best track coach at any American college."

The only better American track team than USC's was the U.S. Olympic squad, and half of those guys were Trojans, anyway. To Hill's way of thinking, the athletes were so good anybody could succeed with them.

"I didn't do much coaching," he said modestly.

Hill, still youthful and coaching his alma mater, had his dream job and may well have gone on to win the 12 national titles that Jesse Mortensen and Vern Wolfe went on to win, plus some Olympic gold.

Instead, Bill Hunter chose him to replace Jeff Cravath as the football coach in 1951. Certainly names like Leahy, Crisler, and Brown, while bandied about, would have made a big splash. But the choice of a great Trojan satisfied the faithful. Hill was as qualified as a rookie major college coach could be, at least in terms of varied experiences: ex-football, track, and baseball star at USC; big league ballplayer; excellent scholar; Navy veteran; head track coach of national champion track teams; head football coach in high school and assistant college experience at 'SC.

Hill was worldly, loyal, smart, and disciplined. His record is not among the all-time greats, his star not as bright as others, but he was a truly great Trojan. After coaching in the 1950s, he became the school's athletic director, hired John McKay, and presided over USC athletics over a period that has never been remotely approached by any other athletic program in the history of American sports.

Hill graciously gave credit to Cravath for the recruiting he had done, leaving him "in great shape" in 1951. His first decision was to get Gifford on his offense. Using a single wing and T formation, Hill turned Gifford into the star everybody expected him to have become.

He also coached Jim Sears, "one of the finest small backs I've ever seen," who played offense, defense, and returned punts and kicks. Hill was the coach of one of USC's all-time superstars, the legendary Jon Arnett.

Hill's teams from 1951 to 1956 were 45–17–1 (.722). He said he found a sense of "defeatism" when he took over and certainly set that back. He went to two Rose Bowls, but in what was a truly major accomplishment, never lost to Pappy Waldorf and California.

Michigan had instituted the platoon system to great effect. Hill modernized with the times, despite the Jones influence, although the Trojans depended on good, old-fashioned power running attacks.

"We had men in motion, flankers and split ends—just like today," he told Ken Rappoport for his excellent 1981 book, *The Trojans: A Story of Southern California Football.*

The "G.I. problem" that plagued Cravath was not a factor during Hill's tenure. The freshman eligibility rule of the war years was also in effect in his day. Like Pete Carroll 50 years later, Hill told incoming high school phenoms that they could compete for playing time.

His greatest moment came in his rookie season, 1951, when USC traveled to Berkeley to take on Waldorf's number one–ranked Cal Bears. They were undefeated and had won 30 straight conference games. This would be the year they would win the national championship, or so it seemed.

"They had us 14–0 at the half," said Hill, "and we beat them 21–14," in what he further stated was "my most satisfying victory."

That game ranks with the 16–14 Johnny Baker game at South Bend as one of the all-time greats, although, of course, Trojan lore is filled with many equally exciting victories in the succeeding years.

DID YOU KNOW . . . That Oakland Raiders' owner Al Davis got his start coaching under Don Clark at USC from 1957 to 1959?

The "Little White-Haired Man"

During pregame warm-ups on September 12, 1970, at Legion Field in Birmingham, a white player from the segregated Alabama Crimson Tide approached Sam "Bam" Cunningham, the black fullback of USC's integrated Trojans.

"I bet you're shakin' in your boots havin' to face the mighty Alabama Crimson Tide," he said to Cunningham, trying to shake him up. Cunningham just pointed to John McKay.

"I'm only scared of one thing: the little white-haired man over there," he replied before rushing for 135 yards and two touchdowns to lead his team to a historic 42–21 trouncing.

McKay was a cigar-smoking, whiskey-drinking, duck-huntin', iconoclastic, conservative Republican, West Virginia Catholic. He was known for his sharp quips to the media. He was a favorite of the writers who came to him for good quotes. In light of his success and great reputation, it seems incongruous that McKay was not enamored with the "Knights of the Keyboard," as Ted Williams had disparagingly referred to the Boston press.

But McKay did not trust the press. This attitude stemmed from his early experiences with them. When he came to USC, McKay installed a revolutionary new offensive scheme called the I formation. It totally veered away from the age-old concept of a "triple-threat" quarterback/running back. It placed a tailback well behind the line. In the eyes of lesser lights in the press box, the "I" in the I formation stood for "incompetent, intolerable, and ineffective." McKay never forgot the barbs.

McKay, who would serve for four years as athletic director, led USC to the ultimate heights of football and athletic glory. The period from 1962 to 1981, the last five years in which McKay's handpicked successor, John Robinson, was at the helm, represent the most dominant 20-year run in the entire history of college football. The Trojans won five national championships

John McKay took over as coach in 1960, and in 1962 began a 20-year era of Trojan dominance.

and earned four Heisman Trophies. But victories are only part of the story. They also became the team of excitement, of last-minute drama, of ultimate glory, and of Hollywood glamour. The prestige of the school itself owes much of that *panache* to the image created, fostered, and led by John McKay.

"He was an extremely competitive man," said his son, John K. "J.K." McKay. "It wasn't that he so much hated to lose, which he did, but he loved to win and he loved to compete."

In 1962 the Trojans would ascend to the heights of glory. McKay would be vindicated. Hollywood front-runners would show up to cheer them on. The season certainly did not hold high hopes in the beginning, though. A mere 26,400 fans showed up at the L.A. Memorial Coliseum for the season opener against eighth-ranked Duke. A national TV audience was surprised to see the Trojans prevail 14–7.

The team was just that, a team. There were no huge superstars, no Heisman hopefuls. Oregon State quarterback Terry Baker won it that year.

The captain of the team was Marv Marinovich, and out of this the Trojan family would expand. Marinovich would go on to marry sophomore quarterback Craig Fertig's sister. Marinovich's brother would become the football coach at Bishop Amat High School, where his star players would be McKay's sons, J.K. and Richie, quarterback Pat Haden, and future UCLA Rose Bowl MVP John Sciarra. Marinovich and Fertig's sister would have a son, Todd, who would break all of Haden's California state passing records, and then all of USC's hearts—but not until after he would lead USC to victory in the 1990 Rose Bowl over Michigan.

Fertig was part of a talented trio of signal-callers: Pete Beathard and Bill Nelsen were the others. Somehow, they were able to work together as a unit without problems.

TRIVIA

Despite USC winning the 1963 Rose Bowl 42–37 to capture the national championship, the MVP of the game was not a Trojan. Who was it?

Answers to the trivia questions are on pages 187–191.

"I remember Pete Beathard and I were the first two quarterbacks he recruited, and he told us we could play baseball," Fertig recalled in *The History of USC Football* DVD. "He's a catcher and I'm a pitcher and, like I said, his first year didn't go so well. But his freshman team went undefeated.

"So one day we're on the baseball field and McKay's secretary comes out and says to Coach Dedeaux, 'Coach McKay'd like to see Beathard and Fertig.'

"Well I just looked at Beathard and said, 'What'd you do?' And he said, 'I'm your roommate, I haven't left your sight.' So we go on up to McKay's office and he's reading the sports section, and all you can see is the cigar smoke comin' from behind it, and he says, 'You guys aren't real good at either sport, *make a decision*.' I cleaned that up for you, too. That's when we decided to be football players."

USC brought an integrated team to Dallas for game two. A mere 14,000 showed up to see them defeat Southern Methodist 33–3. Ranked number six, they won a defensive struggle over Iowa 7–0. Cal came to L.A. and lost 32–6. After winning at Illinois and beating number nine Washington, the peculiar fandom of Los Angeles was aroused.

Ticket manager John Morley found himself rising at 3:00 in the morning to meet the demands of alumni he had not heard from "in 10 years." Typical L.A. The Trojans realized they had something good going on when they made all three columns of the *Los Angeles Times* in one day.

"We knew we had a good football team," said All-American end Hal Bedsole, "but no one felt that it was a national championship–caliber team—you don't think of things like that before a season, anyway."

The Washington victory vaulted them to number two. Wins over Stanford, then Roger Staubach and Navy, had them thinking about it. They were number one heading into the UCLA game. McKay did it in an unusual way, alternating Beathard and Nelsen. Fertig was number three but considered part of the mix, too. As the season wore on, though, Fertig asked and received permission to play some at wide receiver, just so he could get in games.

Both Beathard and Nelsen would achieve success in professional football, Beathard at Houston and Nelsen with Cleveland.

"Beathard was as fine an athlete as played college football," said Bedsole.

The team did not approach games with the expectation of putting a lot of points on the board, although as the offense synchronized, they became much more potent than they had been at the beginning of the year.

"I know we're playing a lot better defense," McKay told the press. "I feel our defense against Iowa forced them into a good many errors. You've got to be stubborn to win against top competition, and stubbornness should begin on defense."

"We beat the Bruins for the Rose Bowl 14–3 with a great comeback," Bedsole said. "They were ahead 3–0 in the last five minutes, and then Brown made a miraculous catch near the goal line and they turned the ball over and we scored again."

DID YOU KNOW . . . That fiery USC assistant coach Marv Goux played a gladiator in *Spartacus*? His speech to the team before the 1967 UCLA game was almost identical to Kirk Douglas's rhetoric in front of the gladiators he urges to initiate a slave rebellion against the Roman Empire in Stanley Kubrick's 1960 classic. This was not an accident. Goux urged the Trojans to "win one for John." He held up a photo of McKay, dejected as he left the field after losing the 1966 UCLA game. "Listen, listen," Goux said in fistic rage. "The worst thing in life is to be a prisoner. Never. I would rather die. We've been prisoners to those indecencies over there for two years. Today's the day we go free." McKay countered Goux by telling the players that the walk back to the locker room after the game would either be the longest or the shortest of their lives.

TRIVIA

What late 1950s Trojan All-American lineman was one of the first great stars of the fledgling American Football League?

Answers to the trivia questions are on pages 187–191.

A crowd of 86,740 watched Troy earn a trip to Pasadena. Of course, beating Notre Dame was still a task that lay ahead.

"It's like the poker player," McKay told his team. "He's won all the money, and then somebody challenges him to a showdown, all or nothing."

On the game's third play, Beathard swung a pass to Willie Brown, who gained 34 yards to the Irish 18. Two-hundred-twenty-eight–pound fullback Ben Wilson went for eight, then three plays later leaped over the pile to make it 7–0. John Underwood of *Sports Illustrated* wrote that the game was USC's from that moment forward. Whenever Notre Dame made an adjustment, USC countered. Notre Dame coach Joe Kuharich's squad kept shooting themselves in the foot with penalties and mistakes. McKay went conservative in the second half.

The 25–0 win set up one of the greatest Rose Bowl shootouts of all time. It would be a game against Wisconsin that totally went against the ebb and flow of USC's season. They would be outplayed, according to some, but they would survive and leave with the national championship.

Fertig-to-Sherman

Nineteen sixty-four would prove to be memorable, yet bittersweet. The Trojan quarterback was Craig Fertig, a senior out of Huntington Park High School. Fertig is a colorful figure in Trojan history who would go on to become an assistant coach under McKay, a head coach at Oregon State, a longtime Fox Sports football analyst with Tom Kelly, a fixture on the alumni banquet circuit, and the host of USC campus tours. He is, in many ways, the "face" of USC.

Fertig was always a guy who liked to have fun, enjoyed partying, and had an eye for the ladies. He had waited his turn while Beathard and Nelsen were draped in the glory of a national title. The stage was set for the anointing of Notre Dame's expected national championship on November 28. The Irish had not captured the crown since 1949. The 1950s and early 1960s had been down years in South Bend, although they had given USC all they could handle. But Northwestern's Ara Parseghian took over that year. At first, little was expected of him.

The Irish quarterback was an unknown senior who had not started. John Huarte and his favorite receiver, Jack Snow, had grown up in Orange County, which is "Trojan country," but they had gone to Notre Dame. In the summers they had worked on pass routes on Orange County's beaches. In 1964 they put the practice to good use.

Notre Dame surprisingly went through their first nine games undefeated, earning them the number-one ranking. Huarte was just dripping with Notre Dame polish. The best quarterback in America that year was Alabama senior Joe Willie Namath, but Namath injured his knee in the seventh game of the season. That gave Huarte the inside track to become Notre Dame's sixth Heisman Trophy winner.

Huarte was Mater Dei High's first Heisman winner (Matt Leinart became their second in 2004). There are only two high schools in the country that have produced two Heisman winners (the other: Woodrow Wilson High of Dallas with Davey O'Brien and Tim Brown).

But on that November day of 1964, the best quarterback in America was not Huarte, Namath, Craig Morton, or any of the other more-heralded signal callers of the year. Fertig certainly did not give indication of this at first.

McKay knew that his reputation would be cemented on this day. Either he could beat Notre Dame or he could not. Beating them when they were ranked number one would prove his place. He had an open date after the UCLA game to prepare.

None of USC's plans or hopes appeared to amount to a hill of beans when Huarte started to shred the USC defense. He hit on 11 of 15 attempts for 176 yards in the first half. He spotted Snow for a touchdown, a field goal was good, and another drive ended with Bill Wolski's run into the end zone.

Notre Dame led 17–0 when the teams broke for their locker rooms, but the greatest *halftime* coach ever may well be McKay. He had a serene confidence, an ability to make adjustments, a way of conveying calmness to his team that is not matched.

TRIVIA

What year was USC's baseball stadium, Dedeaux Field, built, and what great event got it off to a good start?

Answers to the trivia questions are on pages 187–191.

In the other locker room, Parseghian told the Irish, "Just 30 minutes of football separates you from a national championship." While true, the words conveyed a sense of "running out the clock." Parseghian was one of the best coaches ever, but this kind of thinking, which was exemplified on several high-profile occasions, costs him legacy points.

Mike Garrett scored to make it 17–7. The crowd of 83,840 Coliseum faithful exploded with pent-up emotion. Fertig lit up the Los Angeles sky on an 82-yard drive. Fred Hill's catch made it 17–14.

"I knew we had 'em," McKay later said of his attitude at that point. "The momentum was all ours. In a situation like that, the number-one rating is a fairly suffocating thing."

Two minutes and 10 seconds remained. The Coliseum was awash in noise and emotion, a cacophony of sound. There are many large stadiums in America. Ohio Stadium. Michigan Stadium. Notre Dame Stadium. Yankee Stadium. Fenway Park. Crowds that flock to these places are boisterous and crazy. L.A. fans have a well-deserved reputation for being laid back. USC's backers, while loyal and among the best alumni in the world, are often well heeled and quiet compared to the crazies at Florida State, LSU, or any of two dozen other venues. However, with that being said, those who have experienced the Coliseum at full throttle, when all is on the line usually against Notre Dame or UCLA, describe a tidal wave of sound and excitement that matches if not exceeds any atmosphere in America. So it was that day in 1964.

When Fertig nailed Fred Hill on a down-and-out pattern for 23 yards, it was a first down at the Irish 17. For the Trojans, a field goal was not an option on fourth down at the 15 with 43 seconds left.

Receiver Rod Sherman told McKay he wanted to try "84-Z delay." He would split wide to the left, delay one second after the snap, sprint ahead for five steps, fake outside, then cut sharply down and across the middle. Fertig would just have to avoid a sack, trusting that his man would be where he was supposed to be.

"I watched the way their halfback reacted and I figured that I could beat him," Sherman said.

Sherman juked Tony Carey, and Fertig hit him chest high. Fifteen yards. Touchdown. The Coliseum exploded. Sherman and Fertig would live off this moment for time immemorial.

USC's victory over Notre Dame did not earn them a trip to Pasadena, however.

"We beat the number-one team in the country," Fertig said, "and Oregon State, God bless 'em, beat Idaho...so they went."

Mike Garrett: USC's First Heisman Winner

The year 1962 will be looked back on as the year McKay broke the jinx and led USC to the proverbial Promised Land. But in many ways 1965 is a demarcation point in Trojan football history. Mike Garrett was a senior that year. He was one of those great, fast black athletes that McKay knew he needed in order to succeed. But Garrett's Trojan career meant more than just success on the field. He was, in a small yet significant way, a social statement. Certainly he was a guy who had grown up rooting for UCLA because the Bruins did a better job providing opportunities for black players. However, John McKay had impressed him while recruiting the 5'9", 185-pound All-City running back from Jefferson High School.

"When McKay asked you to play for him," Garrett would later say, "you accepted."

At Jefferson, Garrett had averaged 10 yards a carry, earning prep All-America honors. He scored 37 points in one game, 32 in another, and was the L.A. City Player of the Year. He also starred in track in high school and later at USC.

Garrett and the legacy of McKay's I formation system are inextricably linked. While Garrett did not really begin the legacy that McKay may well have taken his greatest pride in, he is perhaps most associated with it. The conservative West Virginian was "totally race neutral," in the words of his son, J.K. McKay. Garrett loved him like a father. McKay loved him like he was J.K.'s and Richie McKay's brother. In the wake of the Watts riots, it was a nice image for a city and a school that meant so much to that city.

Garrett was not the first black Heisman Trophy winner. Jim Brown really could have, maybe should have, won it in the mid-1950s. His

Syracuse successor, Ernie Davis, had earned the statue in 1961 before tragically dying of cancer. When Garrett won it for USC, black athletes around America took notice. The press made note of the fact that USC's Willie Wood had been a black *quarterback* as far back as 1957. Black quarterbacks were all but unheard of. Minnesota had fielded one in the early 1960s, Sandy Stephens who led them to consecutive Rose Bowls, but it just *wasn't done* except at black colleges like Grambling. The pros took those guys and turned them into defensive backs anyway. The Packers had done that with Wood, but of course there is no argument that he was a better quarterback than Bart Starr.

But black athletes in the South, who harbored no illusions that Alabama, Georgia, or Texas were offering them scholarships anytime soon, saw USC and they saw opportunity. Nice weather. Good night life. An accommodating atmosphere. "Pretty girls of all races," as McKay said. Garrett's ascension was that final point in which the black athletes of Los Angeles no longer favored UCLA. It would foreshadow cataclysmic events with national implications.

Garrett himself was insecure.

"It's like you're in a dark alley, and you're running from trouble. You know you can get hurt if you get caught, so you keep running," is how he described his experiences as a running back. "I'm not chicken, though. I keep going into that alley."

Growing up on the tough streets of L.A.'s Boyle Heights, Garrett knew that his key to success would be football, but that it was a means to an end that would be the *real* key to his success: education.

"If it hadn't been for football, I'd have been a bum," he said. Listening to tapes of a young Garrett speak, one finds this hard to believe. Even as a youthful football player, he was comfortable with the press, speaking articulately while handling himself

TRIVIA

In how many Super Bowls did Mike Garrett play?

Answers to the trivia questions are on pages 187–191.

with class. By no means did he ever give off the aura of some guy who could play sports but was out of his element in an academic atmosphere. Garrett was a guy with a social conscience and a slightly rebellious streak.

Mike Garrett wipes a tear from his eye after learning he was the Heisman Trophy winner at a November 1965 news conference.

"I had a long conversation with Garrett and Willie Brown," said former USC assistant coach Dave Levy, who had been Brown's coach at Long Beach Poly High before coming to USC. "I told them that they owed it to other black kids to make the most of the opportunity football gave them, through education, to pave the way for others."

Garrett then decided he wanted to live off-campus. He wanted to rent an apartment in Pasadena. Pasadena was the hometown of Jackie Robinson, but the city—at least the section where Garrett wanted to live—did not "rent to blacks," according to Levy. Garrett vented to his coach.

"I just told him that instead of getting mad at white people," Levy said, "he just had to stay with it, to give people a chance to change, and in time it would happen. He nodded and came to agree with that."

In three years, Garrett rushed for an astonishing 3,221 yards, more than Jim Brown, Ernie Davis, "Mr. Inside and Mr. Outside" at Army (Glenn Davis, Doc Blanchard), or any other collegiate runner.

Garrett also caught passes for 399 yards, occasionally threw the ball (48 yards), and was a potent threat returning punts and kicks. In 1965 he rushed for 1,440 yards.

"I don't think anything is more exciting than winning the Heisman," he said. It turned Garrett into a prized rookie who weighed competing offers from the Rams, who made him their second-round pick, and the Kansas City Chiefs of the AFL.

Garrett, who had never known his father, and whose mother worked as a domestic while raising her son in a $36-per-month housing project, now had the things he had always wanted but never had. Garrett, however, once said, "I didn't know then that I was poor."

Garrett made some runs that McKay said "could [not] be made, yet Mike made it." Garrett was the ultimate team player, too. There was no sense of prima donna to him. He practiced hard, exhibiting leadership qualities as befitting his role as captain. He was not USC's first black captain by any means, however. Willie Wood (1959) and Willie Brown (1962) had helped pave the way for black players like Garrett.

McKay once said that Garrett was a complete football player who would have been his best linebacker, guard, and "might have been my best quarterback" if he had been installed at those positions instead. Garrett never would have complained.

The night before the Heisman Trophy winner was to be announced, Garrett lay in bed thinking it over. The more he thought about it, the more confident he became that he deserved it. Early the next morning he got the call congratulating him from USC's sports information director.

Garrett had just the right amount of bravado. When he won the Heisman, he said that the previous black Heisman winner, Ernie Davis, "was a great man." He later stated that winning it is "like winning a Pulitzer Prize. You don't have to worry about anything else once you've won that Pulitzer." But when held to 57 yards by Notre Dame, he said, "All I was thinking about was getting off the ground. That's where I was most of the time." Garrett was always thanking his linemen, a trait that O.J. Simpson learned from him.

Garrett's records would be broken by O.J., but he had broken the marks set by the likes of Morley Drury (1,163 yards in a season, 1927), Orv Mohler (career total of 2,025 rushing yards from 1930 to 1932), and Jim Musick (219 carries from 1929 to 1931). Garrett had 3,269

DID YOU KNOW . . . That Mike Garrett was also a star baseball player? He was close friends with future Mets' Hall of Fame pitcher Tom Seaver at USC, where he inspired Seaver to lift weights, beginning a trend in baseball. Seaver and Garrett double-dated girls, a practice considered racially groundbreaking in the mid-1960s. Garrett was drafted by both the Pittsburgh Pirates and Los Angeles Dodgers.

yards in total offense, eclipsing the record set by his teammate, Pete Beathard. He was described as being like trying to tackle "a bowling ball." Against UCLA in 1965 he ran for 210 yards. Like other class acts before and after him, he entered the UCLA locker room to congratulate the Bruins after UCLA won.

TRIVIA

Why did John McKay say he wanted to beat Stanford by 2,000 points?

Answers to the trivia questions are on pages 187–191.

"He darn near had me bawling," said UCLA's great halfback, Mel Farr.

"He's the greatest runner I've ever seen," said the Bruins' Dallas Grider. The day had been a tough one, though. Despite his yards, Garrett had coughed up the football at crucial times in the 20–16 defeat, costing Troy the Rose Bowl.

McKay was near tears himself after the game, one of his all-time low moments. Part of his disappointment was for Garrett. Garrett would be smiling, however, when he became the first California collegiate player ever to win the Heisman.

Garrett broke the NCAA career rushing record previously held by Ollie Matson of the University of San Francisco from 1949 to 1951.

Juice

What is there to say about Orenthal James "O.J." Simpson—Trojan legend, NFL record-breaker, Hollywood celebrity, infamous "criminal"—that has not already been said?

O.J. is a source of some, if not the greatest, pride as well as shame in the history of USC sports. For that very reason, his fall from grace caused great anguish, embarrassment, and public humiliation for the school that made him and then suffered because of him.

On October 14, 1967, USC played one of the most important games in its history. They had not defeated Notre Dame at South Bend since 1939, but 59,075 came out to see Simpson and the Trojans. McKay, the coach who watched game film every night for a year, had the All-American superstar he needed to throttle his great foe.

"They had talked about how USC hadn't beaten Notre Dame in South Bend in a long, long time," said quarterback Steve Sogge. "It was a tough place to play in. Great for Notre Dame, of course. Their fans have such tremendous enthusiasm."

Simpson's legend, like many of Notre Dame's opponents over the years, was made that day against the Irish. It turned him into an All-American and a Heisman contender, rare for a junior, unheard-of in a J.C. transfer. Despite the hoopla surrounding him and his team, the

DID YOU KNOW . . . That Bill "Spaceman" Lee emerged from the luggage chute at the Hawaii airport during a USC road trip to the islands?

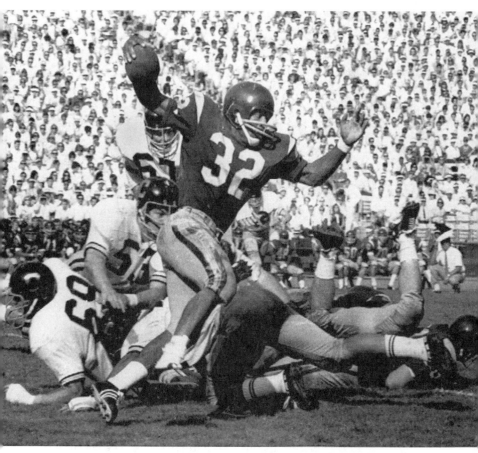

Despite his infamy off the field, no one can dispute that O.J. Simpson was one of the greatest running backs in USC, and college football, history.

"intimidation factor" that is South Bend in autumn; with "Touchdown Jesus" framed behind the goalposts, the crowd noise, and the weight of 28 years of bad memories, was enough to make the Trojans the underdogs.

"Intercollegiate football's most colorful intersectional rivalry will be resumed here tomorrow on another of bizarre notes that have been the rule rather than the exception whenever Southern California and Notre Dame clash," read one Midwestern account.

"Undefeated Southern California, rated number one nationally, is a 12-point underdog. It could happen only in this computer age."

History looked to repeat itself when the Irish jumped out to a 7–0 lead. Then Simpson entered history. He rushed 38 times for 150 yards in a dominating 24–7 victory that left no doubt.

Early on, the game was tentative and dominated by hard defensive hitting. It looked to be a match between linebackers—USC's Adrian Young and Notre Dame's Bob Olson.

"The burly Trojans were just too fast, too quick, and too determined," one account read. "It was a bitter defeat for Notre Dame, made almost humiliating by a genuine Irishman from Dublin, one Matthew Adrian Young. Three times he choked off Notre Dame scoring threats within the 12-yard line by intercepting passes. A fourth threat cracked up on a fumble on the 4-yard line.

"In all, Young, born in Ireland and raised in California, made four of the Trojans' seven interceptions [five thrown by heralded Terry Hanratty]."

Indeed, Young made *his* legend that day, too. He was a Dubliner by birth and a Bishop Amat Lancer by high school affiliation. The coach at Bishop Amat was Marv Marinovich's brother, Gary. The Catholic school in La Puente would later be the staging grounds for J.K. McKay, Pat Haden, and John Sciarra. It was the top prep football power in California in its heyday.

Young, USC's cocaptain in 1967, would earn consensus All-America honors as a 6'1", 210-pound linebacker. He played in the National Football League from 1968 to 1973, with the Eagles, Lions, and Bears.

Hanratty, who would be Terry Bradshaw's capable backup on the Pittsburgh Steelers' Super Bowl champions, spent the day clutching his helmet and throwing his hands up before Ara Parseghian in disbelief.

Simpson had dominated the offensive side of the ball with a one-yard bulldozing through the Notre Dame line, then a 35-yard end sweep for a touchdown. His third touchdown run of three yards in the last quarter clinched it. O.J. had really broken loose in the third quarter,

TRIVIA

What did John McKay say after getting beaten 51–0 by Notre Dame in 1966?

Answers to the trivia questions are on pages 187–191.

eliciting groans and silence from the Notre Dame faithful. Assistant coach Johnny Ray was heard muttering, "Too many yards, too many."

When Simpson broke free for a long touchdown, Ray just shouted an agonizing, "*Nooooooo!*"

McKay was carried off the field by his players saying, "This is my greatest win."

"We just had better football players than Ara did, and that's why we won," was McKay's blunt assessment. "Southern Cal hadn't won at Notre Dame since 1939, and I was getting awfully tired of being reminded of this."

After the game, McKay noted in his usual dry manner that at the beginning of the contest, crowd noise had resulted in several offside penalties assessed to the Trojans. After Simpson took over and USC took command, it "had a quieting effect," he stated.

McKay would always say this was his most satisfying victory. It was the great turnaround, the dividing line, the demarcation point of the rivalry, and that first major step toward establishing the University of Southern California as a football tradition that people could look at and argue was maybe, just maybe, equal or even better than Notre Dame's. It was that little extra ingredient that their fans could point to and say, "Well, Alabama's great, and so is Oklahoma, but we play Notre Dame, we beat the Irish at their place, we win Heismans, we've got the edge."

TRIVIA

In 1968 Trojan senior pitcher Bill "Spaceman" Lee, held out until coach Rod Dedeaux acquiesced to what demands?

Answers to the trivia questions are on pages 187–191.

"We had them figured," said McKay. "Our people were able to get in the right places. Hanratty was off, and we got him to throw impatiently on a few occasions."

Memories of the 16–14 victory of 1931 were stirred up. The papers revisited the comparisons in the sweet days that followed.

A classic line was uttered by Notre Dame sports publicist Roger Valdiserri, when he said, "Simpson's nickname shouldn't be 'Orange Juice.' It should be 'Oh, Jesus,' as in, 'Oh, Jesus, there he goes again.'"

The City Game: "It's Not a Matter of Life or Death. It's More Important than That."

In 1949 UCLA coach Red Sanders said, "The USC-UCLA game is not a matter of life or death. It's more important than that." There have been times when it sure seemed that way, and 1967 was one of them.

O.J. Simpson had sustained a slight injury but recovered in time for the UCLA game. In terms of college football games where everything was on the line, the 1967 City Game ranks above all other so-called "games of the century." The combination of the pregame hype, the special circumstances, the excitement of the game itself, and the results of the season based on its outcome, makes it probably the greatest game ever played at this level. Few if any pro games match it, for that matter. Not until the 2006 USC-Texas Rose Bowl game has a single game had so many bells and whistles, then lived up to the hype.

The old saw is that "Hollywood couldn't write a better script." The truth is, the script at the Coliseum on November 18, 1967, was Oscar-worthy. First, there was the Heisman campaign. Gary Beban was the preseason favorite. As a sophomore, he had engineered a stirring 14–12 "gutty little Bruin" win over Michigan State in the Rose Bowl. Now a senior, he was the perfect Heisman contender— smooth, polished, poised on and off the field. He was the epitome of what UCLA had become: first class all the way.

Simpson had entered the season a heralded junior college transfer. Heralded, for sure, but still a J.C. transfer. The idea of a J.C. transfer winning a Heisman trophy was, if not ludicrous, certainly never contemplated. In all the years since, it has never happened, and no other J.C. transfer has ever even been a serious contender in his first year.

That the seeds of the 1970 USC-Alabama game were planted in the minds of Bear Bryant and John McKay when they appeared together at a California coaching clinic run by Pete Carroll's high school coach, Bob Troppmann, in the mid-1960s? Serendipitously, 14-year-old Carroll was a "camper" who "coached" the younger kids. "It was his first gig," said Troppmann.

Heisman voters *did* see what Simpson did that day, which really makes one wonder, "What were they thinking?"

Aside from the Heisman race, the game was for the national championship. Whoever won would be number one, there was no doubt about that possibility. Notre Dame, Alabama, Michigan State—the usual suspects of the past few years were out of the picture by November 18.

Of course, while people said it was "for the national championship," they really meant that it would be for the *opportunity* to win the title, and that opportunity would come in the Rose Bowl. This meant that it was for just that...the Pacific-8 Conference title and with it the Rose Bowl, too. Then again there were all the usual nuggets of this game: city pride, bragging rights, family versus family, brother versus brother, husband versus wife, office boasts, schoolyard shouts, neighborhood yelling, the whole nine yards. The closeness of two schools in the same city playing for such a thing gave it an aura *unavailable* to any other rivalry.

"Never in the history of college football have two teams approached the climax of a season with so much at stake," wrote Paul Zimmerman in the *Los Angeles Times*.

"It was not too many years ago the Trojans owned this town," wrote Jim Murray in the *L.A. Times* of the fact that UCLA had won eight of the preceding 14 match-ups. "More than the Rose Bowl is at stake. The town is. The Trojans want it back."

McKay the Brooder also yearned to shut up those critics who had taken to saying that UCLA coach Tommy Prothro was smarter than he was.

"Well, we pushed 'em all over the field in 1965, but we fumbled on their 1, 7, and 17," McKay said, responding to media speculation that Prothro "had his number." "I guess he planned that."

A crowd of 90,772 packed the old stadium. When the thing finally started, Beban, who had bruised ribs, engineered a long drive topped by Greg Jones's 12-yard touchdown run. USC's defense saved the day early, though. After the half, Beban was effective, but kicker Zenon Andrusyshyn was not. Tall Bill Hayhoe blocked his field-goal try. Later, Andrusyshyn began to enter the pantheon of all-time goats when his other kicks were blocked.

The teams battled in the pits. Then Beban took over again. He nailed four straight passes, covering 65 yards. Dave Nuttall hauled in the last for the score, but Andrusyshyn was having one of the worst days in kicking history. Kickers dread such a day. They have nightmares about it.

Up 20–14, he kicked a low one. Hayhoe got his hand on it again. McKay told the press that even though Hayhoe was tall, the purpose was to get Andrusyshyn to rush, which he did.

"I call that brilliant coaching," McKay would say.

For every goat, there is a hero. In a game in which Simpson and Beban worked with equal brilliance, and Beban's team was a little better, O.J. was the difference. Amid the tensions and noise of a one-point game in the fourth quarter, with everything that can possibly ride on a college football game at stake, with fans in the stands looking at each other and saying, "This really *is* more important than life or death," O.J. separated himself from normal. He entered the shrine of immortality.

In the huddle, quarterback Toby Page saw Simpson's hangdog expression. He decided to try something that might net seven or eight yards for a needed first down. Simpson didn't seem to have it in him at this point in the afternoon. At the line of scrimmage, Page saw

IF ONLY . . . O.J. Simpson had won the Heisman Trophy he deserved in 1967, USC would have eight (if not more) Heismans, instead of being tied with Notre Dame and Ohio State for the most of any college with seven. The fact is, they should have nine. O.J. should have won in 1967 (meaning he would have preceded Archie Griffin, the only player to win it twice, since O.J. won it in '68), and Anthony Davis in 1974.

both of UCLA's linebackers eagerly anticipating his predictable play selection. He audibled: "23-blast."

"That's a *terrible* call," Simpson said to himself. But Page had called for O.J.'s favorite play. It meant running between the tackles, not always the best method for gaining eight yards, but it caught the Bruins flat-footed. Simpson took the handoff, hit the line, juked, and *ran to daylight!*

TRIVIA

When did USC's song girls debut?

Answers to the trivia questions are on pages 187–191.

It was the most memorable run of his career, pro or college. It is probably the most famous in USC history, and one of the most well-remembered in collegiate annals. Guards Steve Lehner and tackle Mike Taylor opened the hole. Center Dick Allmon knocked down a befuddled Bruin linebacker. Simpson headed towards the left sideline, benefited from *another* block that eliminated two Bruins in one fell swoop, then swerved back up the middle. Olympic-class sprinter Earl McCullouch hung by his side like the Marines protecting the flank against an invading army. Simpson was off to the races.

All the commentary about the game could not match Prothro's priceless, exasperated lament to an assistant coach while the play was still in progress. "Isn't but one guy can catch Simpson now," said Prothro as McCullouch whizzed by him stride-for-stride with the ball-carrying O.J., "and he's on the same team."

It was a variation on something Phillies' manager Gene Mauch said when Willie Mays had hit a home run over the fence, just beyond the outstretched glove of one of his outfielders.

"The only guy who could have caught it," mused Mauch, "hit it."

Simpson's dash beat UCLA 21–20. It ranks with The Play, the famous returned-kick-lateral-through-the-band run that gave California an improbable 1982 win over John Elway and Stanford. *Sports Illustrated* gave it its front cover: "Showdown in L.A."

"All on one unbearable Saturday afternoon is strictly from the studio lots," wrote *SI*.

Before his 64-yard run, Simpson was "tired," having told Toby Page to "give me a blow. It was third and 7, and we had a passing play called. But he switched to a running play at the line of scrimmage. I was so surprised," said Simpson.

When Page did that, "UCLA went into pass mode on defense," he continued. "When I broke outside, I could hear McKay yelling for me to go, and I was trying to zigzag. I was tired and knew that I didn't have that burst...I was so oblivious to the crowd. I just remember that I almost collapsed when Earl McCullouch hugged me in the end zone."

"To this day that USC-UCLA game was the biggest college football game I've ever seen," said Steve Bisheff on *The History of USC Football* DVD.

"When you sat back and looked at it, the game was everything you ever dreamed of," said Beban. "It was O.J. over there, he was established, and me, we received so much attention. It was bigger than anything we ever dreamt of, for the city, the Rose Bowl, and the national championship."

"We went into formation, and I had told our quarterback that if we walk out and they don't got a guy on Simpson, then run the blast and give it to Simpson," said McKay. "People always asked me was I afraid somebody would catch him, and I say the only guy who could've stopped him was on our team, Earl McCullouch, an Olympic-caliber hurdler."

The 1968 Rose Bowl game was almost anticlimatic after the UCLA thriller. Simpson scored both touchdowns and gained 128 yards in Southern California's 14–3 win over Indiana. He was named the MVP. His 1,543 yards led the nation. The game clinched another national championship for McKay. The victory had none of the Hollywood dramatics of the City Game.

"The idea is to win, isn't it?" McKay asked rhetorically.

Woody vs. McKay

The 1969 Rose Bowl between Ohio State and USC was one of the most anticipated college football match-ups of all time. It posed a clear on-field battle for the national championship, with no room for pollsters to interject upon the result. Ohio State coach Woody Hayes wanted the national championship for his program, his conference, and himself. He knew USC posed an enormous challenge to this desire. He was relentless in his pursuit of it.

It would be incorrect to say that McKay took the game anything but seriously. He wanted it just as badly. He no longer approached it with the laissez faire attitude of the 1963 Wisconsin contest. He saw in Woody a natural rival, in many ways his opposite number in terms of approach, style, offensive strategy, and overall philosophy. Woody was a strict disciplinarian. McKay was of course the "little white-haired man" who instilled fear in his charges. Marv Goux was a martinet figure. But their exhortations had Southern California panache attached to it; flair, a touch of humor, and wit. McKay and his staff dealt with off-field issues such as hair length, curfews, partying, and the like in the L.A. manner. Woody was Columbus, Ohio, all the way.

It was not Richard Nixon versus Dr. Timothy Leary. It was a little more like the Greatest Generation versus the Age of Aquarius, although nobody ever accused John McKay of being a free love–advocating hippie.

Woody's plan was to give USC's defense the outside lanes, utilizing his strong inside running attack and the efficient curl-in passes of quarterback Rex Kern. The 1968 Buckeyes may not have beaten some of the other strong teams of the 1960s, namely the 1966 Notre Dame Fighting Irish and Michigan State Spartans, but in terms of the

This group shot of the 1969 USC quarterbacks (plus coach Craig Fertig) includes two backups who later found glory as National Football League head coaches: Jim Fassel (6) and Mike Holmgren (7). Others in the picture are Jimmy Jones (8), Jim Heuman (9), and Greg Briner (5).

complete package, they may well rate as the decade's best team, when one compares the records and their performance from the season's beginning to its end.

They were young and promised only to get better, which was scary. Kern was a sophomore, as was their tremendous All-American safety, Jack Tatum. Woody had recruited great black athletes, as Duffy Daugherty had done a few years earlier at Michigan State. His team was fully integrated with the very best talent available.

Ohio prep football was legendary. Paul Brown had coached at Massillon High School. A number of Massillon players dotted Woody's roster. They were loaded. Other stars included Jan Hayes, Jim Otis, Jim Stillwagon, Leo Hayden, and Jim Roman.

"I measure a good back by how many men it takes to bring him down," Woody said in typical Midwest-speak, "and O.J. certainly qualifies in this." Woody, however, qualified his statement by saying that he did not fear "a damn thing" about USC.

The two teams battled it out in the trenches, but in the second quarter Simpson showed why he was the very best. First, USC drove into the red zone, setting up Ron Ayala's 21-yard field goal. Later in the quarter, Simpson went wild. His 80-yard touchdown romp is, aside from the 64-yarder against UCLA, one of his best-remembered runs. At 10–0, the Trojans could taste another national championship.

"Now we knew he was for real," Ohio State tackle Dave Foley said of Simpson's run, as if it had taken that to convince them. Either way, Ohio State went into high gear.

"That run was beautiful," said Ohio State defensive tackle Paul Schmidlin. "I was pursuing all the way, so I had a clear view of it. The run was simply great, and it was just what we needed."

"We decided we'd better wake up," said fullback Jim Otis, "or this guy was going to blow us off the field."

Ohio State did wake up, and quickly. They engineered drives behind Otis's power running between tackles. Before the half was over, they had tied the score at 10–10. It had taken the air out of the confident Trojans, deflating the partisan L.A. crowd.

IF ONLY . . . Unbeaten USC had not tied Notre Dame in 1969, they would have won another national championship. Nicknamed the "Cardiac Kids" because they won so many games in the last minute, they defeated unbeaten UCLA 14–12 on a desperation Jimmy Jones–to–Sam Dickerson touchdown pass after an earlier interference call kept their drive going. A teenage Pete Carroll was in the Coliseum stands. Jones hit Bob Chandler for a long sideline touchdown run in their 10–3 victory over Michigan in the Rose Bowl.

"Tying before the halftime gun was a big lift for us," said Rex Kern. "It gave us the momentum, and it took that away from them."

The third quarter was blood sport, with Ohio State breaking through to take the lead for the first time on a late-quarter Jim Roman field goal, 13–10. When quarterback Steve Sogge fumbled deep in his own territory, the tide had turned. Ohio State converted the turnover into the game-winning touchdown. Kern would hit Ray Gillian for another touchdown. Sogge connected with Sam Dickerson, but it was over. The final score was 27–16. It was a game of mistakes. Ohio State played a perfect game. USC lost three fumbles, two by Simpson. Sogge was intercepted twice.

TRIVIA

USC's 1969 defensive line was known as the "Wild Bunch." Where did that nickname come from?

Answers to the trivia questions are on pages 187–191.

"It wasn't a game for girl scouts and cookie eaters," said McKay, adding that despite Simpson's 171 yards gained, eight passes caught for 85 yards, a 20-yard kickoff return, and an 80-yard touchdown romp, his two fumbles had detracted from his performance. Some critics expressed concern over O.J.'s running style, in which he would carry the ball with one hand when in the open field. Woody, however, had only high praise for the Trojan legend.

"It was damn near inhuman for a guy to do that," he remarked of the touchdown run, in which O.J. had cut behind eight Buckeye defenders in a sprint for glory. Sogge said he thought the team was "complacent." Some "experts" conceded that if the team played six times, USC would get some wins, maybe even a majority of them, but Ohio State earned their place in history.

Simpson, the 1968 Heisman Trophy winner, had combined junior college and USC statistics that have never been approached: 90 touchdowns and 5,975 yards. None of that mattered to him in the locker room, where he fought back tears, acknowledging Ohio State's greatness but questioning his own errors. Just as Beban came into the USC locker room in 1967, O.J. went over to congratulate Ohio State, telling several of them, "You're the best team in the nation and don't let anyone tell you differently."

He told reporters that coming off the field for the last time as a Trojan was "strange," but that, "I can't help thinking how much the school and the other guys have done for me."

Ohio State of course won the national title, with USC placing fourth in the AP and second in the UPI polls.

TOP 18

1964 to 1981: USC vs. Notre Dame Games Impacting the National Title Race

Year	Team Competing for National Title
1964	Irish
1965	Irish
1966	*Irish
1967	*Trojans, Irish
1968	Trojans
1969	Trojans
1970	Irish
1971	Irish
1972	*Trojans, Irish
1973	*Irish, Trojans
1974	*Trojans, Irish
1975	Trojans
1976	Trojans
1977	*Irish
1978	*Trojans, Irish
1979	Trojans
1980	Irish
1981	Trojans

*Won national championship

Turning the Crimson Tide

Craig Fertig was not yet 30 years old in the spring of 1970. He had engineered that miraculous victory, coming from 17–0 down at the half to defeat Notre Dame in 1964, thus denying Ara Parseghian his first national championship. In so doing, he had earned his eternal place in the glory halls of Troy.

Now, however, he was a lowly assistant coach. He had made it past the graduate assistant stage, but not by a whole lot. He was assigned bed-check duty. When McKay had his fill of whiskey at Julie's, a nearby watering hole, Fertig (whose unofficial duties included keeping up with the old man) was tasked with driving him home to Covina.

On this smoggy spring day, Fertig again found himself playing taxi driver.

"Come on, Craig, let's go" McKay barked.

"Yes, sir," said Fertig. No questions asked. No details inquired of or given.

Out the door they went, to the parking lot, where McKay handed Fertig the keys to his car, a big, old, gas-guzzling Cardinal Toronado.

"Well, I get in the car, I'm born and raised in L.A., you tell me where you wanna go, and I'll get you there, but he doesn't say anything," Fertig said on *The History of USC Football* DVD. "And I never speak unless I'm spoken to."

They edged out onto the freeway. No small talk, just directions.

"So I turn here, turn there," continued Fertig.

Traffic coming off the Hoover entrance.

"Ten west," says McKay. Traffic clearing up around San Vicente, boxing them in again around the interchange with the San Diego Freeway.

"Four-oh-five south," says McKay.

Clear to Washington, then airport traffic the rest of the way.

"LAX," says McKay.

Los Angeles International Airport, their home away from home. How many times had they flown in and out of this place, for games and recruiting?

"And finally we get to the airport, so I said, 'Short term or long term?' and he says, 'Short,' and I said, 'Aah, short flight.'"

"Western Airlines," McKay said, directing them.

They parked and made their way to Western Airlines, and found a table in the Horizon Room.

"And I never forget," said Fertig, "at 10:00 in the morning, we go to the Horizon Room of Western Airlines, and he says, 'I'll have a cocktail here,' and he's still not talkin' to me, and he looks at his watch and he says, 'We'll have another one here,' and he says, 'He'll be here in about five minutes.'"

"Scotch on the rocks," said McKay.

"Vodka," said Fertig. "With O. J. Just like Simpson."

"One drink, then two," Fertig recalled 35 years later, "then three, then four."

"He'll be here in four minutes," said McKay. "I don't know who 'He' is. In 'He' walks with his hound's tooth hat on. It's *Paul Bear Bryant*. Like Mt. Rushmore with legs."

"Hi, Paul."

"Hi, John."

Sunburned from days on the Palm Desert Golf Course, where he had been a participant in the Bob Hope Desert Classic, Bryant extended his hand. Fertig had never met him before and was like a child.

"Martini," mumbled the Bear.

Another round, small talk. Another round. Nice weather. More drinks. Love California. How's *Corky?* How's *Mary Harmon?* Another round. Then...

"What do you wanna see me about, Paul?"

"Well, John—we'll have one more round here—John, I'm gonna offer ya $150,000 if y'all come down to Birmingham to help us open up the season—we'll have another one," says Bryant, according to Fertig's recollection.

McKay tugs at his cigar and says, "Okay, I'll tell you what I'll do, Paul, I'll give you $250,000 if you come out the following year and play us in the Coliseum."

McKay knew what to expect.

Fertig just stared as the two men shook hands.

Bear's integratin' his program, he thought to himself. *Jesus, Mary, and Joseph.*

"They shook hands, and that's what started that football game," said Fertig.

Fertig was "sitting in on a historical moment," he told author Allen Barra. "Coach McKay and Coach Bryant both understood what had just happened, but I didn't catch on right away. They had just agreed to play the first integrated college football game in Alabama."

Details were worked out, pleasantries exchanged, more drinks to toast the occasion, and finally Fertig had to get the old man home.

About six months later, on September 12, 1970, the integrated Trojans traveled to Legion Field in Birmingham to play the segregated Alabama Crimson Tide. It was a replay of 1956, when integrated USC took on all-white Texas in Austin. This time, Sam "Bam" Cunningham took on the C.R. Roberts role, scoring twice and rushing for 135 yards in a 42–21 thrashing in front of a capacity crowd of shocked white Southerners. The impact was much different, though.

In 1956 Texas players had changed their tune, shaking Roberts's hand after the game, but the fans remained hostile. Nothing changed in the South. This time, the Alabama players were relatively polite during and after the game. The fans were numbed into silence, with the exception of a small contingent of black spectators behind the end zone. During periods of silence, the only sounds heard were USC's players and coaches whooping it up, until the fourth quarter. Black people from Birmingham gathered *outside* the stadium. Their cheers for the visiting Trojans provided an eerie backdrop, and in many ways were like angels heralding a new day!

TRIVIA

Aside from Bryant's "This here's what a football player looks like" quote, what other famous statement was made that day and by whom?

Answers to the trivia questions are on pages 187–191.

After the game, black fans by the thousands met USC's players as they boarded the bus, lining the road as the team left Legion Field. In the warm night air, they carried Bibles and candles, sang hymns, prayed, and thanked the Trojans as if there were a modern Moses leading them to the Promised Land.

TRIVIA

What was the headline of Jim Murray's next-day column of September 13, 1970, in the *Los Angeles Times*?

Answers to the trivia questions are on pages 187–191.

Unlike the 1956 USC-Texas game, *this time* the game had a profound impact on society. Bear Bryant and John McKay had planned the game to help Bear ease the transition of his first black recruit, Wilbur Jackson, as well as a black J.C. transfer, John Mitchell, who had been ticketed for USC until McKay boasted of him, prompting Bear to "steal" him for his program.

Jackson, Mitchell, Sylvester Croom, and other African American players were seamlessly integrated into the Alabama program. After 1970, thousands of black athletes made smooth transitions to Southern sports teams at every level. Society as a whole—politics, education, culture, religion—completely changed. The laws were ratified by changing hearts and minds. When one hears the grim descriptions by the tiny handful of blacks playing basketball in the Southeastern Conference in the late 1960s, then compares that with the memories of Jackson, Mitchell, and Croom, who were treading in this same territory just a year or two later, one considers the distinct possibility that what occurred was nothing less than an act of God!

"If I had any bad memories of my time at 'Bama," said Jackson, "I never would have sent my daughter there. I was voted team captain in 1973. There were only eight black players, so obviously I had support among my white teammates. When I went to the reunion of that team, it was the best time I ever had."

Mitchell and Croom, who both coached on Bryant's staff, had similar good things to say and were insistent that Bryant did not have a racist bone in his body. The change that occurred between 1969 and 1971 was seismic, a paradigm shift in the hearts and minds of ordinary folks. The 1970 USC-Alabama game was a big part of it, and certainly sits in the middle—historically, geographically, chronologically, and culturally—of these momentous times.

After the game, Bryant supposedly took Sam Cunningham into the Alabama locker room and told his team, "This here's what a football player looks like." The problem is, nobody in the Alabama locker room says it happened. In truth, Bryant probably took Cunningham into the hallway and made overheard remarks in and around media, alumni, and faculty, while a few 'Bama players probably ventured out to shake his hand. While the story is as much myth as truth, 'Bama quarterback Scott Hunter summed it up best by saying, "No, it didn't happen, but it should have."

The Greatest College Football Team Ever Assembled

"We never had a game in doubt," stated McKay's son, J.K., who along with his high school friend Pat Haden was a back-up sophomore on the 1972 national champions. "We never had a close game all year. We dominated in every way you can. It was the best football team ever."

From the 1972 team, 13 players would be All-Americans.

"We were a *team*," said Manfred Moore, "who wanted to win every game, and for sure we always knew when the Monday review of the game was on, and we didn't want to be ridiculed, so we performed at our best."

The 1972 Trojans were the greatest collegiate football team in history.

The season opened at War Memorial Stadium in Little Rock, Arkansas. The Razorbacks were fourth in the country, USC eighth, but Southern California dominated them 31–10.

USC returned home to dismantle Oregon State 51–6.

Sophomore tailback Anthony Davis scored twice in a 55–20 thumping of Illinois.

Lynn Swann ran a punt back 92 yards to power the 51–6 rout of Michigan State at the Coliseum.

The following week was the one McKay had been waiting for: Stanford.

"They're the worst winners I've come up against," McKay said of the 1970–1971 Stanford victories over his team, which propelled them to two straight Rose Bowls. "They've shown no class against us. I'd like to beat them by 2,000 points."

The 30–21 win was the closest of the season and still rankles players who felt they owed Stanford a beating.

Sam Cunningham, Mike Rae, and Charles Young keyed the 42–14 victory over Cal.

Washington had quarterback Sonny Sixkiller. They were ranked 18th, but their star was hurt, and they lost 34–7.

Against Oregon (the only game they were "pushed," said Pat Haden), USC won 18–0. The rain fell on the slippery artificial turf.

The press started to focus on Davis, who, like Reggie Bush in the 2000s, was becoming a national star but was not even the starting tailback yet. Davis's brash personality made him a perfect quote-meister. McKay smiled when he thought about the young man now dubbed "A.D."

"I coach 'em not to get tackled," McKay joked.

With Davis finally in the starting lineup, Washington State fell 44–3. A.D. ran the opening kick back 69 yards, setting up a 23-yard field goal.

"USC isn't the top team in the country," joked Washington State coach Jim Sweeney. "The Miami Dolphins are."

A huge crowd filled the Coliseum on a hot November evening for the USC-UCLA game. *Sports Illustrated* duly noted that the L.A. crowd left behind more trash than any stadium in America, a reference to their propensity for alcohol consumption during night contests.

Rae engineered a first-quarter drive culminated by a field goal. After holding UCLA's veer, USC drove again. A.D. swept around into the end zone for 23 yards, 10–0.

A UCLA touchdown drive and a Davis fumble had the Bruins back in the game, 10–7, but UCLA missed a game-tying field-goal try before linebacker Richard "Batman" Wood took over. He chased down Bruin tailback James McAlister and harried UCLA's Mark

IF ONLY . . . USC and Notre Dame did not schedule each other every year, both schools might have more national championships. The 1964 USC–Notre Dame game started, and was part of, the greatest period in the intersectional rivalry's history. Sometimes the games were close, sometimes they were blowouts. A couple were classics—games that those who saw them call the "best ever played."

John McKay poses for a photo with his son, sophomore J.K. McKay, during USC's dominant 1972 season.

Harmon badly. With the outside lanes shut down, UCLA had to go up the middle. Batman Wood was there every time.

Rod McNeill capped an 80-yard drive with a one-yarder to make it 17–7. Mike Rae led a 96-yard third-quarter march, capping it with a keeper to make it 24–7. USC shut it down offensively for some strange reason, but Wood kept dominating, finishing with 18 tackles. Harmon was a pitiful 3-for-9 for 38 yards. Davis gained 178 yards on 26 carries, almost a seven-yard average.

Despite averaging 34 points a game coming in, some UCLA players actually admitted later to being scared of USC.

Two weeks later Ara Parseghian and Notre Dame were looking for revenge. They had not beaten McKay since 1966, when of course McKay said "a billion Chinamen could not care less who wins," and was supposed to have also vowed "never to lose to Notre Dame again."

Since then he had *not* lost to Notre Dame. In the past two seasons his underdog charges had knocked Notre Dame out of the hunt for a number-one ranking. Ranked 10th, the Fighting Irish had lost only to Missouri and were already Orange Bowl–bound.

A review of USC's 1972 wins reveals a team averaging a little over 40 points a game, posting one shutout, usually winning by about 30. It was never close. But what's most impressive is that, in several of their games, they held it back a little instead of laying it on thick. The UCLA game was an example. The 45–23 victory over Notre Dame was another.

Anthony Davis became the legendary "Notre Dame killer" that day in front of 75,243 sun-soaked Los Angelenos. Many recall his game two years later, but his 1972 sophomore performance is very possibly the finest college football game any individual has ever played. He broke five school records, including most touchdowns in a game (six), touchdowns in a quarter (three), points (36), longest scoring kickoff return (97 yards), and kickoff return yardage in a season (an astonishing 468). He had 368 total yards, rushing for 99 to finish the season over 1,000. The numbers are only part of the story. He ran back two kicks, a 96-yarder in addition to a 97-yard return.

Davis opened the game with the 97-yard kickoff return for a touchdown. With USC leading 6–3 in the first quarter, A.D. scored from the 1. Then Dale Mitchell recovered Eric Penick's fumble at the Irish 1, setting up another Davis score from the 5 to make it 19–3.

USC let Notre Dame back in it, 25–23, but no sooner were the Irish eyes smiling when A.D. ran his second kick back to give them a dose of reality. After Notre Dame kicked out of bounds, trying to keep the ball away from him, Cliff Brown tried again. This time A.D. gathered it in at the 4, headed straight up the field into the blocking wedge, squeezed through, and made for the left sideline. He evaded one good shot. From there he was off to the races.

"Whichever way they go, I go the other," he explained.

In the end zone A.D. went into his patented "knee dance."

"Davis is the greatest I've ever seen on kickoff returns in college," noted Parseghian.

When Southern California led 32–23, the 75,243 began to chant, "We're number one!" In the fourth quarter A.D. ran it in *again*, from the 8 for touchdown number six. Cunningham wrapped up the scoring with a one-yard leap to make it 45–23. Had McKay let A.D. score, it would have tied an NCAA record.

"I've never seen a greater single day shown by an individual than Davis gave today," said McKay. "I

TRIVIA

What did John McKay say after USC returned to the Rose Bowl in the 1972 season after a two-year absence?

Answers to the trivia questions are on pages 187–191.

know he could have tied the record by scoring one more touchdown, but we don't worry about NCAA records."

It was quite apropos that Sam "Bam" Cunningham, who started his career so spectacularly against Alabama, would end it as the headliner against Ohio State. Sam is a Trojan legend, a Hall of Famer, and an all-time great, but his career is overshadowed by some of his more flamboyant teammates and events. Not on New Year's Day, 1973.

USC scored the first five times they had the ball in the second half. Cunningham scored four times, which included his patented "over-the-top" tumbles into the end zone.

Rae completed 18-of-25 for 229 yards, six to Swann and six to Young. Davis rushed for 157 yards, but Cunningham was named Player of the Game.

"I owe Sam something," said McKay. "He was a great runner, but I made him a blocker for three years. He's the best runner I ever ruined."

John Bledsoe gave Ohio State a little dignity with a touchdown late to finish it at 42–17.

"Is there anybody else the Associated Press would like us to play?" asked McKay. The Bears, the Jets, the Eagles; there were a few NFL teams that probably were not as good.

Woody Hayes could not say anything bad about USC when it was over.

"Yes, they are the best college football team I've ever seen," Hayes admitted. "We stuck it to a team that was supposed to be great," said A.D. "If Ohio State is the third best team in the country, and we beat them like this, we must be unstoppable."

Media pundits said USC was not only number one, but numbers "two through three," as well. That was how great the discrepancy was between the Trojan dynasty and the rest of college football in 1972. Very few collegiate teams have ever swept through their schedule the way USC did.

The national media took McKay's assessment one step further, positing the notion that it was not USC's best team ever, but rather the best team ever, *anywhere.* McKay would eventually make this same statement. He was still saying it when interviewed in 2000.

"I've never seen a team that could beat it," he stated.

Superlatives describing Rae, Young, tackle Pete Adams, defensive tackle John Grant, linebacker Richard "Batman" Wood, as well as Davis, McNeill, Cunningham, Swann, and others, had a sublime quality to it. The general feeling was that words alone could not accurately depict how much better they were not just of the 1972 competition, but the 1869 to 1971 competition.

They captured both polls as the first two-poll unanimous selection, as well as the Bob Zuppke Award presented to the "best team playing the toughest schedule" in 1972.

It Wasn't a Football Game.
It Was a Sighting!

It was not a sporting event, it was a Roman orgy. USC was not a football team, they were Patton's Army moving through the Low Countries, Grant taking Richmond, the Wehrmacht during the Blitzkrieg.

For 'SC coach John McKay, it was not about coaching, it was about destiny.

"If I was in control," he says, "we would have scored more than six points in the first half."

For Trojan fans, it was not a game, it was a sighting. It was Fatima, Lourdes, and the Burning Bush combined.

For Notre Dame coach Ara Parseghian, it was the Seventh Circle of Hell, the Twilight Zone, "Chef's head" in *Apocalypse Now*.

For the Irish, it was their worst disaster since the potato famine.

It was a 17-minute Southern California earthquake, epicentered at the Los Angeles Memorial Coliseum on a fall Saturday in 1974. It was felt as far away as South Bend, Indiana, and the aftershocks reverberate to this day.

The Notre Dame Fighting Irish were the defending national champions. En route to an undefeated 1973 season, they had smoked Southern Cal at South Bend. Notre Dame gave up 2.2 yards per rush and eight touchdowns in their previous 1974 games, and victory over USC would put them in a position to finish number one again. USC was playing for the top slot, too. A national television audience tuned in to the biggest game of the year, and 83,552 filled the Coliseum.

A typical USC–Notre Dame game.

In the first half, Notre Dame outclassed USC in every way, breaking out to a 24–0 lead, and their fans were in Full Gloat.

'SC managed a touchdown on a swing pass from quarterback Pat Haden to tailback Anthony Davis with 10 seconds left in the first half, but the extra point failed, 24–6.

"I told them that if Davis runs the second-half kickoff back for a touchdown, we would win the game," said McKay. Over the years, McKay's remarks were changed to "Davis *will* run the second half kickoff back for a touchdown," but like everything else that day, his words are now legend and myth.

The first 17 minutes of the second half were the most exciting in college football and Los Angeles sports history.

Kickoff to Davis, who ran it 102 yards for a touchdown, the two-point conversion failed. 24–12.

Anthony Davis breaks into the clear and races 102 yards for a touchdown against Notre Dame to start a 49-point second half that gave USC a 55–24 victory in the Los Angeles Coliseum on November 30, 1974.

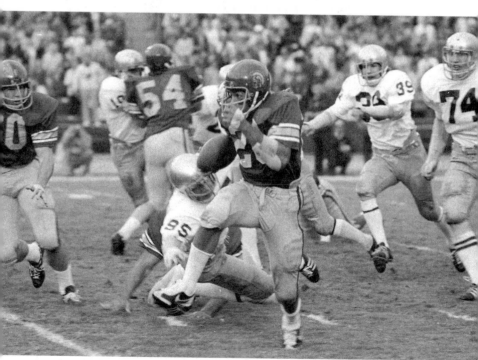

Haden to J.K. McKay for 31 yards, followed by Davis for a six-yard touchdown scamper, kick good. 24–19.

Kevin Bruce recovered a Notre Dame fumble, two Haden pass completions, Davis four yards, touchdown, then Davis dove in to complete the two-point conversion. 27–24, USC, 6:23 gone in the quarter. Madhouse.

TRIVIA

How many Trojans were drafted off the 1974 national champions?

Answers to the trivia questions are on pages 187–191.

Marvin Cobb returned a punt 56 yards for Troy, Haden to McKay. 34–24, 9:23 gone in the third.

Charles Phillips intercepted Irish quarterback Tom Clements's pass, Haden hit McKay from 44 yards out, period over: 41–24.

Bruce recovered another fumble, Haden to Shelton Diggs, 16 yards: 48–24.

Phillips's third interception is returned 58 yards for a touchdown. Seventeen minutes after it started, 55–24.

McKay normally stood calmly amid the bedlam, arms crossed like a commuter waiting for the 5:30 to Larchmont. This time, he lost control, hugging Haden (who lived in his house his senior year at Bishop Amat High), his son, J.K. (Haden's best friend), and Davis, all at the same time. None of the players weighed more than 183 pounds.

"There have never been three smaller kids who have done so much so often," he said, managing to sound like Winston Churchill.

Up in the broadcast booth, Ohio State coach Woody Hayes must have felt like a Prussian military commander with a binocular-view of Napoleon's Italian campaign, knowing he would have to face them down the road. The USC rooting section started chanting, "Woody, you're next!" in reference to the upcoming Rose Bowl.

With 13 minutes left, the Trojans had conquered Ireland, but before they could roll over Austria, Poland, and Denmark, McKay pulled his starters in favor of Vince Evans and Rob Adolph.

Davis proved himself the best college football player in America that day, but because it was played on a late date, ballots for the Heisman Trophy were mailed prior to his performance. Ohio State's Archie Griffin won it instead.

The game left Notre Dame at 9–2. Southern California was not as phenomenal in their New Year's Day game with the Buckeyes. In keeping with the comeback theme, though, Haden combined with McKay and Diggs to bring his team down the field for a touchdown and a two-point conversion, good for the 18–17 victory, a 10–1–1 record, and the national championship. In those days, not only was USC unbelievably good, but they were as exciting as any team ever.

Parseghian never coached after that season. Rumors have it he sees a therapist to combat visions of a white horse constantly running around a field. McKay left for Tampa Bay and pro doldrums.

IF ONLY . . . John McKay had stayed on at USC instead of going to Tampa Bay in 1976, he may well have approached Amos "Alonzo" Stagg's all-time career win record (since broken by Bear Bryant and Joe Paterno), and therefore been considered the best college coach ever.

McKay's successor, John Robinson, beat Notre Dame six of his seven years (1976 to 1982) and won one national championship. If McKay had equaled J.R.'s record and coached into the late 1980s or even early 1990s, the program might have attained unmatched glories instead of going through a down period.

Alabama Redux

Nineteen seventy-eight. Legion Field, Birmingham, Alabama. A day game in September, hot and muggy. National television. Two undefeated teams, the winner would have the inside track at finishing number one.

As Marv Goux would say, "The best of the West versus the best of the East." Eight years prior, in a game that by no means had been forgotten in 'Bama, John McKay's Trojans waltzed into Birmingham for a night game against the Crimson Tide. Southern California was cocky, arrogant. Maybe the greatest program ever assembled over a 19-year period (1962 to 1981). They featured a black sophomore fullback from Santa Barbara named Sam "Bam" Cunningham. Phenomenal black athletes, some from the South, had long been a staple at USC. Their first All-American in 1925 had been a black man.

Coach Bear Bryant's Alabama team was 100 percent white when USC walked into their house in 1970 and administered a whuppin', led by Cunningham with two touchdowns.

Now, in 1978, the men of Troy were back. This time, they were led by a new coach, John Robinson, and he had a team that was possibly more talented than the best of McKay's juggernauts. USC had won the national championship in 1972. In '74 spectacular comebacks against Notre Dame and Ohio State propelled them to the crown.

All-American tailback Charles White led USC in '78. Anthony Munoz opened holes for him. Junior quarterback Paul McDonald had as much brains and ability as Pat Haden. Cornerback Dennis Smith succeeded Dennis Thurman as the second straight All-American to come out of Santa Monica High. A young safety named Ronnie Lott was hitting people with the force of a major earthquake.

Alabama was not their father's Tide. This time they came to play with black athletes. Extremely talented ones. Lots of them. The era of the USCs and Michigan States picking off the Bubba Smiths of the South was over. Now Alabama, Tennessee, Florida State, and the others would reap the harvest sown in their backyards. For this reason, USC no longer enjoyed that quiet advantage that nobody really wanted to talk about in 1970. They would have to play it even up in the other guy's stadium.

It was no contest. White ran for 199 yards and a couple touchdowns. The Trojans dominated from the first snap, taking the huge crowd out early, and the final score, 24–14, did not reflect Southern California's superiority.

A few weeks later the Trojans had a letdown. It was one of those radio-only Saturday night games against a tough Sun Devil squad, fired up to prove themselves in the new Pacific-10 Conference. In L.A., sports fans making the disco scene at the Red Onion or Flanagan's missed Tom Kelly's broadcast of ASU's 20–7 upset win.

That was it, though. The rest of the conference fell like Eastern Europe under Stalin. Terry Donahue's UCLA Bruins could play anybody else even up in 1978, but against their rivals they were boys facing men.

Then came Thanksgiving weekend.

With Alabama already having been knocked off, the game, played on an overcast day at the Coliseum and before a full house in an electric atmosphere, promised to be for the national championship. In

IF ONLY . . . John Robinson had stayed at USC instead of going to the Rams, the Trojans all-time football tradition might have surpassed Notre Dame's in the 1980s instead of "waiting" until the Pete Carroll era to reach those heights. After beating Notre Dame for the fifth consecutive year, in 1982, a rivalry that had been fairly dominated by Notre Dame was now dominated by USC, and the all-time record between the two was almost even. In the pecking order of college football supremacy, Southern California had ascended to an equal historical footing with, and possibly even was now above, Notre Dame. After J.R's departure, though, Notre Dame ran up a 13-year unbeaten streak against Troy.

1977 Joe Montana and the green-shirted Irish derailed USC's winning streak in front of a more-deranged-than-usual Notre Dame crowd. That earned them an eventual national title, but the victory was an exception during that era. In those days, USC beat Notre Dame like a redheaded stepchild.

Mays going all out. Brando emoting. Reagan communicating to the camera. Some people are naturals, and anybody lucky enough to have been at the Los Angeles Memorial Coliseum that day could recognize that Montana had it, too. Absolute charisma. Undeniable magic.

Still, in the beginning, USC moved Notre Dame off the line with ease, Lott was in Montana's face, White ran crazy, and McDonald threaded passes like a southpaw surgeon. Well into the third quarter, 'SC led by three touchdowns.

Then came Joe! If you were there, you saw Montana wake up the echoes and single-handedly silence the home crowd. He was everything that he would be against Dallas, Cincinnati, or Denver.

Still, those were the halcyon days of the University of Southern California. They got the ball back with about a minute on the clock, and McDonald moved them up the field. With two seconds left, Frank Jordan, a history major from Riordan High School in San Francisco, calmly broke Joe Montana's heart with the game-winning field goal, 27–25. Montana walked off the field, a defeated warrior bathed in the kind of respect reserved only for the rarest of champions.

In an anticlimatic Rose Bowl game, Southern California toyed with an out-manned Michigan team, holding the score down like Ali letting his opponent save a little self-respect.

When the sun set in Pasadena on New Year's Day to the chant of "We're Number One," it seemed a foregone conclusion that USC had indeed captured the national championship. They were 12–1 in a year that saw no undefeated teams. Alabama's one loss had come at the hands of 'SC.

What those "number one" chanters had not taken into consideration was the popularity of Paul "Bear" Bryant. The next day, the Associated Press (the writers) voted Alabama number one. United Press International (the coaches) voted 'SC number one. Twelve years earlier, Bryant's unbeaten team had lost the "Catholic vote" to

DID YOU KNOW . . . That Marv Goux gave legendary pep talks in the old "dungeon" (before Heritage Hall was built) prior to road trips? "Cardinal is the color of blood," he told his players, "which we all are on the inside. Gold is what every man wants to be—rich—and will shed blood for. Gentlemen, a conquest is the act of going into another man's stadium and destroying him. We will use their living guts to grease the treads of our tanks. We'll crush their will to live! Their faith in themselves will be taken from them on their own field. We'll rob them of their pride! Why? Because we *are* the University of Southern California! *We are!* USC! *We are!* USC! It is our destiny to rape, pillage, to take no prisoners. After the game, if they still have anything left, we'll beat 'em in any setting available."

Notre Dame; backlash against their segregated roster. The 1970 USC-Alabama game had ushered in cataclysmic change, and now Bryant was a heroic figure.

Had USC not blown a 21–0 halftime lead against Stanford at the Coliseum in 1979, they would have won back-to-back national championships. The 1979 and 2005 Trojans might be considered the best college teams not to win national titles. Coach John Robinson's '79 team featured Heisman winner Charlie White, offensive lineman Anthony Munoz, and safety Ronnie Lott.

Robinson took USC to four bowls in his first four years, including three Rose Bowls, winning them all. His teams broke a 47-year record at USC for most consecutive games without a loss, 28.

USC safety Lott later spearheaded the San Francisco 49ers to four Super Bowl titles. He earned All-America honors and may well be the noblest Trojan of them all. He played on the 1978 national champions and the 1979 Rose Bowl champs. A member of the College Football Hall of Fame and the team's 1980 MVP, Lott also won the Davis-Teschke Award as the most inspirational Trojan.

Anthony Munoz
Goes Hollywood

Anthony Munoz, a surefire All-American, was hurt in 1979. He did not play until the Rose Bowl. Had he been healthy, he might have won the Outland Trophy and unquestionably would have been an All-American. Munoz, who starred at Chaffey High School in Ontario, was a towering specimen at 6'7", 280 pounds. The third pick of the 1980 draft (he was selected ahead of Brad Budde, despite his injury) by Cincinnati, Munoz became one of the greatest offensive linemen in NFL history. In his second year, 1981, he led the Bengals to the Super Bowl. Unfortunately, both of the perennial All-Pro's Super Bowl appearances, 1982 and 1989, were losses to Bill Walsh and the San Francisco 49ers.

An exceptionally handsome, articulate, and charismatic figure, Munoz made a brief foray into acting. He played the indomitable Gonzales in the 1984 classic, *The Right Stuff*, which told Tom Wolfe's story of the Mercury space program. Many who watched his performance found him to be a memorable, albeit minor, character. Audiences may well not have known who he was, thinking, "Whatever happened to that big Hispanic guy who played the male nurse in *The Right Stuff?*"

DID YOU KNOW . . . That USC All-American quarterback Paul McDonald hit 56.7 percent of his passes in 1978 for 1,690 yards? In 1979 he set school records with 2,223 yards and a 62.1 completion percentage. His 2,223 yards were an all-time single-season record, to go with 4,138 career yards and a 59.7 completion percentage.

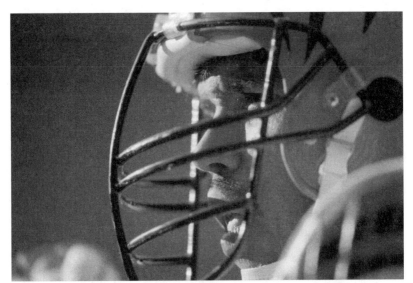

Anthony Munoz had an exceptional career at USC and in the NFL, which would eventually lead him to the Pro Football Hall of Fame.

Director Philip Kaufman may just have wanted to create a visual spectacle that would jolt audiences. Gonzales indeed was a male nurse. The dark-haired, dusky-featured 280-pounder appears in a starched, white nurse's uniform, stationed at a military hospital in New Mexico in the late 1950s, when all the "fighter jocks" were being tested for a shot at becoming astronauts.

Scott Glenn plays Alan Shepard. At the time, a comic was making the rounds as a politically incorrect faux-Mexican "astronaut" with a whiny Spanish accent, riffing on space terminology like "blast off" and "crash helmet" ("oooh, I *hope nooot!*"). Shepard apparently loved the character, making a pest of himself imitating "Jose Jimenez." In the film, these efforts at humor are met by classic scowls by Munoz/Gonzales, whose imposing presence would frighten George Patton, much less a fighter pilot.

Munoz-as-Gonzales uses Glenn-as-Shepard's moment of weakness to lecture him on his depiction of Mexicans.

"Me 'n' my friends think your Jose Jimenez imitation is A-okay," he says in a booming voice that sounds like thunder, "but what you're doin' with it is B-A-D *baaad!*"

"You're absolutely right, Mr. Gonzales," Shepard says.

TRIVIA

What was the 502 Club?

Answers to the trivia questions are on pages 187–191.

Finally Glenn gathers himself, venturing a question to Gonzales. In reality, an orderly likely would not have had the answer, but for dramatic effect, it works.

"Mr. Gonzales, how'm I doin'?" asks Glenn.

"I think you're gonna make it, man," says Munoz in one of the deepest voices in Hollywood history. "I think you're gonna be an astronaut."

It is a truly memorable scene. Munoz's performance is not amateurish, albeit unusual. Had he chosen to pursue it, Munoz could have had a career on the screen. One could easily have pictured him partnered with or trying to kill "Dirty Harry" Callahan, for example.

Anthony Munoz wore No. 79 on the USC baseball team, just as he did in football. Baseball recruit Phil Smith recalled his visit: "The game was on. Munoz must have been hurt or something, but he's sitting in the stands. I'm introduced to this guy and told he's on the baseball team. He's about 7'7", 392.5 pounds, wearing a cowboy hat and huge 'shit kicker' boots. He's got the voice of God and looks like Pancho Villa on steroids. I'm a lowly high school player from Canyon High, this is the first baseball player I met at USC, and I naively think to myself, 'This is what every Trojan baseball player looks like!' "

Munoz was part of what turned out to be a last hurrah of Trojan glory, until Pete Carroll arrived.

DID YOU KNOW . . . That Charles White rushed for 2,050 yards in 1979, the first time any USC back had done so? His 6,245 career yards would be a school and Pac-10 record (still behind Tony Dorsett). His 5,598 career regular season yards were second in NCAA history. He set or equaled 22 NCAA, Pac-10, USC, and Rose Bowl records.

"Young Juice"

Life was gooooooood in 1981! USC tailback Marcus Allen was doing things nobody; not Simpson, Tony Dorsett, or Charles White, had done. Number-one USC beat number-two Oklahoma at the Coliseum on a last-second pass by quarterback John Mazur to tight end Fred Cornwell from two yards out to give Troy a dramatic 28–24 win.

They prevailed over Notre Dame, 14–7, followed by easy wins over Washington State and Cal. At that point the third-ranked, 8–1 Trojans, featuring the sure Heisman winner, looked to have the inside track at the national championship.

On November 14 in Seattle, however, 47,347 watched the Huskies knock Southern California out of the Rose Bowl and the national championship, 13–3.

USC found themselves in the role of spoiler against UCLA. Allen came in with a gaudy NCAA record 2,123 yards and seven 200-yard games.

After three quarters, the Bruins were ahead 21–12. Allen just pounded and pounded and pounded until USC went ahead 22–21 with 2:14 to go on his five-yard run. When USC cornerback Joe Turner intercepted Tom Ramsey with 1:19 on the clock, it seemed to be over, except for a flag thrown on 'SC linebacker August Curley, charged with roughing the passer.

UCLA drove to the 29 before calling on kicker Norm Johnson with four seconds left and Southern California holding on by the skin of their teeth. Nose guard George

TRIVIA

How many home runs did USC's Mark McGwire hit in setting the single-season Pac-10 record?

Answers to the trivia questions are on pages 187–191.

141

Achica etched his name in the marble annals of Trojan memory by breaking through Dennis Edwards and Charles Ussery to block the 46-yard try, returning the Victory Bell to Figueroa and Jefferson. Curley awarded his first-born son to Achica, and is still seen washing his car on Sundays.

Allen rushed for 219 yards on 40 carries. It was USC's 11th win over UCLA in 15 seasons, and redemption after the ignominious loss in the 1980 "Probation Bowl" between the Trojans and Bruins, in which Marcus had been held to only 72 yards.

Joe Paterno and Penn State ended USC's year on a sour note, though, with a 26–10 win in the Fiesta Bowl. At 9–3, USC finished 12th (AP) and 13th (UPI).

It was a strange year, one in which USC had beaten Notre Dame on the road and UCLA, played on New Year's Day, and their record-

Marcus Allen goes over the top of the pile to give the Trojans' 28–24 last-second victory over Oklahoma in 1981.

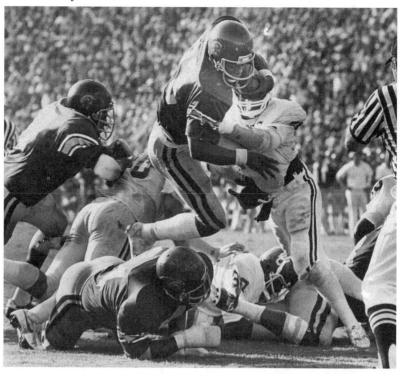

DID YOU KNOW . . . That in the 1990s, the two most dominant, intimidating major league baseball players were Mark McGwire and 6'10" Randy Johnson, one-time Trojan teammates? Incredibly, USC never even made it to the College World Series with these players.

setting tailback won the Heisman. But the loss to Penn State was a devastating one, leaving their supporters with an uneasy feeling. There was no outward hint that the empire was on the verge of collapse, but something was amiss.

Allen was nicknamed "Young Juice" for his physical resemblance to O.J. He employed a similar style in the open field. He was the second leading rusher in the nation as a junior through 10 games, but missed the 20–3 win over Notre Dame with an eye injury. When Allen broke all the national rushing records, earning the 1981 Heisman, combined with his good looks and natural charm, he became an iconic figure at Troy.

"That particular time when I won the award, I was very happy because I'd achieved something I wanted to achieve, but I was really happy for my family," said Marcus in *The History of USC Football* DVD. "It was more important for my parents than it was for me, because it was a reflection of all the hard work they'd put in—years ago, all the Pop Warner experiences, my mom being the team mother and my dad being the coach running back and forth and really giving up their lives for their kids' lives. So for me, it was like the first time I had an opportunity to pay back my parents. I remember, my dad is a very loquacious guy, talks nonstop, but for the first time in my lifetime, he was just quiet. He was speechless, and I know he was nothing but proud, it was *his son*. He could say, 'My son,' and my mom could say, 'My son is known as the best college player in the country.' That's for them, what it's all about. And for me, that's what it was all about."

The captain of the 1981 team, Allen set 16 NCAA records and was the first collegian to break 2,000 regular-season yards. He won the Walter Camp and Maxwell trophies, averaging 212.9 yards a game in his senior year. In 1982 the Raiders, in the process of moving from Oakland to L.A., made him their first pick.

All Right Now

When USC recovers a fumble, their band plays "All Right Now," a popular rock song by Free from the 1970s. When Pete Carroll took over in 2000, it really was all right now. Finally.

By 2002, there was a strong sense that Southern California faced a make-or-break year. Despite the loss in the 2001 Las Vegas Bowl, Carroll had some people excited that perhaps he could right the ship. However, other coaches had gotten the fans' hopes up in the past, only to let them down.

The Associated Press ranked Troy 18th coming in. The main source of optimism came via reports that Norm Chow was making major progress with quarterback Carson Palmer. One of the most celebrated high school quarterbacks California has ever produced, in four years he had shown sparks of brilliance interspersed with terrible glimpses of Sean Salisbury. Palmer was not an all-conference player, much less an All-American. *StreetZebra* magazine's 2000 speculation that the 6'6", 230-pounder would win a Heisman seemed a cruel joke by 2002. USC, whose marketing machinery is as adept at promoting Heisman candidates as any in the country, did not even see fit to put Palmer on the cover of their 2002 football media guide. Troy Polamalu graced it instead.

After five games, Palmer was better but not great. All-American safety Polamalu was spectacular. Freshman receiver Mike Williams, while showing flashes of brilliance, was still very unreliable. Close losses to Kansas State and Washington State left Carroll's team at 3–2, on the verge of mediocrity.

USC then carried a modest winning streak to Pasadena to take on a solid 7–3, 25th-ranked UCLA squad before 91,084. The 52–21

Carson Palmer helped lead a Trojan resurgence in the early 2000s.

trouncing they put on the Bruins in their house was the most impressive single performance in the history of the City Game (until Reggie Bush in 2005). Palmer's "watch-me-win-the-Heisman" performance was impressive. He dominated the Bruins in an unstoppable offensive extravaganza.

Williams caught six passes for 66 yards. Kareem Kelly caught four for 94, Keary Colbert four for 84. Palmer had four scoring strikes. Justin Fargis scored a touchdown. Hershel Dennis made a

TRIVIA

Mike Gillespie's daughter, Kelly, married a catcher who played for Gillespie with the North Pole Nicks of the Alaskan Summer League in 1983. Who was it?

Answers to the trivia questions are on pages 187–191.

38-yard run. Mike Patterson, Antuan Simmons, and Matt Grootegoed spearheaded the defense. Kenechi Udeze made four stops for losses with two sacks.

If there was any doubt in anybody's mind, Palmer secured the Heisman Trophy the next week before 91,432 at the Coliseum in a totally devastating, 44–13 annihilation of seventh-ranked Notre Dame. His numbers were nothing less than gaudy: 32-of-46 for 425 yards and four touchdowns. The contrast for Notre Dame coach Ty Willingham's offense was embarrassingly dramatic. Irish quarterback Carlyle Holiday was held to 70 yards in the air. Fargis ran for 120 yards and added 41 on receptions. Williams caught 10 for 169.

Troy was the co–Pacific-10 Conference champion for the first time since 1995. The 10–2 Trojans were invited to the Orange Bowl against number-three Iowa. They featured a quarterback who had been touted for the Heisman himself, Brad Banks. Palmer was 21-of-31 for 303 yards, earning MVP honors. Mike Williams set an NCAA freshman record for receptions (81), receiving yards (1,265), and touchdowns (14). His improvement since the Kansas State and Washington State debacles directly correlated with the team's—and Palmer's—success. Matt Grootegoed had six tackles.

After the 38–17 thrashing of Iowa, USC finished fourth in the polls. They averaged 35.8 points a game while allowing an average of 18.5.

That ex-Trojan baseball coach Mike Gillespie, who played at USC, attended Hawthorne High School with members of the Beach Boys?

The Promised Land

One of Pete Carroll's favorite expressions, which he often exhorts to his team in the locker room just before taking the field, is, "It's a good day to be a Trojan!" Perhaps it is because he rooted for USC as a kid, or because his wife's father was a Trojan, or because his daughter chose to play volleyball for the women of Troy before he took over as head coach—whatever the reason, Pete has never been a mercenary coach. In 2003 he became a national championship coach.

Sophomore quarterback Matt Leinart took to the challenge posed to him in the spring and summer of 2003.

"I was actually third-string going in to the spring and I just remember it being a battle," Leinart said on *The History of USC Football* DVD. "But I remember working very hard that whole off-season. My whole mindset was that it kind of miraculously shifted from March to the three months before the first game, to where this is my opportunity, and my confidence kind of built as the practices went on because I could see the coaches gaining confidence in me, and I was gaining confidence in myself. From then on out, I just took the reins and went with it and then slowly the players started respecting me and gaining confidence in me. And that's when I knew it was my team and that I could actually play here and be successful."

There were 86,063 fans for the opener at Auburn. Very few were Trojan supporters. The weather was hot and steamy, but in front of a national CBS audience, USC quickly took the crowd out of the game. They never let them in, shutting out *Sports Illustrated*'s number-one team in the nation 23–0.

Mike Williams caught Leinart's initial toss for the score. The defense simply shut down Carnell Williams (40 yards), Ronnie

Brown (28), and quarterback Jason Campbell (121 yards). USC dominated the turnover game. In truth, they could have won by a bigger margin but chose to keep things simple for their sophomore quarterback.

A few weeks later, USC dealt with a setback when California defeated the Trojans 34–31 in overtime at Berkeley to make them 3–1.

Naturally, the Berkeley faithful descended on the field afterward, tearing down the goalposts as if they had won their first national championship since 1937. It dropped Troy to 10th. At that moment *their* national title hopes were dim. There was some consolation, since the game was early in the season. The theory is that if you are going to win a title with a loss, that loss better come early. The theory would prove true.

The turning point came the following week at Arizona State. Leinart injured his knee and ankle in the second quarter. At the half, the score was tied, 10–10.

"Matt was limpin' around," Carroll recalled. "I just challenged him to play through it because we needed him."

Leinart responded, with a little help from his friends. LenDale White rushed for 140 yards off the bench. Ryan Killeen kicked three field goals. Overall, Leinart hit on 13-of-23 attempts for 289 yards and two touchdowns. He led Troy to 27 unanswered points and an ultimately convincing 37–17 win.

Now 4–1, USC proceeded to go on a roll that few teams have ever matched. Meanwhile, across the country, teams ahead of them lost, allowing USC to move up and up and up in the polls.

USC smoked Notre Dame at South Bend en route to a 9–1 mark, right where many preseason prognosticators thought they would be. When UCLA entered the Coliseum, 93,172 fans watching the modern version of Christians being eaten by

TRIVIA

What teams have won the national championship playing at home?

Answers to the trivia questions are on pages 187–191.

lions. Reggie Bush earned conference Special Teams Player of the Week, returning a kick 96 yards and officially entering the pantheon of Trojan lore. Leinart methodically hit 23 passes out of 32 attempts

Matt Leinart continued the Trojans' march through the 2000s and won the 2004 Heisman Trophy.

for 289 yards (273 in the first half), with Williams snaring 11 for 181. Final score: Trojans 47, Bruins 22.

Oklahoma was still unbeaten, but to all observers of the college football scene, USC had the earmarks of being the nation's finest team, with little doubt. Two weeks later, that doubt was erased when the Trojans vaulted into the number-one position in both the Associated Press and *USA Today*/ESPN polls, utterly annihilating Oregon State 52–28 at the Coliseum.

Oklahoma lost in ignominious fashion to Kansas State in the Big 12 title game, making it easy to decide who was number one entering the bowl season. In the final regular-season game, Leinart tossed five touchdown passes, with Williams and Bush (who was now regularly catching the ball almost as much as he was running it) grabbing two each. Beaver quarterback Derek Anderson was able to throw for over 400 yards, but Oregon State, after opening the game with a touchdown, never got close after that.

Ranked number one in both polls, Southern California advanced to the Rose Bowl against Michigan. The Rose Bowl seating capacity had been reconfigured, and the stadium no longer held 100,000 people. The 93,849 who saw the Trojans beat Michigan 28–14 had one of the hottest tickets in L.A. sports history. In the game, Leinart threw three touchdown passes and caught another. The defense recorded nine sacks. The truth is, it was like so many games Pete Carroll has coached: not as close as the score. USC could have won 45–14 or by more. There was a sense that USC dictated and dominated to such an extent they were essentially just writing the game story according to their whim.

TRIVIA

Coach Carroll is big on honoring tradition. What did he do prior to the 2003 opener at Auburn to honor USC's tradition?

Answers to the trivia questions are on pages 187–191.

It marked USC's 21st victory in 29 Rose Bowls, the most wins and the best percentage of all Rose Bowl teams. 'SC led 21–0 until late in the third quarter. Defensive lineman Shaun Cody blocked an early Wolverine field goal. Four plays later Leinart had USC in the end zone with a 25-yard aerial to Keary Colbert.

Carroll accepted the Rose Bowl trophy and told the multitudes that his team "just won a national championship." USC and their fans left the Rose Bowl having won their 10th national title since 1928, and their first since 1978. If USC did not have a loss on their record, the 2003 Trojans may very well have gone down in history as the greatest team ever, instead of just one of them. *Sports Illustrated* featured Matt Leinart scoring on his touchdown *reception*, trumpeting the 2003 national champions with the headline, "USC's the One!"

Five 2003 Trojans made All-American. They included wide receiver Mike Williams, offensive tackle Jacob Rogers, defensive end Kenechi Udeze, punter Tom Malone, and quarterback Matt Leinart.

Re-Pete

Occasionally in college football, all the stars are aligned. A team enters the season with a chance to be a little more perfect than other so-called perfect teams. Perfect is not merely going unbeaten, untied, and winning the national title. Many teams have accomplished that.

"Perfect" in the sense discussed herein means running the table ranked number one from the preseason polls (or, in USC's case, since the previous regular season) until the bowls have been played and the title decided. It means winning the Heisman Trophy and having the best recruiting class. It means that people start using words like "dynasty," and begin positing the notion that the team may just be the best ever. Thus was the case for the 2004 Trojans.

USC's star-studded team was also reminding people of legendary champions of the past, which included: Cal's Wonder Teams of the early 1920s; Knute Rockne's Four Horsemen of Notre Dame (1924); Howard Jones's Thundering Herd at USC (1928–1932); Army's Mr. Inside and Mr. Outside champs (1944–1945); Frank Leahy's 1947 Fighting Irish; Bud Wilkinson's Sooners of 1955–1956; the 1971 and 1995 Cornhuskers; 1979 Alabama Crimson Tide; and 2001 Miami Hurricanes. Members of USC's '72 national champions, considered the very best of the best, were torn between defending their record and extolling that of their younger brethren.

In 2004 USC was looking to be only the second team ever to be ranked number one in the preseason AP poll, then hold it right through the trophy ceremony. Florida State had pulled that off in 1999.

USC's marketing people came up with a slogan inspired by the 2004 George Bush/Dick Cheney presidential campaign. They distributed T-shirts that read, "Bush/Leinart '04 Championship Campaign."

IF ONLY . . . USC had brought in Randall Cunningham instead of going with Sean Salisbury at quarterback back in 1981, their fortunes might have changed after Marcus Allen left. Cunningham's older brother, Sam, was a Trojan legend, but when he asked if Randall would play he was told the program was committed to Salisbury, a prep phenom from San Diego. Salisbury was a Trojan bust; Cunningham a UNLV All-American and Philadelphia Eagles star.

Matt Leinart's love life was a big part of his persona. He befriended pop singer Nick Lachey and his then-wife Jessica Simpson. He was supposed to have hung out with tennis sensation Maria Sharapova and dated actress Alyssa Milano, who had a thing for Trojan left-handed athletes (previously seeing then–A's lefty Barry Zito). Actress Mandy Moore's name surfaced, but many noted that at USC, where beautiful coeds are legendary, Leinart saw girls as pretty as Alyssa and Mandy every day walking from Heritage Hall to Howard Jones Field.

USC opened with a hard-earned win over Virginia Tech in the Black Coaches Association Classic at FedEx Field in Landover, Maryland. On a humid night, "Bush carried Southern California," ESPN joked, in reference to the upcoming election.

Wins at Stanford, over Cal at home, and in the fog at Corvallis, Oregon, were also difficult.

Notre Dame arrived, and 92,611 sat in a slight drizzle. It was a night game at the Coliseum, nationally televised on ABC. For the second time ESPN's *College GameDay* broadcast from outside the stadium.

If there was any doubt Matt Leinart was deserving of the Heisman, like Palmer in 2002, he sealed the deal with his best game ever against Notre Dame. He hit five touchdown passes and 400 yards on 24-of-34 passing in a dominating 41–10 trouncing. It left no doubt who the best team in the land was, at least until the bowls. It was USC's 20th straight win and 21st in a row at home. They were 11–0.

The UCLA game showed that Leinart's Heisman competition would not just be Oklahoma's Jason White and Adrian Peterson. Reggie Bush would be one of his main rivals for the award. On December 4, before a sold-out Rose Bowl crowd of 88,442 and another national television audience, Bush put himself on the cover of *Sports Illustrated* with two dazzling touchdowns, 335 all-purpose yards, including 204 on the ground. Bush went down in USC-UCLA history along with O.J. Simpson. He made 65-yard and 81-yard touchdown runs. He added 73 yards on six catches, 39 on kickoff returns, and 19 on two punt returns. His combination of running and kick returning was reminiscent of Anthony Davis's great 1972 and 1974 games against Notre Dame.

USC had a total of 477 total yards. White rushed for 75. Leinart connected on 24-of-34 for 242 yards. Dwayne Jarrett caught five passes. Lofa Tatupu made 10 tackles. UCLA's Drew Olson was 20-of-34 for 278 yards. His touchdown pass to Marcedes Lewis late in the game created some Trojan tension, though. Visions of an onside kick followed by a "Miracle in the Arroyo Seco," which Bruins fans could talk about until 2099, did not happen. USC won 29–24 to remain number one heading into the BCS national championship game.

The five Heisman finalists at New York's Downtown Athletic Club included two Trojans (Leinart and Bush) and two Sooners, quarterback Jason White and freshman running back sensation Adrian Peterson. In the end Leinart won the Heisman balloting in a landslide. This meant the winner, the runner-up (Peterson), and four of the top five finalists would face each other in the national championship game on January 4 in Miami.

There have been many great games played over the years. Some would live up to the hype, some would not. When it came to pregame expectations, the 2005 Orange Bowl was far and away (up until that time) the most anticipated, built-up game ever played by college teams.

Lee Corso went on record saying that the greatest *single performance in a game* that he ever saw was USC's 55–19 annihilation of Oklahoma in the Orange Bowl. What the University of Southern California did to Oklahoma was a game for the ages, one of the *most dominating* if not *the* most dominating performance—certainly considering the opponent, the setting, and the stakes—ever. In 'SC annals, it ranks with the 55–24 win over Notre Dame in 1974. While the game was important for other reasons, it is to be included with the 42–21 win at Alabama in 1970.

Game MVP Matt Leinart was 18-of-35 for 332 yards and five touchdowns. The statistics of the game do not lie. The greater meaning of what happened at Pro Player Stadium is that USC achieved Carroll's admonition to "Leave no doubt!" that they were without question the finest team in the land. Beyond, the Trojans reached for and made a bid for history; they put themselves on that short list of teams who must be mentioned when historians argue the identity of the best single-season team ever.

Furthermore, when combined with the 2003 juggernaut (not to mention the 2002 "best in the country if there had been a play-off" team), Troy established themselves as the best back-to-back national championship team of all time.

A sign of USC's overall class was found when an Oklahoma fan posted the following on a fan's blog after the 2005 Orange Bowl:

I was in New Orleans for the Sugar Bowl between OU and LSU in January 2004. That whole week in the French Quarter, we'd run into LSU fans, and it was a donnybrook. Fights, foul language, insulting each other's women. These LSU fans would just go around saying, "Tiger meat, Tiger meat!" like they had nothing more intelligent to say. It was mean-spirited from both sides. The next year, I was at the BCS Orange Bowl, OU versus USC. These 'SC people were a whole different breed. Beautiful women, well dressed, professional demeanor, classy. We'd run into them, and they'd just tell us how much they admired our team, thought Jason White was a fine quarterback, how much respect they had for Sooners football tradition. On and on like that. We're exchanging business cards, they were just as nice as can be. USC has class!

The re-Pete titles thrust USC even further into the national spotlight. Spike! TV ran a reality show called *Super Agent*. It featured Shaun Cody, in preparation for the draft, choosing his representation from among five hopefuls. One scene was shot at Heritage Hall. As the agents gazed at the Heismans, the national championship trophies, the All-America plaques, immersed in the imprimatur of excellence, one of them simply said, "Wow. If I'm a player, I'm comin' here!"

National sportstalk host Jim Rome said of Pete Carroll's program after they won a re-Pete national title in 2004, "This guy's got it goin' on like John Wooden at UCLA. I don't see why Carroll can't win five or 10 national titles."

Carroll followed the national championship with his third straight national-best recruiting class (2003, 2004, 2005; the 2005 class was considered the best in history).

Marv Goux had once described recruiting at USC.

"USC is unique," he said. "It's in the middle of a huge city, with a giant population base. You don't have to travel all over the land to recruit guys, they live close by, they can just drive to campus, it's easy to see them play, visit with their families. The thing of it is, at the University of Southern California, once you start winning, it's a snowball effect. They'll just come to you. You hardly have to recruit anymore. And when the guys who want to play for you come out of the biggest population base in the country, comprised of traditionally the best high school athletes in the nation...*watch out!*"

TRIVIA

In 1998 USC ended a 20-year drought in which they never won the College World Series. Who did they have to beat twice to get to the championship game, and what Trojan later sparked Houston into the 2005 World Series?

Answers to the trivia questions are on pages 187–191.

Three-Pete

The first big recruit of 2005 was Leinart. The NFL experts were in virtual unanimous agreement. If he declared, he would be the very first pick in the upcoming NFL Draft. To the surprise of some, but not all, Leinart chose to stay. When he did that, he turned himself into a hero on campus and in Los Angeles, an athlete of legendary status.

Carroll hugged Leinart. The 2005 repeat national championship seemed all but assured. While Leinart was the team's MVP as a 2003 sophomore, following that up with a Heisman campaign in 2004, it was Reggie "the President" Bush who earned the team MVP award for 2004. Entering the 2005 campaign, all the other awards—Heisman, Maxwell, Unitas, O'Brien—promised to be less competitive than this singular honor, which spoke volumes about what Pete Carroll had built in Los Angeles. In addition to being an almost-guaranteed New York finalist for the 2005 Heisman, Bush also was a Doak Walker Award contender with a chance at breaking various USC records.

As a sophomore, he had finished fifth in the nation in all-purpose running yards (179.2 a game). His 2,330 all-purpose yards were the most by a Trojan since Marcus Allen. He averaged 10.1 yards each time he touched the ball. In addition to finishing fifth in the Heisman vote, in which he was a finalist in New York City, Bush was named the 2004 College Player of the Year by the Touchdown Club of Columbus. He was a consensus All-American and, along with Leinart, the conference co–Offensive Player of the Year. When the 2003 national champions visited the White House, the real President Bush singled Reggie out for his last name.

He earned Freshman All-America and all-conference honors in 2003 after coming out of Helix High, where the local prep media alternated between calling him the best high school football player to come out of San Diego since Marcus Allen, or the best high school football player *ever* to come out of San Diego.

That is quite a compliment. Aside from Bush and Allen, Ricky Williams, Rashaan Salaam, Junior Seau, Terrell Davis, and Cotton Warburton played high school football in San Diego County. Bush's teammate at Helix High, quarterback Alex Smith, had been a Heisman finalist with Reggie in 2004 and the number one pick of the NFL Draft by San Francisco.

"I expect great things out of myself," said Bush, a religious young man from a tight-knit family (albeit one that got into trouble over possibly accepting an agent's gift in 2005). "I expect to make great plays, great moves. In my mind, I can never be good enough....It just comes with the territory of making the most of what God has given you. I'm just trying to make the most out of a blessing I was given."

Where Bush was "Lightning," 6'2", 235-pound powerhouse LenDale White, his alternate at the tailback position, was "Thunder." White was All-American, all-state for three years, and the Gatorade Colorado Player of the Year as a senior at Chatfield High in Denver. He gained a state record of 7,803 yards as a four-year starter (the first three at Denver's South High).

As a 2003 freshman, White ran for 754 yards, earning Freshman All-American, All–Pacific-10, and Pac-10 Freshman Offensive Player of the Year honors. In 2004 he made All–Pac-10 and collegefootballnews.com's Sophomore All-America team.

DID YOU KNOW . . . That after 46 years at the Sports Arena, USC basketball moved into the Galen Center on campus in 2006? With a view from *inside* of downtown L.A., the Galen Center is part of the revitalization of the corridor between the school and Staples Center, where the Lakers play. ESPN announced plans to build a huge new Hollywood movie and production studio, complete with entertainment complex, shopping centers, and a pedestrian mall, near the site. All of this promises to be a huge boon to USC, the neighborhood, and the city.

Reggie Bush followed up Leinart's and Palmer's Heisman Trophies by winning one himself in 2005.

Despite his reputation for running inside the tackles, White insisted, "I'm shifty, but I have the power when I need it. I used to be a scatback, but I got to USC and gained some weight."

White actually was the starter in 2004, although Bush started in the Orange Bowl against Oklahoma. White, with the exception of one reported flare-up that may not have happened or may have been overblown, accepted his sharing role as a complete team player.

"There's not even competition between us," he said of Bush and, in 2003, Hershel Dennis. "Our competition is how we can push each other to be our best....All of the tailbacks here believe we're great, and great as a group."

Entering the 2005 season, USC was in a position to:

- pass Notre Dame as the greatest collegiate football tradition ever
- become the greatest single-season team ever
- become the greatest half-decade dynasty of all time
- have quarterback Matt Leinart become the best college football player in history
- have the Leinart-Bush duo pass Army's "Mr. Inside and Mr. Outside" Blanchard-Davis combo to become the most ballyhooed teammates ever

As the season approached, the natural talk about "three-Petes" became inevitable, along with the ridiculous notion that the school, despite the spelling differential, could not market the theme "three-Pete" because former Laker basketball coach Pat Riley had patented the term "three-peat"—a peculiar, only-in-L.A. oddity.

It was the most loaded, talented, hyped collegiate football team of all time: prep All-Americans *everywhere*; a Heisman winner; Heisman contenders; All-Americans; Lombardi, O'Brien, Unitas, Maxwell, Biletnikoff, Ray Guy candidates. The only thing that could stop USC was USC.

The chance to win an unprecedented third-straight title, something no team had ever done, and to do it at the Rose Bowl, added to the perfection of the situation.

"It's an exciting challenge to be the returning national champion, and we look forward to dealing with everything that goes with that," said Carroll. "We'll handle it well. Our approach will be the same as it always is. Our goal always is to win the Pac-10 and the Rose Bowl."

USC had 11 first-team All-Americans, two of three Heisman winners, winning 22 straight and 33 of the last 34 over the previous three years.

Fourteen starters returned (eight on offense, five on defense, and the punter) along with 75 squadmen (58 of whom had seen playing

TRIVIA

How did an ESPN football analyst describe the USC–Notre Dame rivalry before the 2005 game?

Answers to the trivia questions are on pages 187–191.

time, 49 who had lettered, and 28 on the two-deep chart). Twenty-four players started in the past. Nineteen new scholarship players joined the roster.

"We have grown comfortable with being in this environment, with all this attention on us," said Carroll.

Leinart came in with gaudy numbers: 65.3 percent completion rate, 3,322 yards, 33 touchdowns against six interceptions in 2004. His 71 career touchdowns in two years was one behind Palmer, who needed the better part of five seasons. He was 25–1 as a starter with a 22-game winning streak.

"If USC pulls off a three-Pete," former quarterback Rodney Peete was asked on ESPN Classic, "will they be the greatest team of all time?"

"I think so," replied Peete. "In today's era, with the competition, the scholarships, the national level of the game; yes, they'd have to be."

After opening with easy wins over Hawaii and Arkansas, USC traveled to Eugene to take on the 24th-ranked Oregon Ducks (3–0). A capacity crowd of 59,129, par for the course whether the Trojans were at home or on the road by now, filled Autzen Stadium. It was a hard-fought first half, but Oregon was no match. The Trojans closed it out at 45–13.

TRIVIA

How does Austin Murphy, who attended both Notre Dame and USC, describe the rivalry?

Answers to the trivia questions are on pages 187–191.

Leinart, 12-of-25 in the first half, finished 23-of-39 for 315 yards and three touchdowns.

"We know you can't win a game in the first three quarters," he said. "It's how you finish." But when Troy fell behind 21–3 at Arizona State, all bets were off. Best team ever? Dynasty? How about plain survival?

A crowd of 71,706 fans yelled, screamed, and stomped. The stifling midday heat was 100 degrees with no abatement, giving special meaning to the name Sun Devil Stadium.

Maybe it was all hype. Or, maybe it was just a chance for the Trojans to show that they were not only a great team, but also a team of heart, of guts, of great will.

"They didn't try anything fancy in the second half," said Arizona State coach Dirk Koetter. "They just ran the two tailbacks at us."

In the third quarter, Southern California decided to separate the boys from the men. No more screwin' around. In the beginning, they looked as if they had spent the previous night partying in the *Girls Gone Wild* atmosphere of the nearby Scottsdale bar scene. Then it was time to go to work. After White's 32-yard scamper and Bush's 24-yard scoring run, Arizona State, a team that had not trailed all day, entered the fourth quarter with a 21–17 lead, but felt more like a guy who just busted open an indoor beehive, only to realize the room was locked.

A 34-yard burst by Bush gave USC the lead, 31–28, with a mere 3:44 left. That was followed by a 46-yard explosion by White to secure it, 38–28.

The Four Horsemen of Southern California

Outlined against a blue-gray October sky, the Four Horsemen rode again. In dramatic lore they are known as famine, pestilence, destruction, and death. These are only aliases. Once named Stuhldreher, Miller, Crowley, and Layden, the gladiators of the New Millennium are men of youth, color, and American diversity. Their real names are: Leinart, Bush, Jarrett, and White. These new Four Horsemen of Southern California came to the land of destiny, riding their famed white steed Traveler, that dreaded Coliseum sight of Irish past. They relegated the old Notre Dame ghosts to their place and time, a time when the only color was white, myths were protected, lies told as truths. They formed the crest of the South Bend cyclone before which another Fighting Irish team was swept over the precipice at Notre Dame Stadium on the afternoon of Saturday, October 15, 2005. A crowd of 80,795 spectators peered down upon the bewildering panorama spread out upon the green plain below.

These fans observed the changing of the guard, the team of the New Age, the University of the 21st century. For the better part of the previous century, their team held that loftiest position on the grid landscape. No more. Their ancient rivals arrived at their house of worship, paid homage to their shrines, and honored their traditions.

Their skill, class, and guts emanated like water pouring forth upon a barren valley, informing all whose eyes saw that truth, when witnessed in an American arena, is never misunderstood.

The truth of October 15, 2005, in that most perfect of settings, was that the Trojans of Southern California had taken over from the previous title-holders, the Fighting Irish of Notre Dame, the lofty moniker Greatest Collegiate Football Tradition of All Time! They did as their legendary old coach, Marv Goux, advised countless legions to do. They did as Goux's beloved granddaughter asked them to do. Four games in four years passed since Kara Kanen advised that future Trojans, "Win one for the Goux!"

For four years now they took on the Irish at home and away. Each time they left them heartbroken in noble defeat. On this day they would take more than a shillelagh back to Heritage Hall. There was no plaque, no crystal football, nothing inscribed.

There was only pride and knowledge that what they did secured for them everlasting glory. Legends were made. Expectations had been met. Eighty years of excellence had not only been lived up to, but exceeded by a new generation. They took the foundation laid brick by brick by decades of Trojans, erecting a higher statue than ever before.

A modern Lancelot led them, for indeed the times he was living in were those of a Camelot quality. His name was Leinart. The similarity to "Lion Heart" was not insignificant. It was, rather, cosmic, for he did not lace his cleats in a land of mere mortals. He was part of something ancient and utterly sacred The standards this tallest and sturdiest of the new Horsemen set under that blue-gray October sky, with the wheat of an Indiana harvest swirling about like so much stardust, were standards that nobody will ever be expected to meet. To strive for, but not to meet.

The second new Horseman's name was Bush. On a field of play where 81 years ago he would have been invited to leave, this stepson of a lay preacher man stepped up and took a nation, a Trojan Nation, and with his loyal partner, the "Lion Heart," he thus moved mountains on the flat Midwestern plains.

TRIVIA

What was Grantland Rice's famed description of the "Four Horsemen of Notre Dame" in 1924?

Answers to the trivia questions are on pages 187–191.

The third new Horseman's name was Jarrett. A babe in the woods, a child desperate to return to his Jersey roots rather than accept the challenges that God graced him with the ability to meet, he did meet them on the green plains of South Bend. He met them;

soft of hands and swift of feet did he meet them as he raced through the gauntlet set forth before him. His was a moment of mystery and wonder, a Shakespearean marvel: "There are more things on Heaven and earth, Horatio, than can be dreamt of in your philosophy."

Finally, in the "most Gracious" Shakespearean of seasons, did the fourth new Horseman emerge. His name was White, a famous last name and one he lived up to, as he had taken the previous man's number, 12, and turned it around: 21. In the glare of the spotlight, Mr. White did what made him splendid. He sacrificed for his team. His name will not be synonymous with the glory and memory of this challenge met under the watchful eye of Touchdown Jesus, but his mates knew that they would not have been there without his sacrifice.

Thus was history made. Leave no doubt? Thus was the statement made. USC was not tested, they were outplayed. But championship teams do what championship teams do. On the game's final play, Leinart pushed into the line, then did a spin move that looked like something he learned in a Tuesday night ballroom dancing class. With three seconds left, he found a seam to score the winning touchdown. Number-one USC escaped with its 28th straight victory, 34–31 over the ninth-ranked Irish. The game more than lived up to expectations. It was the greatest game in the history of the storied rivalry that went back to 1926. Depending on one's perspective, and considering the pressure, the stakes, and the atmosphere, it may have been the greatest football game ever played, college or pro. It was watched by the largest TV audience of any regular-season college football game in a decade. To say it meant the rivalry was revived was as obvious as saying Pamela Anderson possesses sex appeal. The college football world, increasingly complaining about Trojan hegemony, now saw a reason to tune back in.

TRIVIA

How did USC's Fred Matua describe the USC–Notre Dame game?

Answers to the trivia questions are on pages 187–191.

When the teams lined up as Leinart approached the line for the last play, Carroll could be seen making the "spike it" motion. Apparently it was a deke. In the NFL, Miami's Dan Marino

LenDale White was among the Four Horsemen of Southern California that also included Leinart, Bush, and Dwayne Jarrett.

approached the line against Carroll's Jets, looking to spike the ball to stop the clock, luring the Jets off-balance before throwing a touchdown pass.

Leinart looked at the stack of Notre Dame defenders. The play called was a sneak. He turned to Bush.

"What should I do?" he screamed. "I don't think I can make it, Reggie, what should I do? You think I should go for it?"

"Go for it, Matt!!" yelled Bush.

Then the Irish crowded the line. Bush had second thoughts.

"NO! NO! NO! NO! NO!" he screamed. Leinart never heard him.

Leinart took the snap, heading into the line. It was not even close. He had no chance to muscle through the pile. But it was all in one place. He pirouetted. The ball was precariously held halfway tucked against his shoulder and halfway in the air, where it could be swatted away. He somehow found a hole. The Trojans, like Daniel in the lion's den, had found glory in enemy territory.

DID YOU KNOW . . . That in an effort to slow up USC, Notre Dame coach Charlie Weis allowed the grass to grow like tall stalks? It looked like the cornfields out beyond Kevin Costner's baseball field in *Field of Dreams*.

2005: Quest for History

Many people say that the single greatest game ever played by a college football player was Anthony Davis against Notre Dame in 1972. Perhaps the best competition for that comes from A.D. two years later. But Reggie Bush was superhuman against Fresno State. Maybe better than A.D. had been.

Five hundred thirteen all-purpose yards. 294 yards on just 23 carries. Two touchdowns. Three receptions for 68 yards, 151 on kick returns. Second all-time in NCAA Division I history for all-purpose yardage. Broke A.D.'s old school record of 368 in 1972. But the numbers do not tell the whole story.

On this night, Bush was so unstoppable, so unreal, that he won the Heisman Trophy. Matt Leinart, the golden boy with the Hollywood friends, would be in New York, and deservingly so. So would Vince Young. The UCLA game would be played on national TV and would give everybody one last chance to shine. But Bush did it on this night. When the harrowing 50–42 win was finally, safely in the books, the big question around Heritage was, *Why'd we schedule these guys? What's wrong with U.C.–Davis? Aren't the New Mexico Lobos available?*

Against UCLA at the Coliseum, there was no tension. It was a matter of dictatin' and dominatin' in Troy's 66–19 stomping.

Saturday, December 3, blew in clear and sunny, one of those unbelievable Southern California days that leave the rest of the world in awe. It had rained slightly the day before. The breezes were up, but that served only to clear the air of any smog on a cloudless, Pacific blue afternoon.

From the Coliseum press box, the view was nothing less than spectacular. To the east, the San Gabriel Mountains stood proud,

DID YOU KNOW . . . That Giles Pellerin was a USC graduate who saw every single USC game, home and away, beginning in the 1920s and stretching into the 21st century? His brother saw almost as many, missing a few for World War II. Francis Benavidez is the "successor" to Pellerin. Except for three years in the Navy and a year teaching overseas, Benavidez attended every home game since enrolling as a student in 1933.

although they had yet to be draped in their winter snowcaps. Straight ahead lay the downtown skyscrapers, tall and majestic. Just to the left of that, the Hollywood Hills. The Hollywood sign was clearly in view.

Considering USC's near-total hold on the City of the Angels, it seemed apropos to send a construction crew above Lake Hollywood to install a giant "USC" underneath the iconic Hollywood symbol. Actual homes in the Hollywood and Beverly Hills could be picked out. To the west, the tall buildings of the Miracle Mile and Century City could easily be seen.

From the veranda adjacent to the press box, the view stretching across the basin spread out from behind the Coliseum's shadows was equally impressive. As the day droned on, with the early setting December sun descending behind the Palos Verdes Peninsula into the Golden West, the whole image was utterly surreal. It was a dream day—for the Trojans. Right from the very beginnings, it was a day of total conquest. The old "half USC, half UCLA" nature of the City Game was no more. It was obvious just walking to the stadium, and especially once inside it, that this was 'SC's house. It was a sea of Cardinal and Gold, reminiscent of Nebraska's "Big Red." A small, quiet contingent of UCLAns bravely clung to their little corner of the Coliseum. The Trojan Nation were the Allies—92,000-strong (completing USC's sixth sell-out in six home games and 11th of 12 overall) descending on the Normandy beaches. Their opponents: a beaten, doomed crew. After Troy's beyond-imagination thrashing, there was nothing left but to send out condolences, because USC took no prisoners. All the drama was in the pageantry, the ceremony, the symbolism. The crowd was star-studded: Kirsten Dunst, USC grads Will Ferrell, Henry Winkler, Tom Selleck...

USC secured its chance to call themselves the greatest college football team ever if they could win the Rose Bowl. It was Bush who vaulted into a new pantheon of Trojan—and college football—history. He had 228 yards at the half. There was talk of beating Ricky Bell's record of 347. Bell had set the NCAA record against Washington State in 1976. Carroll went to the pass in the second half, ostensibly to get Leinart back in rhythm, and also to prevent an unnecessary injury to Bush. He finished with 260 yards on 24 carries, a 10.8-yard average. Like so much of USC's season, the only thing preventing him from running for as many yards as he chose to run for was the decision not to try it.

LenDale White showed no ill effect from a shoulder bruise, averaging even more yards (11) than his partner (14 carries for 154 yards). Bush made a spectacular, leaping 13-yard touchdown run and later a 10-yard TD scamper to send Troy into halftime with a 31–6 lead.

"Let me tell you something," said *Long Beach Press-Telegram* sports columnist Doug Krikorian, who has seen 'em all, "when USC gets focused, *nobody* can beat 'em. They have the best offensive line in college football history. All 11 offensive starters can play in the NFL right now. Reggie Bush is the greatest running back in history. Matt Leinart is the most successful college quarterback ever. What more can you say?"

"Reggie Bush will be the number-one pick in the draft," said Mel Kiper Jr. "Matt Leinart will be number two. LenDale White will be drafted in the late first round if he comes out."

Talk about the all-time greatest teams was in the air. USC was now the prohibitive favorite to replace their own 1972 version.

"They've done it despite injuries, early defections to the NFL, graduation, coaching departures, and the law of averages," wrote Gene Wojciechowski of ESPN.com.

They had done it in the age of the BCS, the television age, the age of cable, Fox Sports, ESPN, the Internet, big money, gambling, steroids, total integration of whites, blacks, Pacific-Islanders, even Chinese-Americans (two of whom, the Ting brothers, were significant defensive contributors to Troy). They had done it in the age of the newest coaching, training, and diet techniques; in an age in which the best coaches were spread throughout the land, lending a sense of egalitarian fairness to competitive sports at all levels and in all regions. They had done it when the best juniors leave for the NFL, and they had the best juniors (in Mike Williams's case, the best sophomore). They had done it amid the white-hot glare of a Hollywood spotlight. No college sports team had ever attracted so much attention, all in the media capital of the world.

There was simply no comparing the 1947 Irish, the 1956 Sooners, nor even the 1995 Cornhuskers or the 1972 Trojans. Nobody was a match for this team if they could survive number-two Texas.

By the end of the evening on Saturday, December 3, it was almost too much. Even for Trojan fans.

Almost.

Reggie Bush left the competition behind, as was his and his team's usual custom, in winning USC's seventh Heisman Trophy. This tied Troy with Notre Dame for the most Heismans. If they could beat Texas, it would push them ahead of the Irish 12–11 for the most national championships.

"It's truly an honor to be elected to be in this fraternity of Heisman winners," Bush said.

By the NUMBERS

The Longest Modern Era, Major College Winning Streaks

Streak	Team	Dates
47	Oklahoma	Started 10/10/53 vs. Texas, snapped 11/16/57 vs. Notre Dame
34	USC	Started 10/4/03 at Arizona State, snapped 1/4/06 vs. Texas (Rose Bowl)
34	Miami	Started 9/23/00 at West Virginia, snapped 1/3/03 vs. Ohio State (2 OT, Fiesta Bowl)
31	Oklahoma	Started 10/2/48 vs. Texas A&M, snapped 1/1/51 vs. Kentucky (Sugar Bowl)

By the NUMBERS

The Longest Modern Era, Major College Winning Streaks (con't)

30	Texas	Started 10/5/68 vs. Oklahoma State, snapped 1/1/71 vs. Notre Dame (Cotton Bowl)
29	Miami	Started 10/27/90 at Texas Tech, snapped 1/1/93 vs. Alabama (Sugar Bowl)
28	*Alabama	Started 9/21/91 vs. Georgia, snapped 10/16/93 vs. Tennessee (tie)—extended to 31-game unbeaten streak, snapped 11/6/93 vs. LSU
28	Alabama	Started 9/30/78 vs. Vanderbilt, snapped 11/1/80 at Mississippi State
28	Oklahoma	Started 10/6/73 vs. Miami, snapped 11/8/75 vs. Kansas—part of 37-game unbeaten streak started 10/28/72 vs. Kansas State (tied USC on 9/29/73)
28	Michigan	State Started 10/14/50 vs. William & Mary, snapped 10/24/53 at Purdue
25	*USC	Started 10/3/31 vs. Oregon State, snapped 10/21/33 vs. Oregon (tie) —extended to 27-game unbeaten streak, snapped 11/11/33 by Stanford's "Vow Boys"
23	USC	Unbeaten streak started 10/23/71 at Notre Dame (tied UCLA 11/20/71 and Oklahoma 10/29/73), snapped 10/27/73 at Notre Dame

Among other streaks, Toledo started a 35-game winning streak on 9/20/69 vs. Villanova, snapped 9/9/72 at Tampa. Records are sketchy, but Washington had a 63-game unbeaten streak, which included 39 straight wins between 1908 and 1914, but it is not considered the modern record due to rules changes and the playing of rugby instead of football.

By the NUMBERS

National Champions by Year
(where Heisman winner played for the champions, shown in parentheses)

1869 Princeton	1896 Princeton
1870 Princeton	1897 Pennsylvania
1872 Princeton	1898 Harvard
1873 Princeton	1899 Princeton
1874 Princeton	1900 Yale
1875 Princeton	1901 Harvard
1876 Yale	1902 Michigan
1877 Princeton	1903 Princeton
1878 Princeton	1904 Minnesota
1879 Princeton	1905 Stanford, Chicago
1880 Yale	1906 Yale
1881 Princeton	1907 Yale
1882 Yale	1908 Harvard
1883 Yale	1909 Washington
1884 Princeton	1910 Harvard
1885 Princeton	1911 Princeton
1886 Princeton	1912 Harvard
1887 Yale	1913 Washington
1888 Yale	1914 Texas
1889 Princeton	1915 Washington State
1890 Harvard	1916 Pittsburgh, Oregon
1891 Yale	1917 Georgia Tech
1892 Yale	1918 Michigan
1893 Princeton	1919 Texas A&M
1894 Yale	1920 Notre Dame, California
1895 Pennsylvania	1921 California

By the
NUMBERS

National Champions by Year (where Heisman winner played for the champions, shown in parentheses, cont'd)

1922 California

1923 Michigan

1924 Notre Dame

1925 Alabama

1926 Stanford, Alabama (tied each other in Rose Bowl)

1927 Illinois

1928 Southern California

1929 Notre Dame

1930 Alabama

1931 Southern California

1932 Southern California

1933 Michigan

1934 Minnesota

1935 Minnesota

1936 Minnesota

1937 Pittsburgh, California

1938 Tennessee, Texas Christian (Heisman: Davey O'Brien)

1939 Southern California, Texas A&M

1940 Minnesota, Stanford

1941 Minnesota (Heisman: Bruce Smith)

1942 Ohio State, Georgia (Heisman: Frank Sinkwich)

1943 Notre Dame (Heisman: Angelo Bertelli)

1944 Army

1945 Army (Heisman: Doc Blanchard)

1946 Notre Dame

1947 Notre Dame (Heisman: John Lujack)

1948 Michigan

1949 Notre Dame (Heisman: Leon Hart)

1950 Tennessee

1951 Michigan State

1952 Georgia Tech

1953 Maryland

1954 UCLA, Ohio State

1955 Oklahoma

1956 Oklahoma

1957 Auburn, Ohio State

1958 Louisiana State

1959 Syracuse

1960 Mississippi

1961 Alabama

1962 Southern California

1963 Texas

1964 Arkansas, Alabama (lost to Texas in Orange Bowl)

By the NUMBERS

National Champions by Year
(where Heisman winner played for the champions, shown in parentheses, cont'd)

1965 Alabama

1966 Notre Dame

1967 Southern California

1968 Ohio State

1969 Texas

1970 Nebraska

1971 Nebraska

1972 Southern California

1973 Notre Dame

1974 Southern California, Oklahoma (NCAA probation, no bowl game)

1975 Oklahoma

1976 Pittsburgh (Heisman: Tony Dorsett)

1977 Notre Dame

1978 Southern California, Alabama

1979 Alabama

1980 Georgia

1981 Clemson

1982 Penn State

1983 Miami

1984 Brigham Young

1985 Oklahoma

1986 Penn State

1987 Miami

1988 Notre Dame

1989 Miami

1990 Colorado, Georgia Tech

1991 Washington, Miami

1992 Alabama

1993 Florida State (Heisman: Charlie Ward)

1994 Nebraska

1995 Nebraska

1996 Florida (Heisman: Danny Wuerffel)

1997 Nebraska, Michigan (Heisman: Charles Woodson)

1998 Tennessee

1999 Florida State

2000 Oklahoma

2001 Miami

2002 Ohio State

2003 Southern California, Louisiana State

2004 Southern California (Heisman: Matt Leinart)

2005 Texas

2006 Florida

2007 Louisiana State

The Ring of Fire and Those Most Worthy of All Foes, the Texas Longhorns

The weeks leading up to the Rose Bowl were filled with greater hype and anticipation than any collegiate sporting event in history—more so even than the ballyhooed 2005 USC-Oklahoma Orange Bowl.

Texas came in with a 12–0 record, averaging over 50 points per game, with one of the nation's best defenses. Vince Young, the star of the 2005 Rose Bowl when he led the Longhorns to a stunning 38–37 victory over Michigan, was the face of their team. As great as he was, it was felt that it would be too much for him to carry Texas on his shoulders alone. USC, also averaging 50 points a game, was installed not only as a seven- to eight-point favorite, but was anointed as the greatest offensive team ever, as well as the greatest college team in history. ESPN ran a series of polls and "fantasy games," using computers and expert analysis, comparing the Trojans to the greatest teams ever. It was determined that indeed the 2005 team was the best ever assembled.

The Longhorns arrived in Los Angeles amid all the Hollywood hoopla. Day after day, on TV, radio, and in the papers, they were subjected to pagan idolatry heaped upon their opponents, as if Texas were the Washington Generals, set up as opponents for the Harlem Globetrotters to trounce. The pressure to live up to their star billing worked on USC and spurred Texas to establish their own place in history.

On Wednesday, January 4, 2005, in the "ring of fire" known as the Rose Bowl in Pasadena, the Longhorns did just that. Vince Young played what may have been the greatest game any player has ever played. That is what it took to break USC's hearts.

USC in its history has played a number of games that might be considered the "game of the century" or "the best college football game ever played." The 1931, 1974, and 1978 Notre Dame games come to mind because of what happened on the field, but they were great mostly from USC's point of view. The 1988 Notre Dame game and the 2005 Oklahoma Orange Bowl were steeped in pregame hype but failed to live up to the billing. The 1967 UCLA game was unique in many ways and may have been the best college game ever played, considering everything, but the 2006 Rose Bowl topped them all. It was the greatest of all time.

After Vince Young sprinted nine yards for a touchdown with 19 seconds remaining to give Texas the 41–38 win and the national championship, those Trojans who were able to put it all in perspective felt that it had been an honor just to play in such a game.

Yes, USC lost more than just a football game. Their place in history was more than merely the '05 national title. A laundry list of records and accomplishments, most of which would have separated them from Notre Dame and Alabama, clearly delineating them as the greatest of all traditions, became suddenly a closer call when Young crossed the goal line.

Symbolically, USC failed to win its 12th national championship, which, aside from pushing them from the 11-all tie with Notre Dame, would have passed UCLA's 11 hoops championships, not to mention tying the 12 won by the Trojan baseball team over the years. In an eerie coincidence, Rod Dedeaux, who coached 11 of those baseball titles between 1948 and 1978, died at 91 the day after 'SC's loss. USC also remained far behind their 26 NCAA track titles.

Also lost was the quest for an unprecedented third straight title; their attempt to break Oklahoma's 47-game winning streak; the end of their 33-week record of AP number-one rankings; and the chance for returning seniors to win four national championships in as many years. But Matt Leinart's claim to be the "greatest college football player of all time" was still a valid argument, while Reggie Bush remained the favorite to be the number-one pick in the 2006 NFL Draft.

The loss could not help but shed new respect on the accomplishments of a Bruin, John Wooden, who had won 10 of their national titles in 12 years. The game held some similarities to the 1974 Final Four match-up between UCLA and North Carolina State. Substitute Matt Leinart and Reggie Bush for Bill Walton and Keith Wilkes, then Vince Young for David "Skywalker" Thompson. USC, like the Bruins 32 years earlier, held the lead late in the game. Victory, firmly within their grasp, was allowed to slip away, and with it the chance to sail in uncharted waters of sports greatness.

USC made errors that cost them victory, just as they had done with Ohio State in 1969, and just as UCLA had done with North Carolina State in 1974. They made a plethora of unusual errors and mental failures. For those who saw the game in person, ESPN Classic's TV replay three days later was a bitter pill to swallow because it revealed multiple mistakes that went against Troy time and time again, usually by a matter of inches that the fan in the stands could not see.

There had been a sense that USC could not lose. Leinart himself had said, "This team doesn't know how to lose," after the Notre Dame game. They had won for so long, usually in dominating fashion, that defeat seemed foreign. There was a sense that this was a team of destiny, that their coach lived under a lucky star. They had dodged bullets, in South Bound mostly. In the back of some nervous Trojan minds there may have run the uneasy thought that if all their good luck turned around, they could be upset, but Carroll was so full of confidence and bravado, the team wrapped in such glory, that this unease was quickly dispelled. As White had said at the end of the Arizona State game, they were just "too dominant."

There was that carry-over effect from the UCLA game, too. Such a perfect day, all the way around; a sense that the championship had been won that day without proper regard for the fact that Texas had beaten Colorado by a bigger margin that day than USC beat the Bruins.

Despite all of that, however, they led by 12 with six and a half minutes to go. They had it won. They could not stop Young and Texas. In the end, the credit must go to the Longhorns and their fabulous quarterback. Furthermore, the credit must go to the Texas defense, which was better than USC's. Defense wins championships. USC had won in 2003 and 2004 on the strength of that very axiom.

Despite having all their star power, all their historical baggage that, after everything was said and done, left them 19 seconds away from being the greatest collegiate football team of all time. In the end their defense was exposed, and it was all ripped away from them.

White finished as USC's all-time career touchdown leader. Bush and White passed Blanchard and Davis for most combined teammate TDs. Jarrett broke the single-season USC touchdown record.

Bush was named 2005 Pac-10 Offensive Player of the Year. Carroll was voted conference co–Coach of the Year (along with UCLA's Karl Dorrell). Nine Trojans, including six on offense, made the All–Pac-10 first team. It was Carroll's second such honor in his

Vince Young runs in for a 17-yard touchdown against USC during the fourth quarter of the Rose Bowl, the national championship game, on January 4, 2006.

five years at USC. In all, 21 Trojans made All–Pac-10 first team, second team, or honorable mention.

It was the second consecutive Pac-10 Offensive Player of the Year honor for Bush. He shared the 2004 honor with Leinart. Bush became just the fifth player to win the offensive award in back-to-back seasons, joining USC's Charles White (1978–1979), Stanford's John Elway (1980–1982), Washington State's Rueben Mayes (1984–1985), and Leinart (2003–2004). Bush was the first non-quarterback in 20 years to win it consecutively.

It was also the fourth year in a row that a Trojan was the conference Offensive Player of the Year. Quarterback Carson Palmer started the streak in 2002, the year he won the Heisman.

Bush, Leinart, Dwayne Jarrett, Darnell Bing, Taitusi Lutui, LenDale White, and Sam Baker were all named to the Associated Press All-America team. Bush was the AP Player of the Year. Leinart won the Johnny Unitas Award as the nation's best senior quarterback.

Bush won the Doak Walker Award as the nation's top running back as well as the Walter Camp Award as the best player. The Pigskin Club of Washington, D.C., named Bush its Offensive Player of the Year. He made the 2005 Football Coaches, Football Writers, Walter Camp, ESPN.com, SI.com, and CBSSportsline.com All-America first teams. Leinart was named the "Sportsman of the Year" by *The Sporting News.*

Reggie was USC's team MVP (for the second consecutive year) and won USC Player of the Game versus Notre Dame, co–Player of the Game versus UCLA, and Co-Lifter and Jack Oakie Rise and Shine (for longest run) awards.

Bush, Leinart, Jarrett, and Lutui were named to the Football Coaches All-America first team. That made 139 Trojan All-America first teams. It was the first year since 1931 (and only the second time ever) that USC has had four offensive players named to an All-America first team.

Leinart became just the second USC player ever to be a three-time All-American, joining linebacker Richard Wood (1972–1974).

Carroll, USC, and the Future

Entering 2008, Carroll is 76–14 in five seasons, but wait. Of those 14 losses, only one has been by more than seven points (27–16 at Notre Dame in 2001). Eleven of them have been on the road or in a bowl game.

As stated earlier, with luck and a few good bounces, Pete Carroll's record could be 89–1. If so, he could have six or seven national championships, not two.

Nevertheless, all the "close but no cigar" scenarios could not overshadow reality. Reality, as of January 2006, was that despite their accomplishments, and despite coming close by the slimmest of margins, Carroll and USC had to look at Knute Rockne's Irish of the 1920s, Frank Leahy's Notre Dame teams of the 1940s, and Bud Wilkinson's record at Oklahoma in the 1950s, and face the fact that they still had work to do.

The fact that Rockne (with the exception of the 1925 Rose Bowl win over Stanford) and Leahy had done it without the hassle of an end-of-the-season bowl challenge, while Wilkinson's 1956 national champion Sooners were also spared a bowl en route to 47 straight wins, did not assuage Trojan pain. The BCS system, in place since 1998, had created a higher standard. In the past the number-one Trojans would have annihilated Big 10 champion Penn State in the Rose Bowl, while Texas would have beaten some lesser light in the Cotton Bowl, then offered indignation at the voters anointing Southern California with their 12th national championship instead of earning Texas's third post–World War I title (1963, 1969, 2005) fair and square.

While USC could not yet establish clear evidence that they were the best two-year, three-year, short-term, and single-decade dynasty ever, they were clearly contenders. They were now tied with Notre

Dame for the most national championships and (along with Ohio State in 2006) Heisman winners, with more success and momentum in the modern era than the other great traditions. The failure to close the deal at Pasadena had denied them clear claim to have surpassed all other collegiate records, but the edge was still theirs with plenty of optimism that the next years would provide further opportunity to get those bragging rights.

The 2006 Rose Bowl may go down in history as the greatest collegiate football game ever; a game that will mark the times in a manner similar to the 1979 Larry Bird/Indiana State–Magic Johnson/Michigan State NCAA basketball title game. The 2005 Trojans were a collection of talent that probably will never be seen again, together on one team, in our lifetimes, or at least in our generation. A game featuring the college talents of Leinart, Bush, White and Co. versus a player of Vince Young's attributes—with both teams and all their stars playing at the top of their respective games—is a sports rarity. It is possible that, just as Bird and Johnson defined pro basketball in the 1980s after their Final Four match-up, so too will the players from USC and Texas define the NFL over the next decade. The 2004 and 2005 seasons will be remembered as a true Golden Age of college football—the 2005 season may well be the best of all time, and this will carry over.

Future matches or teammate combinations involving Leinart and Young, or Bush teamed with Young, or White and Carson Palmer—the ghosts of the '06 Rose Bowl will reverberate on the sports landscape for years to come.

It is a testament to the unusually high standards set by Carroll that in 2006 and 2007 USC was 11–2 in each season; won their fifth and sixth consecutive Pac-10 Conference titles; won two Rose Bowls in impressive fashion; won their fourth and fifth BCS bowl games out of six BCS bowls in as many seasons; finished in the top five of the AP poll for the fifth and sixth straight seasons; set the all-time record with six straight 11-win seasons; and were disappointing!

The 2006 Trojans were one win away from a date with Ohio State (probably a 30-point USC win, in retrospect) but were derailed in an improbable upset by UCLA. Quarterback John David Booty was an

All–Pac-10 star, and USC outclassed one-loss Michigan in the Rose Bowl 32–18. They finished fourth in the nation.

In 2007 Southern California entered the season a consensus number-one pick. Many pundits felt they were the greatest college football team of all time. Booty was the Heisman front-runner. Despite going 11–2, capturing the conference, destroying Illinois 49–17 (tying the record of 49 points in the Rose Bowl onslaught), and finishing number two in the *USA Today* poll, it was probably Carroll's worst team since his first year.

By season's end, however, USC was the best team in the nation. However, an avalanche of injuries early in the year had made them vulnerable. A 24–23 loss at home to 41-point underdog Stanford; the loss of Booty for the Oregon game, a 24–17 loss at Eugene; and a sense of lethargy served to derail Troy from ultimate greatness. What cost them in the end, however, was something beyond their control.

The BCS computers did not look kindly at USC's strength of schedule component. Nobody could have predicted before the season that traditional powerhouses Nebraska and Notre Dame, both of whom were soundly beaten by Troy, would experience brutal seasons. Normally, these non-conference opponents would have added luster to the Trojans' power ratings, but when they faltered all season, this did not happen. Furthermore, Pac-10 opponents California, Oregon, and UCLA were all ultimately disappointing, meaning that USC's victories over the Bears and Bruins (and loss to Oregon) were unimpressive to both voters and computers. A huge road win on Thanksgiving night at Arizona State was not enough to overcome all of this.

Whether it was Carroll's worst team since 2001 or not, it *was* generally felt that they were the best team in America at season's end (just as they had been in 2002). Booty, a major preseason Heisman candidate, missed key midseason games, costing him a shot at USC's eighth statue. However, his performance down the stretch was as impressive as any quarterback in the country, which the fifth-year senior from Shreveport, Louisiana, hoped would impress some NFL scouts.

"I just want people to think of me as a winner," he said on the Rose Bowl turf after beating the Illini, and he indeed had accomplished that task.

Pete Carroll reacts to cornerback Cary Harris's interception against Illinois during the Trojans' blowout win in the Rose Bowl game on January 1, 2008.

In the bowl season, USC's blowout of Illinois was easily the most impressive of any team in the land. Booty shined in the Pasadena sunshine for the second straight year. USC's 2007 defense was the best it had been since the 2003 and 2004 campaigns. A comparison of USC with other traditional powers also favored the Trojans from a larger perspective.

LSU "won" the BCS title over Ohio State, but with two losses they were probably the most unimpressive national champion in history (with the exception of teams that had won titles prior to losing bowl games, as Alabama had done in 1964 prior to the polls closing only after the bowls). It would be arrogant and unwise to state that, had USC played LSU, they would have beaten them. It would not be untrue to state that, had they played, even at the Superdome, USC would have been favored. The Tigers were better than the Trojans in October. They were not better in January.

Ohio State was bidding to catch USC as the "team of the decade" for the 2000s, but in losing in ignominious fashion in their second straight BCS title game, the Buckeyes fell far, far below that standard.

Oklahoma fans would like to think the Sooners' program is close to USC. Their embarrassing 48–28 loss to West Virginia in the Fiesta Bowl was a continuation of poor bowl performances in the decade, thus eliminating any chance that OU can lay any semblance of claim to parity with the Trojans.

The future looks bright at Southern California, where, as ESPN's Kirk Herbstreit said, the "Trojans are like the old Lakers—rock stars in L.A." Pete Carroll openly stated that his goal is not merely to win the national championship, or even to have the best program in the nation. Rather, his goal is to make USC the greatest historical college football tradition of all time. It appears, upon examination of the evidence, that this is not a contemplated future prospect, but rather an accomplished past act.

May God bless America, and may the Trojans continue to "Fight On!"

ALL-TIME
USC FOOTBALL TEAM

Offense

Position	First (Honorable Mention)
QB	Matt Leinart (Pat Haden, Carson Palmer, Paul McDonald, Rodney Peete)
TB	O.J. Simpson (Charles White, Mike Garrett, Ricky Bell, Frank Gifford)
FB	Marcus Allen (Sam "Bam" Cunningham)
WR	Lynn Swann
WR	Mike Williams (Keyshawn Johnson, Erik Affholter, Bob Chandler, Dwayne Jarrett)
TE	Charles "Tree" Young (Fred Davis)
OT	Anthony Munoz
OT	Ron Yary (Tony Boselli, Ernie Smith, Don Mosebar, Pete Adams, Keith Van Horne, John Vella)
OG	Brad Budde (Taitusi Lutui)
OG	Bruce Matthews (Aaron Rosenberg, Roy Foster, Johnny Baker)
C	Stan Williamson (Ryan Kalil)

Defense

T	Marvin Powell (John Ferraro)
DT	Shaun Cody (Sedrick Ellis)
DT	Ron Mix (Mike Patterson, Tim Ryan)
DE	Tim Rossovich
DE	Willie McGinest (Mike McKeever, Charles Weaver, Kenechi Udeze)

Defense (cont'd)

LB	Junior Seau
LB	Richard "Batman" Wood
LB	Clay Matthews (Dennis Johnson, Chip Banks, Adrian Young, Charles Phillips, Chris Claiborne)
DB	Ronnie Lott
DB	Tim McDonald
DB	Troy Polamalu (Dennis Smith, Dennis Thurman, Joey Browner, Mark Carrier)

Special Teams

KR	Reggie Bush (Anthony Davis)
P	Tom Malone
PK	Frank Jordan (Ron Ayala)

Offensive Player: Matt Leinart

Defensive Player: Ronnie Lott

Coach: John McKay (Pete Carroll, Howard Jones, John Robinson)

ANSWERS TO
TRIVIA QUESTIONS

Page 3: Notre Dame (11) has won only three in the "modern era" (1960–present), while USC (11 overall) has won seven. During this period, Notre Dame has won two Heismans to USC's seven. Alabama claims 12 or 13, but many of those are illegitimate (USC has been awarded 16 titles but unlike other schools they do not recognize all of them). In 1964 the polls voted before the bowls. The Tide lost to Texas. In 1973 UPI voted before the Orange Bowl, which 'Bama lost by a point to the legitimate national champion, Notre Dame. They split the 1978 title with 'SC, despite losing to Troy at Legion Field. 'Bama has zero Heismans. Their valid national titles number eight or nine, depending on how lenient one's standards are. More telling, each of USC's national championships came in years in which they won the Rose Bowl (except for 1928, when they did not play in a bowl, and 2004, when they won the BCS Orange Bowl). Seven of Notre Dame's titles came in years in which they did not play in a bowl. Logic dictates that of those seven years, strong bowl opponents would have beaten them one, twice...three times?

Page 8: In 1994 Professor George Olah won the Nobel Prize in chemistry.

Page 9: It is the USC Health Sciences Campus, northeast of downtown L.A. Also, the USC/Norris Comprehensive Cancer Center is among the finest of its kind in the world.

Page 25: In 1961. Traveler I's progeny have been riding the sidelines at USC football games ever since.

Page 29: Five in a row. From 2003 to 2007, at least one, several (or a consensus) of the various ratings systems (Student Sports, rivals.com, ESPN, Athlon Sports College Football Preview, among others) have rated USC number one. The 2005 recruiting class was at the same considered the greatest ever.

Page 32: In the 1950s, the band began playing "Conquest," originally heard in the 1947 motion picture, *Captain from Castile*.

Page 34: From the 1960s until the early 1990s, the top four film schools in America were NYU and Columbia in New York, and UCLA and USC in California. Over the past 15 years, the USC School of Cinematic Arts has emerged head and shoulders above the competition.

Page 47: In 1888 the university fielded its very first football team. According to the late, great *Los Angeles Times* sportswriter Mal Florence's 1980 book, *The Trojan Heritage*, much of USC's early football history was compiled by Harry C. Lillie, a Los Angeles attorney. Lillie was a "125-pound end on the first rag-tag USC team," wrote Florence. "The only available opposition was a club team which carried the name of Alliance," said Lillie. "Our first game was November 14, 1888, right at the University and we won by a score of 16–0."

Page 50: Brice Taylor in 1925. Taylor was African American and part Native American, a relative of Indian Chief Tecumseh. He was also born without the use of one of his hands.

Page 51: At a track meet between Stanford and USC in 1912, *L.A. Times* sports editor Owen R. Bird wrote that USC's athletes "fought like Trojans." USC's unofficial nicknames, the Methodists and sometimes the Wesleyans and even the Puritans, officially became the Trojans. "The term 'Trojan'; as applied to USC means to me that no matter what the situation, what the odds, or what the conditions," Bird later recalled, "the competition must be carried on to the end, and those who strive must give all they have and never be weary in doing so."

Page 53: USC is the largest private employer in L.A., employing 40,000 people.

Page 55: USC and Notre Dame have won 11 football national championships. USC's baseball team has won the College World Series 12 times. UCLA has 11 NCAA basketball titles.

Page 58: At Rome (1960), Tokyo (1964), and Mexico City (1968), USC captured 12 gold medals and 37 overall medals. Bob Seagren set a world record in winning the Mexico City pole vault competition. Parry O'Brien won the shot put silver medal at Rome. Lennox Miller won 100-meter silver at Mexico City. Jim Hines also was a USC track star.

Page 60: The USC baseball team has won five consecutive national championships (1970 to 1974).

Page 65: Twenty-four Olympic gold, five silver, and three bronze medals. At Berlin in 1936, USC scored 37 points, placing them, if they had been a country, in the top five in the world. Dean Cromwell coached the 1936 and 1948 U.S. teams. His legends included sprinters Charles Paddock, Frank Wykoff, and Mel Patton; jumpers Al Olson and John Wilson; throwers Bud Houser, Jesse Mortensen, and Kenneth Carpenter; vaulter Bill Graber; and miler Lou Zamperini.

Page 78: Cravath's nine-year record from 1942 to 1950 was 54–28–8 with four Rose Bowl appearances.

Page 80: The Victory Bell was what UCLA trotted out when they won football games. In 1941 USC students stole the bell. The bell would be hidden in the Hollywood Hills and then in Orange County. The bell would become the iconic prize that went to the winner of the USC-UCLA football game.

Pranks, thefts, and vandalism would mark the intense rivalry in all the decades after that. Humiliations, head-shavings, imprisonments, kidnappings, bombings, wild rodents; the painting blue of USC's horse, Traveler, as well as Tommy Trojan, and fertilizer drops from helicopters, marked some of the hijinks. Spies were sent out. Card stunts disrupted. The other school's fight songs would play on campus loudspeakers. Bogus student newspapers were printed.

Page 85: Twenty-six. Sprinter Mel Patton set a 100-yard dash world record with a time of 9.4 seconds (gold in London, 1948). Diver Sammy Lee earned a gold and a bronze. Parry O'Brien earned gold in both games. The medal count was spread between track, diving, swimming, water polo, and rowing.

Page 89: Marlin and Mike McKeever were Catholic twin brothers and All-American linemen, but Mike caused serious injury to Cal's Steve Bates, creating national furor over "dirty football." Observance of the tape exonerated Mike. The twins belied the "terror" stereotype by making Academic All-America.

Marlin was a star for the Rams. Mike, a College Hall of Famer, died after a car crash in 1967.

Page 94: Wisconsin quarterback Ron VanderKelen set Rose Bowl passing records, leading the Badgers from a 42–14 deficit to within five points before time ran out.

Page 96: Ron Mix with the San Diego Chargers and Oakland Raiders, eventually making it to the Pro Football Hall of Fame.

Page 98: Dedeaux Field was built in 1974. Trojan pitcher Russ McQueen threw a no-hitter in the first game played there.

Page 101: Two. He was a rookie for the Kansas City Chief team that lost to Green Bay in Super Bowl I at the Coliseum, and a star for the Chief team that beat Minnesota 23–7 in Super Bowl IV at New Orleans.

Page 104: "As the team emerged from the locker room," McKay recalled of a game at The Farm in the late 1960s or early 1970s, "my team was peppered with the most vile, disgusting racial epithets that I've ever heard in 30 years of college and professional coaching....I felt that the liberalism at Stanford was an example of academic hypocrisy. These were people who put down those who didn't share their ideals, who told everybody else how to live. But now I was hearing the exact opposite of what that school supposedly preached."

Page 107: "A billion Chinamen couldn't care less who won." That year, 1966, was the first year of Chairman Mao-Tse Tung's decade-long "Cultural Revolution," in which an estimated 40 to 60 million human beings were murdered under communism in Red China. Aside from that quote, McKay vowed to never be "beaten like that again." From 1967 until his retirement in 1975, he not only

was never beaten "like that again," he was almost unbeaten against Notre Dame. Only a 1973 loss to a national champion Irish team at South Bend broke his unbeaten streak against Ara Parseghian. Over time, his statement was revised to "we'll never let them beat us again."

Page 108: The All-American Lee insisted that he play first base in non-conference games.

Page 112: A huge national TV audience got the full treatment of sun, color, and, believe it or not, at the 1967 USC-UCLA game for the first time, the Trojan song girls. Long regarded as the most beautiful and classiest of college football cheerleaders, they have resisted the scantily clad look that marks oversexualized cheerleaders at other colleges.

Page 117: The *Wild Bunch* was a groundbreaking 1969 Western, directed by Sam Peckinpah, starring William Holden and Ernest Borgnine. The Trojan defensive front consisted of ends Jimmy Gunn and Charlie Weaver, tackles Al Cowlings and Tody Smith, and middle guard Bubba Scott. A statue depicting them was erected on the USC campus. Pete Carroll's 2003 national championship defensive line was nicknamed the "Wild Bunch II."

Page 121: "Sam Cunningham did more to integrate Alabama in 60 minutes than Martin Luther King had done in 20 years," Jerry Claiborne, one of Bryant's assistant coaches, is credited with having said. But Marv Goux also said it. He said Cunningham had done more to integrate the South in three hours than Martin Luther King had done in 20 years, probably repeating what he heard Claiborne had said. McKay, Fertig, and Goux, among others, repeated this and the "This here's what a football player looks like" quotes on the banquet circuit for decades.

Page 122: "Hatred Shut Out as Alabama Finally Joins the Union" was the headline. The article read, in part: "The state of Alabama joined the Union. They ratified the Constitution, signed the Bill of Rights. They have struck the Stars and Bars. They now hold these truths to be self-evident, that all men are created equal in the eyes of the Creator.

"Our newest state took the field against a mixed bag of hostile black and white American citizens without police dogs, tear gas, rubber hoses or fire hoses. They struggled fairly without the aid of their formidable ally, Jim Crow.

"Bigotry wasn't suited up for a change. Prejudice got cut from the squad. Will you all please stand and welcome the sovereign state of Alabama to the United States of America?...

"The point of the game is not the score, the Bear, the Trojans; the point of the game will be reason, democracy, hope. The real winner will be Alabama."

Page 127: "Gentlemen, I'd like to announce that the Rose Bowl no longer belongs to Radcliffe." He derisively referred to Stanford, the 1971 and 1972 Rose Bowl champions, as "Radcliffe" or the "Harvard of the West."

Page 132: An incredible 14 Trojans from the 1974 team were drafted.

Page 140: The 502 Club came into existence in the 1970s. The Five-Oh was an off-campus bar, popular on Thursday nights and after Trojan games. The scene on Sundays after L.A. Raiders games in the 1980s was a madhouse: Raiders cheerleaders dressed in slinky outfits; Raiders players and other pro athletes; their model-hot girlfriends; Hollywood celebrities of every kind; groupies, gamblers, thuggish Raiders fans, low-lifes, "gang-bangers," druggies; USC students, alumni, and, of course, USC athletes. Coach Larry Smith's orders that his players stay away was ignored. This was the place where Todd Marinovich found trouble in more ways than one. It closed down in 1993.

Page 141: After he led the 1982 Alaskan Summer League in batting, Rod Dedeaux made him a full-time first baseman. Big Mac responded by leading the nation in home runs and earning All-America honors in his sophomore and junior years (1983–1984). In 1984 McGwire set the Pac-10 home-run record (32, with 80 RBIs) and was named *The Sporting News* College Player of the Year. He played in the 1984 Olympics at Dodger Stadium.

Page 146: Chad Kreuter, the "Forrest Gump of baseball" married Mike Gillespie's daughter. Kreuter was the catcher when many famous events occurred, including Barry Bonds's 71st home run of 2001. He later became an assistant on Gillespie's staff, and in 2006 was named head coach of the Trojans.

Page 148: "Home" is what USC calls the Rose Bowl—their winter residence—despite the fact that UCLA rents the building in the fall. They have won the 1931, 1932, 1939, 1962, 1967, 1972, 1974, 1978, and 2003 national titles on the green plains of the Arroyo Seco. UCLA's only national title in 1954 came in a year in which they did not play in the Rose Bowl. At the time, the PCC instituted the ill-advised "Big 10 rule" of repeat champions not going to Pasadena. Miami won the 1983 national championship at the Orange Bowl. Texas won in 1963 and 1969 at the Cotton Bowl in Dallas, which is 169 miles from Austin. LSU won the 1958, 2003, and 2007 national championships with victories at the Sugar Bowl in New Orleans. But for the most part, the big names of collegiate football—

Notre Dame, Alabama, Oklahoma, Michigan, Ohio State, Nebraska, Penn State, et al—are cold weather schools or are located in small markets where major New Year's bowl games are not played.

Page 150: Since the game was in Alabama, Carroll invited Sam "Bam" Cunningham and John Papadakis, two of the players from the 1970 team that had beaten Alabama at Legion Field, helping to ease the way for integration. They flew with the team, rode the bus, roamed the sideline, and spoke to the team.

Page 155: USC beat two-time defending national champion LSU twice before defeating Arizona State in the title game. Third baseman Morgan Ensberg later starred for the Astros, where teammate Jason Lane was a Trojan, too. In 1999 the Trojan ace was Barry Zito. In 2000 and 2001 Mark Prior dominated, and his '01 season is thought to be the best of all time (15–1, 202 strikeouts in 138 ⅔ innings, and an earned-run average of 1.69).

Page 159: An ESPN football analyst describe the USC–Notre Dame rivalry before the 2005 game, "Like Nick Lachey and Jessica Simpson seeing each other for the first time across a crowded room."

Page 160: *Sports Illustrated's* Austin Murphy described the Notre Dame–USC rivalry, "Like a bunch of rich Republicans trying to win the nomination." A comic once said of the USC-UCLA game, "It's a convention for the Beautiful People. Everybody's tanned and rich."

Page 163: Rice's description of the "Four Horsemen of Notre Dame" was, "Outlined against a blue, gray October sky, the Four Horsemen rode again. In dramatic lore, they are known as famine, pestilence, destruction and death. These are only aliases. Their real names are Stuhldreher, Miller, Crowley, and Layden."

Page 164: Fred Matua described the USC–Notre Dame game as: "It's like USC versus America. Everyone wants to knock us down. But at the same time, what other position would we rather be in? It's the greatest position to be in, when you're on top and everyone else is trying to grab your ankles to pull you down."

Bibliography

Adams, Bruce. "Cal sees the old USC swagger." *San Francisco Chronicle*. November 13, 2005.

Adande, J.A. "Return Could Mean Back-to-Back-to-Back." *Los Angeles Times*. January 5, 2005.

_____. "L.A. Gets a Double Treat With Bush and James." *Los Angeles Times*. Dember 4, 2005.

Albee. Dave. "Keeping his lust for life." *Marin Independent Journal*. August 25, 2004.

_____. "Coach T handed Carroll first gig." *Marin Independent Journal*. November 11, 2005.

Associated Press. "#1 USC 63, Hawaii 17." September 4, 2005.

_____. "USC gets back to normal - scores 51 points." October 23, 2005.

_____. "USC defense finally flexes its muscle." October 30, 2005.

Athlon Sports College Football. "Best of 2005." September 9, 2005.

Baum, Bob. "Trojans turn the tide on second-half surge." Associated Press. October 2, 2005.

Barra, Allen. *The Last Coach: A Life of Paul "Bear" Bryant*. New York. W.W. Norton & Company, 2005.

Brennan, Christine. "Trojans render Sugar Bowl meaningless." *USA TODAY*. January 2, 2004.

_____. "No need for playoff this time." *USA TODAY*. January 5, 2005.

Bolch, Ben. "Leinart Will Take His Time." *Los Angeles Times*. January 6, 2005.

_____. "For Carroll, Dai Is A Family Affair." *Los Angeles Times*. Dember 4, 2005.

Boyles, Bob and Paul Guido. *50 Years of College Football*.

Bisheff, Steve. *Orange County Register*.

Carey, Jack. "Trojans don't horse around." *USA TODAY*. January 5, 2005.

Chavez, Kevin. "No need for nostalgia for Troy." *San Gabriel Valley News*. January 6, 2005.

Chengelis, Angelique. "USC defense overwhelms Michigan." *Detroit News*. January 2, 2004.

Chronicle News Services. "Arizona makes USC work for its fifth victory." *San Francisco Chronicle*. October 9, 2005.

Cole, Gary. "Playboy's 2004 Pigskin Preview." *Playboy*. September, 2004.

_____. "05 Playboy's Pigskin Preview." Playboy. September, 2005.

Collier, Gene. "Mitchell's Tale Still Twisting." *Pittsburgh Post-Gazette*. September 2, 2004.

Collin, Phil. *The Daily Breeze*. December, 2000.

Coyne, Tom. "Notre Dame hopes to rewrite the plot against USC." Associated Press. October 15, 2005.

Curtis, Jake. "USC has offense, schedule to pull off unprecedented feat." *San Francisco Chronicle*. September 1, 2005.

_____. "These teams pass - or fail." *San Francisco Chronicle*. September 1, 2005.

_____. "Pluck, luck benefit lion-hearted Leinart." *San Francisco Chronicle*. October 17, 2005.

_____. "Diverse Trojan offense arguably the best ever." *San Francisco Chronicle*. November 3, 2005.

Dalton, Dennis. *Power Over People: Classical and Modern Political Theory*. Recorded course from Barnard College at Columbia University, New York. Available at www.teach12.com.

Dettlinger, Chet and Jeff Prugh. *The List*. Atlanta: Philmay Enterprises, 1984.

Dilbeck, Steve. "Trojans' undefeated season leaves no doubt." *Los Angeles Daily News*. January 5, 2005.

Dohn, Brian. "Overshadowing Linart?" *Long Beach Press-Telegram*. December 2, 2005.

DuFresne, Chris. "Turnovers Leave Sooners a Shade of Crimson." *Los Angeles Times*. January 5, 2005.

_____. "BCS Obsessed." *Los Angeles Times*. January 5, 2005.

_____. "With simple formula and fresh approach, Carroll builds a potential Trojan dynasty." *Los Angeles Times*. January 6, 2005.

_____. "Weis Leading a Rivalry Revival." *Los Angeles Times*. October 16, 2005.

_____. "Getting to the Point." *Los Angeles Times*. December 1, 2005.

_____. "Putting the 'C' Back in the BCS." *Los Angeles Times*. December 5, 2005.

_____. "Rose Bowl Hype Ballon Could Burst on Game Day." *Los Angeles Times*. December 5, 2005.

Dunnavant, Keith. *Coach: Life of Paul "Bear" Bryant*. New York: Simon & Schuster, 1996.

Dwyre, Bill. "More Like Powdered Blue." *Los Angeles Times*. December 4, 2005.

Elliott, Helene. "Trojans Put Up Tough Barricade to Stop Sooners." *Los Angeles Times*. January 5, 2005.

Farmer, Sam. "49ers to Go After Carroll." *Los Angeles Times*. January 6, 2005.

Feldman, Bruce. "Reaction time." *ESPN The Magazine*. August 30, 2004.

_____."Wanna see that again?" *ESPN The Magazine*. August 29, 2005.

Florence, Mal. *The Heritage of Troy*. 1980.

Fittipaldo, Ray. "Experts: USC could be among greatest teams." *Pittsburgh Post-Gazette*. October 26, 2005.

Friend, Tom. "Finishing School." *ESPN The Magazine*. July 18, 2005.

Gardiner, Andy. "Tennessee, Nebraska top signing charts." *USA TODAY*. February 3, 2005.

Groom, Winston. *The Crimson Tide: An Illustrated History of Football at the University of Alabama*. Tuscaloosa: University of Alabama Press, 2000.

Hammerwold, Walter. "BCS finally delivers the goods." *Long Beach Press-Telegram.* December 5, 2005.

Harris, Beth. "USC's focus: Limit mistakes." Associated Press. October 10, 2005.

Harmonson, Todd. "Trojans run hog wild all night." *Orange County Register.* September 18, 2005.

_____. "Two heads better for Trojans." *Orange County Register.* December 2, 2005.

_____. "BCS will have its perfect game." *Orange County Register.* December 5, 2005.

Hayes, Matt. "Trouble for the Trojans." *The Sporting News.* October 21, 2005.

Himmelberg, Michele. "A workplace divided." *Orange County Register.* December 2, 2005.

Hisermam, Mike. "USC's Win Means a Bit of a Loss for Business." *Los Angeles Times.* December 4, 2005.

Hoffarth, Tom. "L.A. deprived by early start." *Los Angeles Daily News.* January 5, 2005.

Jares, Joe and John Robinson. *Conquest.*

Keisser, Bob. "Bam's imapct not forgotten." *Long Beach Press-Telegram.* September 12, 2005.

_____. "It's an old-school drubbing." *Long Beach Press-Telegram.* December 4, 2005.

Knapp. Gwen. "Finally, BCS gets its 'Magic' moment." *San Francisco Chronicle.* December 6, 2005.

Klein, Gary. "Conquest." *Los Angeles Times.* January 5, 2005.

_____. *Conquest: How Pete Carroll and USC Ascended to the Top of the College Football Mountain.* 2005.

_____. "Cardinal and Bold." *Los Angeles Times.* January 5, 2005.

_____. "USC Does the Grunt Work With Ease." *Los Angeles Times.* September 18, 2005.

_____. "Leinart's Sneak Peak." *Los Angeles Times.* October 16, 2005.

_____. "Chart Breakers." *Los Angeles Times.* December 2, 2005.

_____. "Trojans Go on a Tear." *Los Angeles Times.* December 4, 2005.

Krikorian, Doug. "Pundits way off on USC." *Long Beach Press-Telegram.* January 6, 2005.

_____. "Dennis waiting for his turn." *Long Beach Press-Telegram.* December 1, 2005.

_____. Trojans leave the Bruins Bushed." *Long Beach Press-Telegram.* December 4, 2005.

Los Angeles Daily News. *A Tradition Restored.* Champagne, Ill.: Sports Publishing, 2003.

LeBatard, Dan. "The view from...Miami." *Miami Herald.* January 5, 2005.

McKay, John with Jim Perry. *McKay: A Coach's Story.* New York: Atheneum, 1974.

Michaels, Vicki. "Southern Cal loaded for another shot." *USA TODAY.* January 2, 2004.

Modesti, Kevin. "Routing Oklahoma only the start for USC?" *Los Angeles Daily News.* January 5, 2005.

_____. "Everything went right on this night." *Los Angeles Daily News.* January 6, 2005.

Moore, Leon. "Carroll re-energeizes Trojans." *USA TODAY.* December 31, 2003.

_____. "USC strikes 1st in title race." *USA TODAY.* January 2, 2004.

_____. "Senior Colbert turns in career day." *USA TODAY.* January 2, 2004.

_____. "Junior Leinart easily junks Heisman jinx." *USA TODAY*. January 5, 2005.

_____. "Carroll's Trojans have talent to maintain prime position." *USA TODAY*. January 5, 2005.

Moran, Malcolm. "Dream season ends with nightmare." *USA TODAY*. January 5, 2005.

_____. "Leinart cements legend with late heroics." *USA TODAY*. October 17, 2005.

Murphy, Austin. "Without a Doubt." *Sports Illustrated*. January 10, 2005.

_____. "Danger Is His game." *Sports Illustrated*. August 15, 2005.

_____. "College Football 2005." *Sports Illustrated*. August 15, 2005.

_____. "Can Anyone Beat USC?" *Sports Illustrated*. October 17, 2005.

_____. "Fantastic Finishes." *Sports Illustrated*. October 24, 2005.

Murray, Jim. "Hatred Shut Out as Alabama Finally Joins the Union." *Los Angeles Times*. September 13, 1970.

Nadel, John. "USC steamrolls Stanford."Associated Press. November 6, 2005.

Neal McCready. *Mobile Press-Register*. August 2003.

Newhouse, Dave. "Leinart outshines Bears as USC cruises to victory." *Oakland Tribune*. November 13, 2005.

Norwood, Robyn. "Spotted fever." *Los Angeles Times*. December 3, 2005.

_____. "Trojan Defense Gives the Bruins No Shot." *Los Angeles Times*. December 4, 2005.

Nyiri, Alan. *The Heritage of USC*. Los Angeles: University of Southern California, 1999.

Penner, Mike. "There Are No Big Winners in ABC Booth." *Los Angeles Times*. January 5, 2005.

Perry, Jim. "USC Loses One of Its Legends With the Death of McKay." *Trojan Tail*, 2001

_____. "Alabama Goes Black 'N White." *Los Angeles Herald-Examiner*, 1971.

Peterson, Anne M. "Oregon overwhelmed by USC in secon half." Associated Press. September 25, 2005.

Pierson, Don. *The Trojans: Southern California Football*. Chicago: Henry Regnery, 1974.

Plaschke, Bill. "It's Crystal Clear—No One Can Touch This USC Team." *Los Angeles Times*. January 5, 2005.

_____. "In Run-Up to a Vote, Bush Surely Makes His Case." *Los Angeles Times*. December 4, 2005.

_____. "Good From the Word 'Go.'" *Los Angeles Times*. October 16, 2005.

Pool, Bob. "Rah, Rah - Boo, Hiss." *Los Angeles Times*. December 3, 2005.

Prugh, Jeff. "Trojans Fall on Alabama..." *Los Angeles Times*. September 13, 1970.

_____. "Two Black Students Had Enrolled Before Wallace Showdown." *Los Angeles Times*, June 11, 1978,

_____. Excerpt from *The Herschel Walker Story*.

_____. "The Night They Drove Old Dixie Down."

_____. "George Wallace Was America's Merchant of Venom." *Marin Independent Journal*. September 15, 1998

_____. "Anger boiled within Gerald Ford before this football game." *Marin Independent Journal*. August 12, 1999

Ratto, Ray. "USC is the new Notre Dame; the new 'America's Team.'" *San Francisco Chronicle*. November, 2005.

Rappoport, Ken. *The Trojans: A Story of Southern California Football*. Huntsville, Ala.: Strode Publishers, 1974.

Russo, Ralph, "Bush Runs Off With Heisman Trophy." Associated Press. December 11, 2005.

Schrader, Loel. Long Beach Pres-Telegram.

Schulman, Henry. "Astros win time to watch USC." *San Francisco Chronicle*. October 16, 2005.

_____. www.theuscreport.com.

Simers, T.J. "The Trojans Owe It All to Good Ol' Uncle Pete." *Los Angeles Times*. January 5, 2005.

Sports Illustrated. *USC Trojans*. 2005.

Springer, Steve. *60 Years of USC-UCLA Football*.

Stewart, Larry. "Peete Was Looking for a Special Deliver." *Los Angeles Times*. December 1, 2005.

Thamel, Peter. "Leinart's goal-line dive gives No. 1 USC win in thriller." *New York Times*. October 16, 2005.

Travers, Steven. "It Wasn't a Football Game, It Was a Sighting." *StreetZebra*, November, 2000. Available at www.streetzebra.com.

_____."Dynasty: The New Centurions of Troy." Excerpted from *The USC Trojans: College Football's All-Time Greatest Dynasty*. Boulder, Colo.: Rowman & Littlefield Publishers, Inc., 2006 (based on "2005 USC Trojans: Greatest College Football Dynasty Ever?" available at www.american-reporter.com, July 4, 2005).

_____. "The Four Horsemen of Notre Dame." Excerpted from *The USC Trojans: College Football's All-Time Greatest Dynasty*. Boulder, Colo.: Rowman & Littlefield Publishers, Inc., 2006.

_____. "Is it too early to hype Palmer for the Heisman?" *StreetZebra*. September, 2000.

_____. "He Was a Legend of the Old School Variety." June 2001.

_____. "Legend: A Conversation with John McKay." *StreetZebra*, 2000. Available at www.streetzebra.com.

_____. *One Night, Two Teams: Alabama vs. USC and the Game That Changed A Nation*.

_____. "Rich McKay." StreetZebra, 2000. Available at www.streetzebra.com.

_____. "The Eternal Trojan." StreetZebra, 2000. Available at www.streetzebra.com.

_____. "The Tradition of Troy." 2001.

_____. *The USC Trojans: College Football's All-Time Greatest Dynasty*. Boulder, Colo.: Rowman & Littlefield Publishers, Inc., 2006.

_____. "An unsung hero." *San Francisco Examiner*. April 2001.

_____. "Petros Papadakis: USC's player of the month." *StreetZebra*. October 1999.

_____. "Villa Park wins rivalry game." Los Angeles Times. September 2000.

_____. "When Legends Played." StreetZebra, September 1999. Available at www.streetzebra.com.

_____. *God's Country: A Conservative, Christian Worldview of How History Formed the United States Empire and America's Manifest Destiny For the 21st Century*. 2006.

_____. *Barry Bonds: Baseball's Superman.* Champaign, Ill.: Sports Publishing, 2002.

_____. *Orange Countification: The True Story of How the GOP Helped the South Rise Again.* 2005.

Taylor, Phil. "The Tide gets rolled." *Sports Illusrated.* September 27, 2004.

USA TODAY. "Shake-up in college poll." October 17, 2005.

Walsh, Bill. "Coaching Key to USC's Success." *Los Angeles Times.* January 5, 2005.

Wharton, David. "USC Is Better Than OK for Title Win." *Los Angeles Times.* January 5, 2005.

_____. "Leinart Played Conquest in Clutch." *Los Angeles Times.* October 16, 2005.

_____. "USC Bowls Over UCLA." *Los Angeles Times.* December 4, 2005.

Whicker, Mark. "Many questions abound about USC's defense, but does it matter?" *Orange County Register.* September 18, 2005.

_____. "Perfect touch." *Orange County Register.* December 2, 2005.

Whiteside, Kelly. "Southern Cal could b just warming up." *USA TODAY.* January 5, 2005.

Witz, Billy. "Soon after early lead, OU fell apart." *Los Angeles Daily News.* January 5, 2005.

Wieberg, Steve. "What USA's top prep players are thinking." *USA TODAY.* December 31, 2003.

White, Lonnie. *UCLA vs. USC. 75 Years of the Greatest Rivalry in Sports.* Los Angeles: Los Angeles Times Books, 2004.

_____. "Bruins Outgrow Terrible Twos." *Los Angeles Times.* December 1, 2005.

_____. "Bush Run Over Bruins' Defense." *Los Angeles Times.* December 4, 2005.

Wojciechowski, Gene. "USC setting standard for football dominance." ESPN.com. December 6, 2005.

Wolf, Scott. "It's unanimous: USC captures title in rout." *Los Angeles Daily News.* January 5, 2005.

_____. "Leinart mum about his future." *Los Angeles Daily News.* January 5, 2005.

_____. "Analysis: Can Trojans wins a third title in a row?" *Long Beach Press-Telegram.* January 6, 2005.

_____. "USC future is bright if Carroll stays." *Los Angeles Daily News.* January 6, 2005.

_____. "Route 66 to Pasadena." *Long Beach Press-Telegram.* December 4, 2005.

Appendix: University of Southern California Football Letterwinners

Various standards have been used to determine USC letterwinners over the years, but since 1976, squad members who have played at least 30 minutes have been listed here as lettermen. There have been many exceptions to that rule, including kickers and others who contributed significantly to the team's success without playing 30 minutes. In addition, senior squad members who have been on the team for several years have generally been awarded letters for their senior season, as long as they appeared in at least one game.

A

Abdul-Malik, Sultan (1997–2000) LB-DE

Abdul-Shaheed, Shamsud-Din (1998–2000) DE-DT

Abram, Fabian (1955–56) RT

Abrams, Adam (1995–98) PK

Abrams, Andre (1992, 1994) OT-OG

Achica, George (1979–82) NG

Acker, Frank (1904–05) RHB

Adams, Bill (1967) C

Adams, Gene (1904–05)

Adams, Gordon (1980) QB

Adams, Harold (1923–25) E

Adams, Holly (1922–24) C

Adams, Pete (1970–72) OT

Adelman, Harry (1941–42) LG

Adewale, Jody (2004–06) FB

Adolph, Rob (1973–74) QB

Affholter, Erik (1985–88) SE-PK

Aguirre, John (1941, 1945) LT

Aldridge, Rikki (1967) RHB-K

Alekski, Joe (1925, 1927) G

Alexander, DelVaughn (1993–94) WR

Alexander, Harold (1923)

Allan, Roy (1908–10) C

Allen, Marcus (1978–81) TB-FB

Allmon, Dick (1967–68) C

Allmond, Marcell (1999–2003) CB-WR

Allred, John (1993–96) TE

Almy, J. (1907) QB

Anderson, Brad (1981) WR

Anderson, Chuck (1960–61) LG

Anderson, Norman (1922–24)   T
Anderson, Otto (1922–24)   HB
Anderson, William C. (1937–41)   QB
Ane, Charley (1951–52)   QB-LT
Anno, Sam (1983–86)   ILB-OLB
Anthony, Charles (1971–73)   ILB
Anthony, Frank (1927–29)   T
Antle, Ken (1956–58)   C
Antles, Russell (1944–46)   C
Apolskis, David (1990, 1992–93) C-OG
Apsit, Marger (1928–30)   HB
Arbelbide, Garrett (1929–31) HB-E
Arbet, Kevin (1999–2001, 2003–04) CB-S
Archuleta, Bobby (1987)   S
Arnest, Hal (1961)   RE
Arnett, Bob (1957–58)   LHB
Arnett, Jon (1954–56)   LHB
Arnold, James (1918)   G
Arnold, Paul (1889)   QB
Arrington, Gene (1988)   FL
Arrivey, Jim (1982)   QB
Arrobio, Chuck (1963–65)   OT
Artenian, Mickey (1952–53)   LG
Ashcraft, Walt (1948, 1952)   T
Ashton, Collin (2002–05)   LB
Atanasoff, Alex (1937)   C
Aubrey, Bob (1996–97)   LB
Audet, Earl (1943)   RT
Avery, Ralph W. (1896–97)
Axe, Fred (1919–21)   G
Ayala, Ron (1968–70)   S-K

B

Baccitich, John (1966)   C

Badgro, Morris (1924–26)   E
Bailie, Burt (1903–05)   LE
Bain, Bill (1973–74)   OG-OT
Bain, Marv (1964–65)   LB
Baker, John (1929–31)   G
Baker, Roy [Bullet] (1922–23)   HB
Baker, Sam (2004–06)   OT
Baldock, Al (1949–50, 1953)   LE
Baldridge, Lyle (1925–26, 1928)   G
Bame, Damon (1962–63)   LG-LB
Banks, Chip (1978–81)   ILB-OLB
Bansavage, Al (1959)   RG
Banta, Bradford (1990–93)   TE
Banta, Jack (1938–40)   RHB
Barber, Kurt (1988–91)   OLB
Barber, Richard (1931–32)   FB
Bardin, Oliver (1932–33)   G
Barnes, Dan (1987–89)   OG
Barnes, Mercer (1949–50)   C
Barnum, Terry (1992–95)   RB
Baroncelli, Andy (1984)   C
Barragar, Nathan (1927–29)   C
Barrager (1918)
Barrett (1917)
Barrett, Chris (2004–06)   DE-TE
Barry, Al (1952)   RG-RT
Barry, Joe (1992–93)   ILB
Barry, Nelson (1930)   QB
Barry, Steve (1965–66)   OG
Bastian, Bob (1946–48)   LG
Bastianelli, Mike (1995–98)   WR
Bates, Jim (1960–61)   LE
Battle, Art (1946–49)   RHB
Battle, Mike (1966–68)   DHB-S
Bayley, Eugene (1914)   LT
Beale, John Paul (1918–20)   LT
Beals (1917)

Beard, Francis (1932–34) LG
Beard, Greg (1975) OG
Beathard, Peter (1961–63) QB
Beatie, Eugene (1926–27) T
Beatie, Richard (1995) OT
Beatty, Blanchard (1930–31) QB
Beatty, Homer (1934–36) RHB
Beck, Gene (1948, 1950) C
Becker, Henry (1929) HB
Bedsole, Hal (1961–63) LE
Beeson, Bob (1940) LHB
Behrendt, Allen (1924–26) E
Belko, Max (1934–36) LT
Bell, David (1996, 1998–2000) PK-P
Bell, Howard (1926) G-T
Bell, Joseph A. (1943) QB
Bell, Ricky (1973–76) TB-FB
Belotti, George (1954–56) LT
Beloud, Brett (1993) TB
Bender, Wes (1991–92) FB
Bennett, Frank (1939) RT
Benson, Carl (1939–40) RG-LT
Benson, Jeff (1985) OT
Berry, John (1981–83) ILB
Berry, Mike (1969–70) TB
Berryman, Richard (1936) FB
Berryman, Robert (1939–40) QB
Bescos, Julius (1932–34) LE
Best, Oliver (1904) QB
Bethel, Gary (1975–77) C
Bettinger, George (1935) RE
Betz, Bill (1947–48) FB
Bianchi, Steve (1941) C
Bickett, Duane (1982–84)
OLB-DT-ILB
Bickford, John H. (1903–04, 1906)C
Biggers, Keith (1983–84) ILB

Biggs, Henry (1930–32) E
Bing, Darnell (2003–05) S
Bird, Jim (1947–49) LT
Bird, Richard (1919–20) RG
Black, Rupert (1930) G
Blair, Horace (1922) T
Blake, Samuel R. (1916)
Blanche, John (1966, 1968) LB-OG
Blecksmith, Ed (1964–65) S
Bledsoe, Leo (1941) RHB
Bledsoe, William (1940–41) RHB
Bleeker, Melvin (1940–42) QB
Bocage, Chris (2004) TB-WR-S
Bockman, (1905) LT
Boelter, Grant (1996) OT
Bohlinger, Tom (1972–73) LB
Boice, Winchell (1922) E
Boies, Herb (1949) LG
Boies, Larry (1957–58) RE
Bond, Ward (1928–30) T
Bonds, Marcus (1994–95) DE
Bonham, Herschel (1926–28) FB
Booty, John David (2003, 2005–06)
QB
Bordier, Bing (1954–55) RE
Boren, Charles F. (1925, 1927–28)G
Born, Dennis (1967) OT-OG
Bosbyshell, William (1906) LE
Boselli, Tony (1991–94) OT
Boskovich, Joe (2000–03)SNP-C-TE
Boskovich, Martin (1993) P-PK
Botelho, Rod (1958) LG
Bott, Clyde (1896–97) RG
Bottom, Alex (2002) LB-SNP
Bottom, Jay (2002–03) DE
Boulware, Dave (1971–73) FL-P
Bowen, Ken (1995–98) OT

Bowers, Bill (1950)	HB	Brown, George E. (1934)	LG
Bowie, Wilson (1968)	LHB	Brown, George L. (1889)	T
Bowlin, Brandon (1986–88)	S	Brown, Jeff H. (1986–88)	FB
Bowman, Charles (1939)	QB	Brown, Jeff L. (1980–83)	ILB
Boyer, Mark (1982–84)	TE	Brown, Justin (2002)	OT
Boyle, Johnny (1920–22)	LT	Brown, Luthur (2006)	LB
Bozanic, George (1951–53)	QB	Brown, Marcel (1990)	CB
Bradford, Allen (2006)	TB-S	Brown, Raymond [Tay] (1930–32)T	
Bradford, Joe (1945)	RT	Brown, Rocky (1999)	WR
Bradley, Joe (1895)	FB	Brown, Ron (1954–55)	RHB
Bradley, Mario (1994–95)	CB	Brown, Ron (1985–86)	OLB
Bradley, Otha (1973–74)	NG	Brown, Rory (1990–93)	FB
Brady, Greg (1981)	WR	Brown, Van (2002–03)	DE
Brandt, Harvey T. (1934)		Brown, Willie (1961–63)	RHB
Bravo, Danny (1998–2000)	S	Brownell, Dick (1964)	PK
Braziel, Larry (1977–78)	CB	Browner, Joey (1979–82)	S-CB
Breeland, Garrett (1984–85)	OLB	Browner, Keith (1980–83)	OLB
Bregel, Jeff (1983–86)	OG	Browning, Ward (1932–34)	RE
Brennan, Scott (1985–88)	C	Brownwood, John (1962–64)	RE
Brenner, Hoby (1978–80)	TE	Bruce, Kevin (1973–75)	ILB
Brewer, Tony (1982–83)	S	Brummett, Mike (1983)	OG
Bridewell, Walter (1907)	HB	Brymer, Chris (1994, 1996–97)	OG
Bright, Kenneth (1932–33)	HB	Buchanon, William (2002–05)	
Brittingham, Mike (2004–06)FB-LB		CB-WR	
Brock, Louis (1984–86)	CB	Buckley, Bob (1951–53)	RHB
Brockman, Kenneth (1918)	T	Budde, Brad (1976–79)	OG
Broderson, Charles (1898,1902–04)		Buehler, David (2006)	PK-FB-S
RE		Buford, Don (1957–58)	LHB
Bronson, Dick (1957)	RT	Bukich, Rudy (1951–52)	LHB
Brooks, Bruce (1977)	OG	Buncom, Frank (1960–61)	LT
Brouse, Willard (1931)	QB	Bundra, Mike (1959–61)	RT
Brousseau, Raphael (1935–37)	LG	Bundy, Bill (1939–41)	LHB
Brown, Booker (1972–73)	OT-OG	Bunker, Frank (1907, 1909)	C
Brown, Charles (2006)	OT	Burchard, Gerald (1933–35)	LHB
Brown, Dave (1970–72)	C	Burek, Stanley (1905–08)	FB
Brown, Everett (1928–30)	QB	Burke, Don (1948)	FB
Brown, Frederick (1906, 1908)	RG	Burkett, Red (1916)	

Burnett, C.W. (1893, 1895)	RG	Cameron, Rodney (1933–35)	QB
Burns, Dan (1976–77)	TE	Campbell, Gordon (1921–23)	HB
Burns, DeChon (1989)	CB	Campbell, Jack (1978)	OT
Burns, Mike (1975–76)	CB	Campbell, Jim (1917)	LG
Burruel, Ross (2005)	C	Cannamela, Pat (1950–51)	LB-G
Busby, Marvin L. (1934)	T	Cantor, Al (1948–49)	LHB
Busby, Stuart (1961)	LT	Cantwell, John (1974)	FL
Busch, Ernie (1947)	C	Carey, Mike (1976–77)	S
Bush, Reggie (2003–05)	TB	Carlson, Greig (2002–05)	WR
Bush, Ron (1974–76)	CB	Carmichael, Al (1950–52)	RH
Busick, Steve (1978–80)	ILB	Carmichael, Edward W. (1906)	LT
Butcher, Ron (1961–62)	LT	Carpenter, Kenneth (1934, 1937)	RT
Butkus, Matt (1993)	NT	Carpenter, Roy (1905–06)	LE
Butler, Doyle (2000–02)	DE-TE	Carrier, Mark (1987–89)	S
Butler, Raymond (1978–79)	WR	Carten, Red (1894)	
Butterfield, Clarence (1917, 1919–20)	RHB	Carter, Allen (1972–74)	TB
		Carter, Frank (1996–99)	S
Butts, Tracy (1985–88)	CB	Carter, Kent (1970–71)	LB
Byers, Jeff (2004)	C	Caruthers, Gerald (1993–94)	OLB
Byrd, Dominique (2002–05)	TE-DE	Carver, Thomas Nixon (1889)	FB
Byrd, Glenn (1972)	DT	Case, Frank (1905)	LT
Byrd, Lou (1957–58)	LG	Cash, Chris (2000–01)	CB
Byrd, Mac (1962–64)	LG-LT	Cashman, Pat (1966–67)	DHB
Byrd, Sunny (2001–02)	FB-TB	Cashman, Tyler (1993–95)	TE
		Cassel, Matt (2001–04)	QB-TE
C		Cassell, Curtis (1920–21)	C
Cadigan, Dave (1985–87)	OT	Catoe, Ed (1976–77)	DT
Cahill, Ray (1966)	LE	Celotto, Mario (1974–77)	OLB
Cain, Lynn (1977–78)	FB	Chambers, Mahlon (1927–29)	QB
Calabria, Ron (1954)	RHB	Champlain, Jay (1981)	WR
Caley, Dan (1902–03)	RHB-RT	Chandler, Bob (1968–70)	FL
Caley, Elwin (1902–03)	RHB	Chaney, Chris (1972)	FL
Callanan, George T. (1943)	RHB	Chantilles, Tom (1941)	RG
Callanan, Howard (1942)	RHB	Charles, Ben (1959–60)	QB
Callanan, James F. (1944–46)	RE	Chavez, Sal (1988)	NG
Calland, Leo (1920–22)	G	Chesley, Delmar (1986–89)	ILB
Cameron, Don (1923)		Chesley, J.R. (1990)	OLB

Chesley, Martin (1985, 1988)	TE
Chestnut, Bob (1917, 1919)	LHB
Childers, Matt (1999–2000)	DE
Christianson, Howard (1919)	E
Christy, Charles (1896–97)	C
Chuha, Joe (1957)	C
Claiborne, Chris (1996–98)	LB
Claridge, Travis (1996–99)	OG
Clark, Don (1942–47)	LG
Clark, Gordon (1931–33)	HB
Clark, Jack (1935)	RHB
Clark, Jay (1962–63)	RHB
Clark, Kevin (1993)	FB
Clark, Monte (1956–58)	RT
Clark, Ray (1916–17)	RHB
Clark, Roger (1960–61)	RT
Clark, Stephen (1905–08)	RHB
Clark, Tanqueray (1998–99)	CB
Clarke, Eugene (1930–31)	E
Clarke, Leon (1953–55)	LE
Clayton, Frank (1952–54)	LHB
Cleary, Paul (1946–47)	RE
Clemens, Calvin Jr. (1932–34)	RHB
Clemens, Jerry (1919)	LE
Coauette, Greg (1984–87)	CB
Cobb, Garry (1976–78)	OLB
Cobb, Marvin (1972–74)	S-CB
Cochran, Ernest (1909)	RT
Cody, Shaun (2001–04)	DT-DE
Cohn, Thomas (1910)	QB
Coia, Angelo (1958–59)	LHB
Colbert, Keary (2000–03)	WR
Cole, Ralph W. (1921, 1924)	T
Coleman, Michael (2005)	TB
Colley, Tom (1948–49)	RG
Collins, Pat (1973)	Rov
Collins, Will (2004–06)	SNP

Coloneus (1907–09)	
Colorito, Tony (1983–85)	NG
Colter, Cleveland (1986–89)	S
Conde, John (1949–51)	T
Connors, Rod (1977)	TB
Conroy, Jerry (1965)	RG
Conroy, Jim (1956–57, 1959)	FB-QB
Contratto, Jim (1953–55)	QB
Conway, Curtis (1990–92)	FL-QB
Cook, Andrew J. (1924–25)	QB
Cook, Brian (1982)	CB
Cook, Rashard (1995–98)	S
Coones, Ken (1959)	LG
Cordell, Mike (1973–75)	C-OG
Cordes, Herbert Albert (1919)	
Cormier, Joe (1983–85)	TE
Cornwell, Fred (1981–83)	TE
Corsinotti, Dave (1981)	NG
Cotton, Marcus (1984–87)	OLB
Coughlin, Alvie (1932–34)	RT
Cousins, John (2001)	LB
Covington, Humphrey (1968–69) FB	
Cowlings, Al (1968–69)	DT
Cox, Bob (1951–52)	RG
Cox, Kenneth (1924–26)	T
Cox, Morgan (1918–20)	C
Cox, Tom (1984–85)	C
Coyle, Leslie (1927)	HB
Craig, Gerald (1914–16)	RE
Crall, D. Edwin (1907)	RG
Cramer, Stanley (1947–48)	LE
Crane, Bob (1989–91)	TE
Crane, Dennis (1967)	DT
Cravath, Jeff (1924–26)	C
Crawford, Willie (1977–78)	S
Crayton, Estrus (1991–92)	TB

Crisman, Joel (1990–93) OG
Crisp (1919)
Crittenden, Wallace (1944) G
Critton (1905) RT
Crow, Lindon (1952–54) RHB
Crowther, Jim (1941) LT-RT
Cruickshank, Donald (1924–26) T
Crutcher, Fred (1981–85) TB
Culbreath, Cliff (1972) OG
Cummings, Ralph (1921–23) T
Cunnigan, Donn (1991–94)
  ILB-OLB
Cunningham, Sam (1970–72) FB
Curley, August (1980–82) ILB
Curry, Edsel (1943, 1946–47) RHB
Curry, Willard (1915–16) RT
Curtis, Louis Lane (1944) LG
Cusano, Mark (1995–98) LB
Cushing, Brian (2005–06) LB
Custin, George (1906) LHB
Cutri, Cosimo (1950–51) HB

D
Dabasinskas, Tom (1987–89) OT-C
Dahlgren, (1917) RG
Dale, Ron (1988–91) P
Daley, Jeff (1997) TE
Dalton, Matt (1999–2000) WR-QB
Dandoy, Aramis (1952–54) LHB
Danehe, Richard (1941) C
Danelo, Mario (2005–06) PK
Darby, Byron (1979–82)DT-ILB-
  OLB
DaRe, Mario (1952–54) LT
Davis, Anthony (1972–74) TB
Davis, Clarence (1969–70) TB
Davis, David (1934–36) QB

Davis, David (2001–02) PK
Davis, Ennis (1997–2000) DT
Davis, Fred (2004–06) TE-WR
Davis, George (1934) G
Davis, George (1944, 1947, 1949) C
Davis, Jesse (1994–95) S
Davis, Joe (1940–42) RE
Davis, Joe (1973–75) OG
Davis, Keith (1984–87) ILB
Davis, Michael (1981) CB
Davis, Robert (1922) E
Davis, Steve (1998) DT
Davis, Thomas (1914) RHB
Day, Oliver (1937–38) QB
Daye, Anthony (2002) DT-DE
de Lauer, Bob (1939–41)
Dean, Charles F. (1919–21) RHB
DeArmand, Zolo (1917) LG
DeBord, Benji (1995) WR
Debovsky, Phil (1957) RG-C
Decius, Courtney (1906–07, 1909)
  RG
Decker, George (1929–30) T
Decker, Jim (1953–56) FB-LHB
Deese, Derrick (1990–91) OG
DeGroot, Clarke (1924–26) T
DeHetre, John (1934, 1937) C
DeKraai, Terry (1968–69) LE
Del Conte, Ken (1960–62)
Del Rio, Jack (1981–84)
Delaney, Gary (1960) RG
DeLappe, J.R. (1904)
DeMars, Bobby (2001) DE
Demirjian, Ed (1950) QB
Dempsey, Edward (1938–40) C
Denmon, Eric (1998–2000) C
Dennis, Hershel (2002–04) TB

Denvir, John (1985)	OG	Dunning, Corwin (1932)	C
Deranian, Vaughn (1928–30)	G	Dupuy, Reginald (1922–24)	G
Dhaliwal, Gurjot (1998)	TE	Durkee, Harvey (1928–29, 1931)	E
Diaz, Rigo (1988)	SE	Durko, Sandy (1968–69)	DHB
Dickerson, Kori (1998–2001) TE-LB-DE		Duvall, Gordon (1953–55)	FB
		Dye, George (1929)	C
Dickerson, Sam (1968–70)	SE	Dye, John (1931–33)	G
Diggs, Shelton (1973–76)	FL	Dye, William (1933–34)	G
Dihel, Lawrence (1926–27)	E	Dyer, Bruce (1970–71)	CB
Dill, Dean (1947–48)	QB		
Diltz, Jeff (1994–96)	TE	**E**	
DiLulo, Paul (1978, 1980)	FB	Earle, Raymond (1923–25)	HB
Dimler, Rich (1975–78)	NG-DT	Eaves, Phillip (2001–02)	OT
Dittberner, Art (1933–35)	RT	Ebertin, Chuck (1987–88)	C
Doll, Don [Burnside] (1944, 1946–48)	LHB	Eddy, Andy (1985)	FB
		Edelson, Harry (1927–29)	HB
Dolley, Chet (1922–24)	QB	Edgarton, E.O. (1896)	FB
Dominis, John (1943)	RE	Edwards, Bob (1958–59)	C
Doris, Monte (1972–73)	NG	Edwards, Dennis (1978–81)	DT
Dorsey, Gene (1923–24, 1926)	E	Edwards, Hugh (1925)	E
Dotson, David (1993–94)	TB	Egan, John G. (1920)	RE
Dougher, Harold (1922)	G	Elliott, Carl (1904–06)	LE
Dougherty, Morton (1902)	LE	Elliott, E. (1893)	RHB
Douglas, Don (1957–58)	RE	Elliott, Earl (1904)	FB
Douglas, Rome (1996–98)	OT	Elliott, Howard (1925–27)	QB
Downs, Bob (1950)	G	Elliott, Ian (1941)	RHB
Drake, John (2003–04)	OG-OT	Ellis, Sedrick (2004–06)	DT
Drake, Ron (1966–67)	LE	Ellison, Kevin (2005–06)	S
Draper, Travis (2005–06)	C-OG-DT	Elmore, John Jr. (1914)	FB
Dreblow, Milford (1943–46)	RHB	Emanuel, Aaron (1985–89)	TB-FB
Drury, Morley (1925–27)	QB	Embree, Albert B. (1889, 1892)	G
Duboski, Phillip (1936)	LHB	Emmons, Richard (1922)	E
Dudum, J.J. (1991)	PK	Engle, Roy (1937–39)	RHB
Duff, Pat (1949–51)	FB	Enright, Dick (1954–55)	LT-RG
Duffield, Marshall (1928–30)	QB	Eriksen, Bob (1971)	LB
Dunaway, Warren (1934)	LG	Erskine, Robert (1931–33)	T
Dunn, Coye (1936)	LHB	Ervin, Anthony (1985)	DT

Ervins, Ricky (1987–90)	TB	Fletcher, Ron (1954–56)	RT
Essick, Douglas (1941–42, 1946)	LE	Fletcher, Sandy (2000–03)	WR-S
Evans, Charlie (1969–70)	FB	Flint, Fay (1902–03)	RE-RT
Evans, John (1943)	RHB	Flood, Jeff (1973, 1975)	C
Evans, R. (1917)		Floro, Bob (1960)	RT
Evans, Roy [Swede] (1919–21)	RT	Foley, Shane (1989–90)	QB
Evans, Vince (1974–76)	QB	Follett, George (1971–72)	DT-DG
Exley, Landon (1953)	QB	Foote, Chris (1977–79)	C
		Ford, Cole (1991–94)	PK
F		Ford, Dwight (1974–78)	TB
Failor, Walt (1970)	Rov	Ford, Lonnie (1998–2001)	DE-TE
Faraimo, Salo (2003)	LB	Ford, William (1926, 1928)	FB
Fargis, Justin (2002)	TB	Foster, Roy (1978–81)	OG
Farlin, Mark (1994, 1996)	FB	Fouch, Ed (1952–54)	RT
Farmer, Dave (1974–76)	FB	Fouch, John (1949–50)	HB-FB
Farr, Greg (2003–04)	S	Fox, Jack (1926–27)	C
Fassel, Jim (1969)	QB	Fox, John (1915–16, 1919)	LT
Fate, Steve (1971–72)	Rov	Fox, John (1997, 1999)	QB-LB-TE
Fay, Kenneth (1931–33)	HB	Fraser, Scott (1977, 1979)	OG
Ferguson, Claude (1902)	QB	Freeman, George (1921–23)	T
Ferguson, Jim (1966)	C-LB	Freier, Scott (1987–89)	OG-C-TE
Ferrante, Orlando (1953–55)	RG	French, Martin (1985)	CB
Ferraro, John (1943–47)	LT	Friend, Bill (1924–26)	T
Fertig, Craig (1962–64)	QB	Fruge, Gene (1987–90)	NG-DG
Ficca, Dan (1958–60)	LT	Fuhrer, Bob (1932–34)	LE
Fields, Scott (1992–95)	LB-S-TB	Fuhrman, Seymour (1942)	LT
Finneran, Garry (1957–59)	LT	Funk, J.B. (1894)	
Finney, Hal (1942)	LHB		
Fiorentino, Frank (1956–58)	LG	**G**	
Fisher, Jeff (1979–80)	CB	Gable, C.J. (2006)	TB
Fisher, Robert A. (1936–38)	RT	Gachett, Derrick (1986, 1988)	FB
Fisk, Bill (1937–39)	LE	Gage, Stuart (1993–95)	DT
Fisk, Bill Jr. (1962–64)	RG	Gaisford, Bill (1935–36)	LE
Fite, Gary (1965)	FB	Galbraith, Scott (1986–89)	TE
FitzPatrick, James (1983–85)	OT	Gale, Mike (1961–62)	LT
Fletcher, Oliver (1948)	RE	Galindo, Charles (1925)	FB
Fletcher, Paul (1905–06)	LHB	Gallaher, Allen (1970–72)	OG-OT

Gallaway, Darren (1991–93) DE-OLB

Galli, George (1953–55) LG

Galloway, Amor (1921–22) QB

Galloway, Clark (1927–29) G

Galloway, Harold (1918, 1922) FB

Galvin, Glen (1936–39) LE

Garcia, Dan (1978–79) WR

Garlin, Donald (1944–48) LHB

Garner, Dwayne (1986–89) CB

Garner, Troy (1997) WR

Garratt, Nick (2006) LB

Garrett, Mike (1963–65) LHB

Garrido, Norberto (1993–95) OT

Garrison, Edesel (1971–72) SE

Garzoni, Mike (1943–46) RG

Gaskill, Lynn (1959–61) RHB

Gaspar, Phil (1937–39) RT

Gay, William (1975–77) TE

Gaytan, Michael (1991) OT-OG

Gee, Doug (1945) FB

Gee, Matt (1988–91) ILB

Gelker, Benjamin B. (1943) LT

Geller, Roscoe (1908–09) LE

Gentry, Byron (1930–32) G

George, Ray (1936–38) RT

Gerpheide, Ben (1923) RE

Gerpheide, Louis (1923) HB

Getz, Bob (1932) FB

Gibson, Anthony (1980, 1982) TB

Gibson, Craig (1990–93) C

Gibson, David (1996–99) S-LB

Gibson, Don (1987–90) DG-NG

Giers, Mike (1963–64) LT

Gifford, Frank (1949–51) HB

Giguette, Al (1904–05) RHB

Gill, William J. (1934–35) E

Givehand, James (1972) DE

Glenn, William (1922) E

Goller, Winston (1950–51) E

Gomez, Alex (2005) CB

Gomez, Jesse (1995) C-SNP

Gonta, Stan (1962) RG

Goodenow, Harold (1906–08) RG

Goodrum, Rashaad (2005) DE

Gordon, Clifford (1920–21) E

Gorecki, Len (1992) OT

Gorrell, Ted [Butter] (1924–26) G

Gorrell, Walt (1956) C

Goux, Marv (1952–55) C-LB

Gowder, Robert (1927–29) G

Grace, Ken (1993–94) WR

Gracin, Jerry (1934)

Grady, Steve (1966–67) LHB-S

Graf, Allan (1970–72) OG

Graf, Derek (2002) C

Graham, Aaron (1999–2001) LB

Grain, Jason (1997–99) OG

Grant, John (1970–72) DT-DE

Gray, Riki [Ellison] (1978–82) ILB

Gray, Gordon (1943–47) RHB

Gray, John A. (1889, 1992–93) FB

Gray, Ken (1972–74) FB-ILB

Gray, William (1943) C

Green, Brad (1979) C

Green, Edward (1923–24) HB

Green, Garrett (2006) S-QB

Green, Leonard (1994–95) RB

Green, Max (1940) RHB

Green, Paul (1984–88) TE

Green, Tim (1983–84) QB

Greene, Paul (1920–21) LE

Greenwood, Chuck (1953–54) RE

Griffin, Frank (1988–90) TE

Griffin, John (2005–06)   TB
Griffith, Chuck (1954–55)   RE
Griffith, Homer (1931–33)   QB
Grissum, Jim (1968, 1970)   DE
Grootegoed, Matt (2001–04)   LB
Gueguett, Dan (1903–04)
Guenther, Gregg Jr. (2002–03)   TE
Guerrero, John (1985–88)   OT
Gunn, Jimmy (1967–69)   DE
Gurasich, Walt (1956–57)   LG
Gutierrez, Ed (1976–77)   OLB

H

Haas, Brian (1992–95)   LB
Haas, Earl E. (1936)   RG
Hachten, Boyd (1948–49)   C
Haddock, H. (1895)
Haden, Pat (1972–74)   QB
Haigler, Charles (1905–08)   RT
Haigler, Chester (1905–06)   C
Halderman, Richard (1927)   C
Hale, Chris (1987–88)   CB
Hale, D. (2001–02)   WR
Hall, Frank (1954–56)   QB
Hall, Robert H. (1929–31)   T
Hall, Travis (1996)   TE
Hall, William King (1933–34)   C
Hall, Willie (1970–71)   LB-DE
Halloway, Clayton (1914–15)   QB
Haluchak, Mike (1968–70)   LB
Halvorsen, Ray (1936)   LG
Hamilton, Tom (1948)   C
Hamilton, William (1904–05)
Hamilton, Wright (1917)   RE
Hammack, Harold (1929–31)   HB
Hampton, Clint (1981–82)   NG-DT
Han, Harold (1952–53)   FB

Hance, Brandon (2003–04)   QB
Hancock, Brandon (2002–03, 2005) FB
Hancock, Mike (1972–73)   DT-NG
Hanes, Simeon (1914)   LG
Hannah, Travis (1989–92)   FL
Hansch, H.J. (1924)
Hansell, Ellis (1981)   CB
Hansen, Owen L. (1935–37)   LHB
Hanson, Owen (2004)   TE
Hardy, Donald (1943–46)   LE
Hardy, James (1942–44)   QB
Harlan, David (1932–33)   T
Harlow, Pat (1987–90)   OT-DT
Harper, Hueston (1932–34)   RT
Harper, Michael (1980–83)   TB
Harris, Antoine (1997–2000)   TE
Harris, Antoinne (1999)   CB
Harris, Cary (2005–06)   CB
Harris, Lou (1970–71)   TB
Harris, Will (2005)   CB-S
Harrison, Quincy (1994–95)   CB
Hart, Speedy (1980)   WR
Hartsuyker, Craig (1987–90)   OLB
Hartwig, Carter (1976–78)   CB
Harvey, Clarence (1945)   RHB
Harvey, John (1981–82)   DT
Hasen, H. (1902)
Haslam, R. (1896)
Haslip, Ken (1995–98)   CB
Hatch, William (1908)   LT
Hatfield, Hal (1948–50)   E
Hattabaugh, Clay (1991–95)   OG-C
Hattig, Bill (1950–52)   LE
Havili, Stanley (2006)   FB
Hawkins, John (1922–24)   T
Hawkins, William (1930)   C

Hawthorne, Addison (1952–53) FB
Hayes, Jim (1952–53) RE
Hayes, Luther (1958–60) LE
Hayes, Michael (1977, 1979)TB-WR
Hayes, Windrell (1998–99) WR
Hayhoe, Bill (1967–68) DE
Hayhoe, Jerry (1964, 1966) OT
Haynes, Tommy (1983–84) CB
Hayward, Matt (2001–03) SNP-LB
Hazelton, Vidal (2006) WR
Headley, Blake (1944) RHB
Hector, Zuri (1989–92) S
Heidental, Ed (1949) T
Heinberg, Sylvester (1945) RG
Heiser, Bert H. (1924–27) G
Heller, Ron (1962–64) LH-FB
Henderson, Deryl (1985–86) DT
Henderson, James (1935–36) RE
Hendren, Robert (1946–48) RT
Henke, Edgar (1948) RT
Henry, Jerald (1991–94) CB
Henry, Ken (1985–87) SE
Henry, Mike (1956–58) RT
Herpin, John (1992–94) CB
Herrin, Errick (1994–95) LB
Hershberger, Lloyd (1924–26) G
Hertel, Rob (1975–77) QB
Hervey, Edward (1993–94) WR
Hester, Orie (1917–21) G
Heywood, Ralph (1941–43) LE
Hibbs, Gene (1935–37) LE
Hibbs, Jesse (1926–28) T
Hickman, Don (1955–57) RHB
Hickman, Donnie (1974–76) OG
Hicks, Harry (1923) G
Higgins, Clark (1944) LT-LG
Hill, Arthur (1909–10) LE

Hill, DeShaun (2000–02) S-CB
Hill, Fred (1962–64) LE
Hill, Gary (1962–64) RHB
Hill, Hillard (1956–58) LE-RHB
Hill, Jesse T. (1928–29) FB
Hill, Prentice (1995–98) CB
Himebauch, Jonathan (1994–97) C
Hindley, Lewis (1940) LE
Hinman, C.J. (1893, 1896–97) LT
Hinton, Charles (1971–72) CB-TB
Hinz, Mike (1990–93) NT
Hipp, Eric (1979–80) PK
Hoff, Cecil Wayne (1927–29) T
Hoffman, Robert (1937–39) LHB
Hogan, Doug (1973–75) Rov
Hogue, Jeremy (1993–95) C
Holden, Clark (1957–59) FB
Holden, Dave (1984) OT
Holguin, Jess (1995) RB
Holland, Bill (1970–71) FB
Holland, Thomas (1991–93)DT-NG
Hollinquest, Lamont (1988–92)
  OLB-S
Holman, William (1902)
Holmes (1917–18)
Holmes, Alex (2000–02, 2004) TE
Holmes, Calvin (1988–91) CB-TB
Holt, Leroy (1986–89) FB
Homan, Jim (1965–66) OG
Hooks, Bob (1951–52) RE
Hooks, Roger (1954) QB
Hoover, Phil (1961–62) LE
Hope, Neil (1981–84) ILB
Hopkins, Marcus (1988–90) S
Hopper, Darrel (1982–84) CB
Hopper, Tarriel (1993–95) LB
Hord, Randy (1988–89) DG-NG

Houck, Hudson (1963)   C
Houlgate, Jack W. (1933)   C
Howard, Bill (1957)   RHB
Howard, Chris (2001)   TB
Howard, William N. (1933–35)   QB
Howell, Mike (1975)   TE
Howell, Nick (2006)   C-OT
Howell, Pat (1976–78)   OG
Hubby, Lindsy (1956–57)   LE
Huber, Scott (1999–2001)   TE-FB
Hudson, Tyrone (1969–70)   CB
Huff, Tommy (2003)   P
Hughes, Jack (1904–05)
Hughes, John (1923)
Hull, Mike (1965–67)   FB
Hull, Warren Bruce (1934–35)   LT
Humenuik, Rod (1956–57)   RT
Hummell, Edward (1910)   RT-E
Hunnicut (1918)   LT
Hunt, Loran (1961–63)   LHB
Hunt, Paul (1917)
Hunter, Herbert (1917–18)   FB
Hunter, James (1978–80)   TE
Hunter, Keith (1921)   FB
Hunter, Mike (1965)   S
Hurst, Joe (1933–34)   E
Huyck, Harold (1916)

I

Iacenda, Ted (1997)   FB
Ickes, Sydney (1908–09)   QB
Ifeanyi, Israel (1994–95)   DE-OLB
Ingle, Ray J. (1943)   LG
Isaacson, Bob (1954–56)   FB
Isenhouer, Bill (1919–20)   LE
Isherwood, Ed (1956–57)   FB

J

Jackson, Duaine (1981–84)   CB
Jackson, Jabari (1998–99)   TB
Jackson, John (1986–89)   FL-SE
Jackson, Lawrence (2004–06)   DE
Jackson, Melvin (1974–75)   OT
Jackson, Vic (1976)   FB
Jackson, Yonnie (1989–92)   TE
Jacobsmeyer, Walter (1942)   RE
James, George (1914)   LE
Jamison, Dick (1942)   LT
Jaroncyk, Bill (1966–67)   CB
Jarrett, Dwayne (2004–06)   WR
Jefferson, Cedric (1994–97)   DT
Jensen, Bob (1968–69)   LB
Jensen, Robert (1930)   G
Jesse, John P. (1936–38)   LHB
Jessup, Bill (1948–50)   E
Jeter, Gary (1973–76)   DT
Johnson, Charley (1916)
Johnson, Dennis (1977–79)   ILB
Johnson, Eddie (1971–72)   CB
Johnson, Jahi (1997)   TB
Johnson, Kendrick (1916)
Johnson, Keyshawn (1994–95)   WR
Johnson, Matt (1982–85)   CB
Johnson, Paul (1964–65)   C
Johnson, Ricky (1977, 1979)   FB
Johnson, Rob (1991–94)   QB
Johnson, Skip (1960–61)   C
Johnson, Stafon (2006)   TB
Johnson, Tom (1962–63)   LG
Johnston, C.J. (1904)
Johnston, E. (1918)
Johnston, Rex (1956–58)   LHB
Jones, A.E. (1889)   E
Jones, Bob (1939–41)   RE

Jones, Don (1980) CB
Jones, Ernie (1961–63) FB
Jones, Herbert (1915)
Jones, James (1936–38) RHB
Jones, Jim (1969–71) QB
Jones, Michael (1991–92) FB
Jones, Philo (1895–96) LE
Jones, Randy (1962) RT
Jones, Shannon (1990, 1992–93)
DE-ILB
Jordan (1917)
Jordan, Frank (1977–78) PK
Jordan, Steve (1981–84) PK
Jorgenson, Ellwood (1932–35) LT
Joseph, Vincent (2006) CB
Joslin, Clarence (1917) LE
Joslin, J. Howard (1929–31) E
Jurich, Anthony (1929, 1932) RHB
Justice, Winston (2002–03, 2005)
OT

K

Kaer, Morton (1924–26) HB
Kaiser, Ryan (2000–01) WR
Kalil, Ryan (2003–06) C
Kalinich, Pete (1939) RG
Kamana, John (1980–83) FB-WR
Kaprillian, Michael (1910) LT
Kasten, Don (1958) FB-LHB
Katnik, John (1986–87) C
Katnik, Kurt (2003) TE-C
Katnik, Norm (2001–03) C-OT-OG
Keehn, Ludwig (1956) LE
Keiderling, Jason (1993) OT
Kellar, Stewart (1909–10) RG
Keller, Donald W. (1936–37) QB
Keller, John Theron (1935) FB

Kellogg (1917)
Kelly, Brian (1994–97) CB-S
Kelly, Fred (1914–16) FB
Kelly, Kareem (1999–2002) WR
Kemp, Rockwell (1927–29) QB
Kendrick, Donta (1998–99) OG
Keneley, Matt (1993–96) DT
Keneley, Todd (1999) DT
Kerr, Rob (1977–79) PK
Khasigian, Fred (1967–69) OG
Kidder, Allen (1934–35) LH
Killeen, Ryan (2002–04) PK
Kincaid, Howard [Hobo] (1920–22)
King, Arthur (1921)
King, Eddie (1963, 1965–66)Rov-LB
King, Marty (1977–78) P
King, Oscar [Okey] (1922)
Kirby, Jack (1947–48) LHB
Kirkland, Al (1952) RH
Kirner, Gary (1962–63) RT
Kirtman, David (2002–05) FB
Kissinger, Ellsworth (1954–56) QB
Klein, Bob (1966–68) RE
Klein, Gary (1984–85) S
Klenk, Quentin (1939–40) RT
Knickrehm, Fred W. (1917) LT
Knight, Darryl (1998–2000) LB
Knight, Ryan (1984–87) TB-FB
Knight, Sammy (1993–96) LB-S
Knoles, Tully (1901–02) QB
Knutson, Steve (1973–74) OT
Koart, Matt (1982–85) DT
Koch, Des (1951–53) LHB
Koffler, Matt (1994–96) QB
Koo, Dong (1995) OG
Kopp, Jeff (1991–94) ILB-OLB
Kordich, John (1948) RHB

Kovac, Pete (1934) RG
Kraintz, Rudy (1934) FB
Kranz, Doug (1955–56) LHB-RHB
Kreiger, Wm. Karl (1927–29) E
Kroll, Darrell (1942) FB
Krueger, Al (1938–40) LE
Kuamoo, Gaylord (1984–85) OT
Kubas, John (1957) RE
Kuhn, Gil (1934–36) C
Kurlak, Wayne (1954, 1956) QB-FB
Kurle, Alfred (1910) C-G
Kutchel, Theodore (1921) C

L

Lacy, Darnell (1996–98) S
Lady, George (1932–34) RT
Laisne, Eugene (1927–28) HB
Lamb, Mike (1983) OG-OT
LaMont, Grant (1925)
Landrigan, Charlie (1999–2001) FB
Lane, R.C. (1904–05) RG
Langley, Lawrence (1935–36) RHB
Langlois, Dave (1982) S
Lansdell, Grenville Jr. (1937–39)QB
Lanza, John (2005) OG
Lapka, Myron (1977–79) DT
Laraneta, Manuel (1924–26) FB
Lardizabel, Ben (1945–57) LG
Larrabee, Duane (1933–34) RE
Larry, Lawrence (1995–98) DE-LB
LaVelle, Leslie (1926–27) E
Lavender, Tim (1978) CB
Lavin, Tim (1990–91) FB
Lavoni (1905)
Lawrence, Jim (1966–68) RHB
Lawryk, Gene (1976) C
Leach, Jason (2001–04) S

Leadingham, John (1918–21) FB
Leahy, Ed (1920–22) HB
Learned (1917)
LeDuc, William P. (1936)
Lee, Bob (1924–26) FB
Lee, Jim (1972) DT-OT
Lee, Junior (1974–75) SE
Lee, Phil (1964–66) LHB
Lee, Zephrini (1982, 1985) TB
Lefebvre, Henry (1923–25) FB
Leggett, Brad (1987–89) C
Lehmer, Steve (1967–69) OG
Leimbach, Chuck (1954–56) LE
Leimbach, Joe (1980–83) C
Leinart, Matt (2002–05) QB
Lemos, Matt (2003) S
Lenderman, Ryan (1993–94) WR
Lennox, Walter (1904) QB
Leon, Rich (1966) LE
Levario, Steve Jr. (2002–03) WR
Levingston, Bob (1959–60) RHB
Levy, Dexter (1986) CB
Lewis, David (1974–76) OLB
Lewis, Mike (1958) RG
Lewis, Whitney (2003, 2005)WR-TB
Lillywhite, Verl (1945–47) FB
Limahelu, Chris (1973–74) PK
Lincoln, Irwin (1992–93) CB
Lindley, Logan (1918–21) LG
Lindley, Lowell (1920–22) C
Linehan, Tony (1946–47, 1949) LE
Lingenfelter, Dean (1973) TE
Littlejohn, Leroy (1942) LG
Livernash, Leonard (1914–15) LHB
Lloyd, David (1944, 1947–48) LE
Lloyd, William F. (1896–97) LHB
Lockett, Frank (1919–21) FB

Lockwood, John (1964–65) MG-DE
Lockwood, Scott (1987–91) FB-TB
Logie, Dale (1974–75) ILB
Lopez, Frank (1964–65) OG
Lorch, Karl (1972) DT
Lorentzon, Ray (1907) RE
Lott, Ronnie (1977–80) S
Loustalot, John (1923) QB
Love, Robert (1932–33) E
Lowell, Russ (1947) LG
Lowery, Willie (1993–96) DE
Loya, Robert (1992–95) C-OG
Lua, Oscar (2002, 2004–06) LB
Lubisich, Pete (1961–63) LG
Lucas, Al (1920–21) C
Lucas, Jim (1974) P-Rov
Lucas, Lawrence (1914) RG
Lucas, Pete (1917)
Luce, Rick (1999) S
Luft, Brian (1981–84) DT-NG
Luizzi, Bruce (1989–92) S-OLB
Lund, Le Valley (1914) LHB
Lupo, Tom (1962–64) DE-Rov-PK
Lutui, Taitusi (2004–05) OG-OT
Lynch, Ford (1934–36) FB

M

MacGillivray, Mike (1998–2001) P
MacKenzie, Doug (1980–81) FB
MacKenzie, Malaefou (1997,
1999–2000, 2002) TB-FB
MacMoore, Robert (1935) RG
MacPhail, Peter (1941,42,43) RE
Magner, Gary (1965–67) DT
Mahone, Elic (1990–92, 1994)DE-
TE
Maiava, Kaluka (2005–06) LB

Mailo, Faaesea (1996, 1999–2001)
OT-OG
Malcolm, John (1908–10) G
Malette, Frank [Rabbit] (1915–17)
QB
Maley, Duane (1941) C
Mallory, Thomas (1929–31) HB
Malone, Tom (2002–05) P
Maloney, Al (1930) QB
Malu, Alatini (2005–06) OG
Manker, Robert (1923) HB
Manlove, Ferdinand (1925)
Manning, Dick (1941) FB
Maples, Jim (1959–61) RHB
Marderian, Greg (1971, 1973–74)
DT-DE
Maree, Jeff (1985–87) S
Marincovich, Andrew (1943) RG
Marinovich, Marv (1959–62) RT
Marinovich, Todd (1989–90) QB
Marks, Theodore (1915–16) RT
Marshall, Derrell (1988) OT
Marshall, George (1915)
Martin, Austin O. (1897) RE
Martin, Bill (1948–49) FB
Martin, G. (1895)
Martin, Harry Lee (1893) QB
Martin, Rod (1975–76) OLB
Marxen, Edward (1915)
Matock, Marc (1996–98) DT
Matthews, Bruce (1980–82) OG
Matthews, Clay (1974–77) ILB
Matthews, Clay (2005–06) LB
Matthews, Garland (1932–34) QB
Matthews, Kyle (2003) S
Matthews, Robert (1938–42)
Mattos, Grant (2001–02) WR

Mattson, Don (1957)	RT	McGinley, Francis (1931–34)	LG
Matua, Fred (2002–05)	OG-C	McGinn, John (1944–45)	RG
Maualuga, Rey (2005–06)	LB	McGirr, Mike (1971, 1973)	NG-OT
Maudlin, Tom (1957–58)	QB	McGrew, Larry (1977–79)	OLB
May, Ray (1965–66)	DE	McGuire, Joe (2001)	OT-OG
Mays, Taylor (2006)	S	McKay, John K. (1972–74)	SE
Mazur, John (1981)	QB	McKee, Erik (1984–86)	TE
McArthur, Gary (1969)	DT	McKeever, Marlin (1958–60) RE-FB	
McCabe, Hilton (1926–28)	C	McKeever, Mike (1958–60)	LG
McCaffrey, Bob (1972–74)	C	McKinney, Harry (1944–47)	RE
McCaffrey, Brent (1998–2000)	OT	McLaughlin, Kevin (1997)	WR
McCall, Don (1965–66)	LHB	McLean, Kevin (1984–87)	QB
McCall, Fred (1941–47)	RG	McMahon, Rich (1961–63)	FB
McCardle, Mickey (1942–47)	LHB	McMillan, Walter Dan (1917, 1919)	
McCaslin, Lawrence (1926–28)	E	QB	
McClanahan, Bob (1980–81)	FB	McMurtry, Paul (1948–50)	G
McConnell, Steve (1968)	OG	McNeil, Don (1936–38)	C
McCool, Pat (1980–82)	TE	McNeill, Rod (1970, 1972–73)	TB
McCormick, Walt (1945–47)	C	McNeish, Bob (1931–33)	HB
McCowan, Howard (1990)	S	McNeish, George (1934–36)	C
McCoy, Anthony (2006)	TE	McPartland, Kevin (1976)	DT
McCullouch, Earl (1967)	LE	McShane, Matt (1998–99)	C
McCullough, Sultan (1999–02)	TB	McWilliams, Johnny (1993–95)	TE
McCurtis, Mozique (2006)	CB	Mena, Salvador (1938–40)	RE
McCutcheon, Daylon (1995–98)CB		Merk, Ernie (1954–55)	RHB
McDade, Jack (1986)	ILB	Michels, John (1994–95)	OT
McDaniels, Terry (1990–93)	DT	Mietz, Roger (1958–60)	LG
McDonald, Michael (2005–06)	QB	Miles, Lawrence (2005)	DT
McDonald, Mike (1976–79)	ILB	Miller, Billy (1995–98)	WR
McDonald, Paul (1977–79)	QB	Miller, Bob (1966–68)	LE
McDonald, Tim (1983–86)	S	Miller, Chris (1995–96)	WR
McFadden, Dwight (1992)	TB	Miller, Jimmy (2005–06)	TE
McFarland, Don (1954–55)	LE	Miller, John (1953–55)	LG
McFoy, Chris (2003–06)	WR	Miller, Reed (1902–05)	RG
McGarvin, Tom (1940)	LE	Miller, Rick (1976)	OT-OG
McGee, Bob (1950)	T	Miller, Robert (1917)	LHB
McGinest, Willie (1990–93)DE-OLB		Miller, Ron (1951–53)	LE

Milton, John (1921–22)	E	Mort, C.E. (1894–96)	LT-RE
Minkoff, Cliff (1991)	CB	Mortensen, Jesse (1928–29)	HB
Mitchell, Dale (1972–74)	OLB-DE	Morton, A.O. (1895)	
Mitchell, Jason (2002–04)	WR	Morton, Chad (1996–99)	TB-CB-S
Mitchell, Marc (1980)	DT	Morton, Johnnie (1990–93)	WR-SE
Mitchell, Sheppard (1903)		Mosebar, Don (1979–82)	OT
Mix, Ron (1957–59)	RT	Moseley, Corliss C. (1915)	
Moala, Fili (2005–06)	DT	Moser, James (1925–27)	T
Mohler, Orville (1930–32)	QB	Moses, Charlie (1978)	OLB
Moi, Junior (1991–92)	OLB-DE	Moses, Don (1927–29)	FB
Mollett, Jerry (1959)	FB	Mosley, Jonathan (1997)	LB
Moloney, Jerry J. (1950)	HB	Moton, Dave (1963–65)	LE
Monson, Jim (1948–49)	RG	Moyer, Steve (1980)	OT
Montgomery, Marv (1969–70)	OT	Mozart, Forrest (2001–03)S-WR-CB	
Moody, Emmanuel (2006)	TB	Mullins, Gerry (1969–70)	TE
Moody, Michael (1988–91)	OT	Munch, Arlo W. (1934)	FB
Mooney, Mike (1990, 19–92)	FB	Munoz, Anthony (1976–79)	OT
Moore, Brent (1983–85)	DT	Murieta, Alfred John (1886–89)	
Moore, Darryl (1981–82)	OG-OT	Murphy, George (1944–48)	QB
Moore, Denis (1965–66)	DT	Murray, Joe (1982)	OG
Moore, Jim (1949)	RG	Murray, Philip (1915–16)	QB
Moore, Kenney (1978–80)	S	Murray, Thomas (1934)	T
Moore, Kyle (2005–06)	DE	Murrell, Gidion (1990–93)	ILB
Moore, Malcolm (1980–83)	SE	Musick, Billie (1941)	FB
Moore, Manfred (1971–73)	FB	Musick, Bob (1941–46)	FB-QB
Moore, Rex (1984–87)	ILB	Musick, James (1929–31)	FB
Moreno, Zeke (1997–2000)	LB	Musick, John Elmore (1944–46)	LG
Morgan, Boyd F. (1936–38)	RHB		
Morgan, Dave (1959–61)	C	**N**	
Morgan, John (1999)	S	Nason, Craig (1923)	FB
Morgan, Mike (1970–71)	FL	Naumu, Johnny (1946–47)	LHB
Morovick, Dan (1979)	S	Naumu, Sol (1950)	FB
Morrill, Charles (1938–40)	C	Nave, Sam Doyle (1937–39)	QB
Morris, Patrick (1975)	OG	Nazel, Omar (2000–03)	DE
Morris, Robert (1944)	LHB	Neidhardt, David (1929)	C
Morrison, Robert (1932)	FB	Neighbors, Sid (1910)	FB
Morrow, Alex (2004–06)	DE	Nelsen, Bill (1960–62)	QB

Newbury, David (1999–2001) PK
Newerf, Kenneth (1923) G
Newman, P.H. (1893–95) RG-RT
Newman, Wallace (1922–24) G
Nicholson, Hugh (1905–06) RE
Nickels, Matt (1999–2000) WR
Nickoloff, Tom (1951–53) RE
Nielsen, Ryan (1998–2001) DT-DE
Nix, Jack (1948–49) RE
Nix, Lloyd (1915–16) LHB
Noble, Bill (1941–42) RT
Noor, Dennis (1936–37) LE
Nordstrom, Ron (1951) T
Norene, George (1930–31) C
Norman, Hank (1982–85) SE
Norris, Neil (1930–32) E
Norton, Francis (1928) HB
Norton, Miles A. (1936–37) RG
Nunis, Dick (1951–52) LE-RH
Nunn, Ronald (2002–04) CB
Nunnally, Larry (1975) DT

O

O'Brovac, Nick (1950) G
O'Dell (1920) LHB
O'Grady, Steve (1977) OLB
O'Hara, Pat (1988, 1990) QB
O'Malley, Jack (1968) OT
Obbema, Joe (1968) DE
Obradovich, Jim (1973–74) TE
Obradovich, Steve (1976) SE
Ochoa, Juan (1905) FB
Ochs, Brennan (1997–2000) FB
Odom, Ricky (1976–77) CB
Oertley, Bernard (1915)
Oertly, George (1917–18) FB
Oestreich, Newell (1946) FB

Ohalete, Ifeanyi (1997–2000) S-LB
Olivarria, Tony (1979) FB
Oliver, Jason (1990–93) S-CB
Oliver, Ralph (1966–67) MG
Orcutt, Gary (1969) WR
Orndorff, Aaron (2001) LB
Orsatti, Vic (1925–26) QB
Ortega, Tony (1956–58) RHB
Ossowski, Theodore L. (1943) RT
Ostling, Gerald (1933–34) RE
Otani, Bobby (2001–03) LB
Otton, Brad (1994–96) QB
Oudermeulen, Henry (1924–25)
Owens, Dan (1986–89) DG
Owens, James (1931, 1933) QB

P

Pace, Stephon (1989–92) S
Packard, David (1932) T
Packer, Holmes (1919) RHB
Packman, Whitey (1918) RHB
Page, Charles M. (1943) FB
Page, John (1986–87) OT
Page, Mike (1957) FB
Page, Otis (1976–78) OT
Page, Toby (1966–67) QB
Palmer (1917)
Palmer, Carson (1998–99, 2002) QB
Palmer, Ford (1930–33) E
Papadakis, John (1970–71) LB
Papadakis, Petros (1997–98, 2000)
  TB
Papadakis, Taso (1994, 1996)
  FB-ILB
Pappas, Nick (1935–37) QB
Parker, Artimus (1971–73) S
Parker, Larry (1994–98) WR

Parkinson, Brent (1986–89)	OG	Phillips, Victor (1925)	
Parks, Bruce (1985–86)	OT-C	Phythian, Hayden (1922–24)	E
Parsons, Alex (2006)	DT	Pierson, Chad (1999–2002)	FB
Parsons, Charles (1903–04)	LT	Pierson, Mel (1947)	RG
Parsons, Earle O. (1943)	LHB	Pinckert, Erny (1929–31)	HB
Patapoff, William (1943)	RG	Pinkard, Josh (2004–06)	S-CB
Patrick, Doug (1964–65)	DT	Pitman, George (1894)	LT-QB
Patterson, Mike (2001–03)	DT	Pitts, Devin (2001)	WR
Patterson, Travon (2006)	WR	Pivaroff, Ivan (1960–61)	RE
Paulin, Harold (1908–10)	RHB	Plaehn, Alfred (1930–32)	T
Pavich, Frank (1952–54)	RT	Pola, Kennedy (1982–85)	FB
Peake, Crawford (1925)		Polamalu, Troy (1999–2002)	S-LB
Pearsall, Grant (1994–96, 1998)	S	Pollack, Kris (1991–94)	OG
Peccianti, Angelo (1936, 1938)	FB	Pollard, Marvin (1988–91)	CB
Peete, Rodney (1985–88)	QB	Pollard, Mike (1998, 2000–02)	LB
Pehar, John (1944)	RT	Poole, Will (2003)	CB
Pekarcik, Al (1972)	Rov	Porter, Don C. (1892)	LE
Peoples, Robert (1938–40)	FB	Porter, John (1927–28)	G
Perez, Antwine (2006)	S	Porter, Vincent (1942)	LHB
Perrin, Jay (1947)	RT	Poston, Darryl (2001–02)	TB
Perry (1918)	E	Potter, Gary (1962)	RE
Perry, George (1994–97)	DE	Poulsen, Alfred (1933)	C
Perry, John (1980)	P	Pounds, Phalen (1994–95, 1997)	
Perry, Reggie (1991–93)	S-QB	OG-OT	
Persinger, Jerry (1958)	FB	Powdrell, Ryan (2005–06)FB-TB-LB	
Peters, Ray (1978)	C-NG	Powell Marvin III (1995–98)	
Peters, Volney (1948–50)	T	FB-TE-S	
Peterson, Chuck (1948)	RT	Powell, Ed (1972–74)	OLB-DE
Petrill, Larry (1965–66)	MG	Powell, Marvin (1974–76)	OT
Petty, Dick (1952–53)	C	Powers, Jim (1947–49)	QB
Peviani, Bob (1950–52)	LG	Powers, W. Russell (1934)	LG
Phelps, Arthur (1923)		Pranevicius, John (1940–41)	LG
Phillips, Charles (1972–74)		Pratchard, David (1996–98)	OG-C
Rov-S-LB		Pratt, Parnell B. (1897)	FB
Phillips, Floyd (1938–40)	LG	Preininger, Joe E. (1934–36)	RG
Phillips, Jim (1983)	DT	Premo, William (1895)	LE
Phillips, Micah (1992–95)	S	Preston, Marc (1988–89)	P

Preston, Rob (1978–79) QB
Preston, Ron (1970) LB
Prindle, Bill (1985) S
Propst, Cliff (1933–35) FB
Prosser, Chris (2000–01) LB
Prukop, Al (1958–60) QB
Pryor, Dave (1979–82) P
Psaltis, Jim (1951–52) LH-FB
Pucci, Ed (1951–53) LG
Pucci, Ralph (1948–50) FB-LB
Pugh, Allen (1977–78, 1980
  C-OG-DT
Pultorak, Steve (1970) DT
Purling, Dave (1982–84) NG-DT
Pursell, James (1921–23) G
Pye, Ernie (1962–64) FB

R

Raab, Marc (1990–91) C
Rachal, Chilo (2005–06) OG
Radovich, Bill A. (1935–37) RG
Radovich, Drew (2004–06) OG-OT
Rae, Mike (1970–72) QB
Rakhshani, Vic (1978–80)
  TE-FL-V-Back
Ramey, Theron (1930) G
Ramsay, Kian (1989) OG
Ramsay, Kyle (1992–95) OT-OG
Ramsey, LaJuan (2002–05) DT-DE
Randle, Ken (1973, 1975–76) FL-SE
Ransom, Walt (1978) QB
Rapp, Vivian (1914, 1916) LG
Ratliff, John (1961–63) LG
Ray, Terrel (1968) CB
Rayburn, Gordon (1924)
Rea, John (1945–47) LG
Reade, Lynn (1962) RT

Reagan, Pat (1956–57) RG
Reboin, Al (1932–34) LHB
Redding, Bill (1968–69) DG-C
Reece, Danny (1973–75) CB
Reed, Desmond (2004–06) TB-CB
Reed, Dick (1945) LE
Reed, Robert W. (1936–37) C
Reese, Eric (1999–2001) TB-CB
Rendon, Adam (1995, 1997) PK
Renison, Bill (1964) RHB
Rhames, Tim (1973–75) NG
Rice, Carleton [Cot] (1923) C
Richard, Kris (1998–2001) CB
Richardson, Troy (1983–85) P
Richman, Denis (1964) LT
Rickman, Junior (1994, 1996–97)
  TE-OLB
Riddle, Bill (1951–53) QB
Riddle, John (1922–24) HB
Rideaux, Darrell (1999–2002) CB
Ridings, Gene (1931–33) FB
Rightmire, Harold (1918) RE
Riley, Art (1973–74) DT
Riley, Bernard (1999–2002) DT
Riley, Steve (1972–73) OT
Rimes, Robert (1902)
Ritchey, Bert (1928, 1930) FB
Rivers, Keith (2004–06) LB
Roberson, Ted (1973–75) CB
Roberts, C.R. (1955–56) FB
Roberts, Gene (1935) LG
Roberts, Trevor (1999–2000)
  OG-OT
Robertson, Robert (1939–41) QB
Robertson, Wilbur (1949) QB
Robinson, John (1919–21) T
Robinson, Mike (1976) SE

Robinson, Thomas W. (1889, 1892) RHB
Rodeen, Don (1934–35) LE
Rodgers, Marc (1988) FL-SE
Rodriguez, Francis (1983) SE
Rodriguez, Quin (1987–90) PK
Rodriguez, Ray (1972–73) ILB
Rogers, Don (1948–49) LHB
Rogers, Ed (1934) C
Rogers, Jacob (2000–03) OT
Rollinson, Bruce (1971) FL
Romer, Marshall (1943–44, 1946)LT
Roquet, Russel (1940) LT
Rorison, James (1934–36) LT
Rose, Mason (1935) RHB
Rosenberg, Aaron (1931–33) G
Rosendahl, Bob (1956) RE
Rosin, Ben (1959–61) RE
Ross, Mike (2002–03) S
Ross, Scott (1987–90) ILB
Rossetto, John (1946) FB
Rossovich, Tim (1965–67) DE
Roth, Mike (1982) C
Roundy, Jay (1947–49) RHB
Royster, Mazio (1990–91) TB
Rubke, Karl (1955–56) C
Rucker, Frostee (2003–05) DE
Ruettgers, Ken (1982–84) OT
Runnerstrum, Grant (1989–90) PK
Runyon, George O. (1902–04) RG
Runyon, John (1902–04)
Ruppert, Dick (1970) OT
Rusenhhaupt, Theodore (1908) LG
Russell, Darrell (1994–96) DT
Russell, Lynman H. (1936–37) RHB
Russo, Sam (1923) HB
Ryan, Mike (1970–72) OG

Ryan, Richard (1927) HB
Ryan, Tim (1986–89) DT
Ryus, H.D. (1899) LHB-QB

S

Saenz, Edwin M. (1943) LHB
Sager, Mark (1986–88) OT
Sagouspe, Larry (1962–63) C-LB
Sahlberg, Ted (1925) C
Salata, Paul (1944–47) LE
Salisbury, Sean (1982–83, 1985) QB
Salmon, Mike (1990–93) S-CB
Salness, Ty (1964–67) Rov-DE
Samperi, Brett (1996) OG-OT
Sampson, Ben (1952) C-LB
Sampson, Vern (1953–55) C
Samuel, Jim (1960) LG
Sanbrano, Al (1950–51) G
Sanchez, Armando (1962–63)C-DB
Sanchez, Mark (2006) QB
Sanders, Robert H. (1934–36) RG
Sanford, Anthony (1995–96) DT
Sangster, William (1937–39) FB
Sargent, Hugh (1941) LG
Sartz, Dallas (2002–06) LB-S
Saunders, Russell (1927–29) FB
Scarpace, Mike (1965–67) OG-OT
Schabre, Gus (1922) G
Schaub, Alvin (1926–28) HB
Scheving, Albert (1925–27) T
Schindler, Ambrose (1936–39) QB
Schmidt, Denny (1962) C
Schmidt, Hank (1955) RT
Schneider, Dean (1949–51) QB
Schuhmacher, John (1976–77) OT
Schultz, Bill (1989) OT
Schutte, George (1946–48) RT

Schweiger, Jeff (2004–06)	DE	Shute, Eugene (1905–07)	RHB
Scoggins, Eric (1977–80)	OLB	Sigler, John (1916)	LG
Scott, Dan (1966–68)	FB	Simmons, Antuan (1997–2001)	
Scott, Joe (1945, 1950)	HB	CB-LB-S	
Scott, Joel (1989–92)	SE	Simmons, Jeff (1980–82)	WR
Scott, Walter (1923–25)		Simmons, Melvin (2002–03)	LB
Scott, Willard (1967–69)	MG-DT	Simmrin, Randy (1975–77)	WR
Sears, Jim (1950–52)	LHB-S	Simpson, Edward (1915–16, 1919)C	
Seau, Junior (1988–89)	OLB	Simpson, Orenthal James [O.J.]	
Sehorn, Jason (1992–93)	S-CB	(1967–68)	LHB
Seitz, William (1928–29)	T	Sims, James (1972–73)	OLB
Seixas, John (1932–33)	E	Single, Forrest (1910)	RT
Seixas, William (1942)	LG	Skiles, John (1970–71)	DT
Sellers, Leon (1951–53)	FB	Skinner, J. (1907)	RHB
Selph, Ewald (1909)	FB	Skvarna, Carl (1960–61)	LHB-PK
Sentous, Frank (1918)	HB	Slaton, Tony (1981–83)	C
Sermons, Rodney (1994–97)	RB-FB	Slatter, James (1937–39)	RHB
Serpa, Mike (1985–88)	ILB	Slough, Greg (1969–70)	LB
Seymore, Joseph (1902–03)	RE	Small, Erroll (1993–94)	OLB
Shafer, Don (1985–86)	PK	Smedley, Ron (1961–62)	RG
Shannon, Kenneth (1932–33)	HB	Smith, Ben (1893)	LE
Shannon, Tim (1980)	S	Smith, C.E. (1895)	
Shapiro, Ryan (1999–2000)	LB	Smith, Charles (1889, 1892)	G
Shaputis, Bob (1973)	OT	Smith, Corby (1992)	QB
Shaver, Gaius [Gus] (1929–31)	QB	Smith, Dennis (1977–80)	S
Shaw, Gerry (1967–69)	Rov-S	Smith, Ernest (1930–32)	T
Shaw, Jesse (1928–30)	T	Smith, George (1925)	C
Shaw, Nate (1964–66)	DHB	Smith, Harry E. (1937–39)	LG
Shea, Pat (1960–61)	RG-LT	Smith, Herbert (1917)	
Shell, Joe (1937–39)	LHB	Smith, J.R. (1892)	
Sheppard, Arthur (1916)		Smith, James (1918–21)	RE
Sherman, Rod (1964–66)	RHB	Smith, Jeff (1964–65)	DE
Sherman, Thomas Bert (1931)	FB	Smith, Joe W. (1923–24)	E
Shields, Alan (1959–60)	LHB	Smith, Mike (1973–74)	OG
Shindler, George (1921)	HB	Smith, Pat (1996)	C-SNP
Shipp, Joe (1977)	TE	Smith, R. (1910)	RG
Shuey, Edward (1935)	LG	Smith, Robert (1934)	FB

Smith, Roy (1954) RT
Smith, S. (1918)
Smith, Sid (1968–69) OT
Smith, Stanley (1932) G
Smith, Steve (2003–06) WR
Smith, Tody (1969–70) DT
Smith, Wil (2005) WR
Smutz, Huber (1923) C
Snow, Jim (1966–68) LB
Snyder, Ed N. (1937) E
Snyder, Jim (1947) RG
Sogge, Steve (1967–68) QB
Sohn, Ben (1938–40) RG
Solter, Andrew Ford (1923–24)
Souers, Glenn (1950) FB
Soward, R. Jay (1996–99) WR
Spanos, Matt (2004–05) C-OT
Sparling, Raymond (1930–32) E
Spears, Ernest (1986–89) CB
Spears, Raoul (1990–91) FB
Spector, Irwin (1953–54) RG
Speer, Carl (1916)
Spencer, Todd (1981–83) TB
Sperle, Chris (1985–88) P
Sperling, Ty (1977–79) NG-DT
Spicer, Averell (2006) DT
Spraggins, Edward (1934)
Sprott, C.W. (1914) RT
Stall, Joseph (1946) LT
Stanley, Ralph (1936–38) RE
Stare, Jim (1904) RT
Stark, Newton Calvin (1923–25) E
Stearn (1919)
Steele, Harold (1975–76) NG
Steele, Markus (1999–2000) LB
Steele, Todd (1983–86) FB
Steen, Jason (1997–98) LB-DE

Steinbacher, Nate (2000–01, 2003) OT
Stephens, Barry (1929–31) HB
Stephenson, Warren (1960–61) LE-FB
Steponovich, Tony (1927–29) E
Stevens, Lawrence (1931–33) G
Stevenson, Edward (1936) LHB
Stevenson, Steve (1999–2001) WR
Stever, Bill (1924)
Stewart, George (1973–74) DT
Stillwell, Bob (1947–49) RE
Stillwell, Don (1950–52) LE
Stirling, Bob (1970–71) C
Stoecker, Howard (1937–39) LT
Stokes, Bill (1986–87) OLB
Stonebraker, John S. (1938–39) RE
Stonehouse, John (1992–95) P
Stookey, Byron (1906–07, 1909–10) T
Streelman, Brad (1978–79) NG-DT
Strong, Frank (1998–2001)LB-S-TB
Strother, Deon (1990–93) FB-TB
Strozier, Clint (1975–76) Rov
Stuart, Melvin (1919) LHB
Stuart, R. (1916) RG
Studdard, Howard (1977) WR
Sullivan, J.P. (1987, 1989) DG
Sullivan, Tim (1981–82) ILB
Summer (1918)
Sutherland, James (1934–36) LHB
Svihus, Bob (1962–64) LT
Swann, Lynn (1971–73) FL
Swanson, Pat (1997–99) TE-SNP
Swanson, Steve (1967) LB
Sweeney, Calvin (1977–78) FL-SE
Sweeney, Cordell (1988–89) OLB

Swirles, Frank (1939)	QB		Thompson, Ken (1951–53)	RT
Swope, Jess (1949)	LT		Thompson, P.J. (1892)	
			Thompson, Roderick (1930–31)	T
T			Thurlow, Leavitt (1934–36)	LT
Tancredy, Tom (1949–50)	RG		Thurlow, Toby (1962)	LE
Tannehill, Ted (1945–47)	LHB		Thurman, Dennis (1974–77)	S-FL
Tanner, Randy (1984–87)	FL		Thurman, Junior (1985–86)	S
Tappaan, Francis (1927–29)	E		Tiernan, Phillip (1920–22)	FB
Tarver, Bernard (1976)	TB-FB		Timberlake, George (1952–53)	RG
Tatsch, Herbert (1931, 1933–34)	LT		Timmons, Curt (1971)	CB
Tatupu, Lofa (2003–04)	LB		Ting, Brandon (2003–05)	S-CB
Tatupu, Mosi (1974–77)	FB		Ting, Ryan (2003–05)	S-CB
Taylor, Art (1917)	LE		Tinsley, Scott (1980–82)	QB
Taylor, Arthur (1914)	RE		Tipton, Howard (1930–32)	HB
Taylor, Brice (1924–26)	G		Tobin, Hal (1960–61)	FB
Taylor, Mike (1966–67)	OT		Tofi, Travis (2003–06)	DT
Taylor, Paul (1941)	QB		Tolbert, Dennis (1997)	DT
Tellam, Greg (1994, 1996)	DE		Tolliver, Justin (2004)	CB
Templeton, George (1927–29)	C		Tolman, Ernie (1947–48)	LE
Terry, Tony (1967–69)	DT		Tonelli, Amerigo (1936–38)	RG
Thiede, Cliff (1929)	QB		Toolen, Andy (1919–21)	LE
Thomas, Alonzo [Skip] (1971) CB-WR			Torgan, Spencer (2002–03)	C-DT
			Torres, Eric (2000–03)	OT-OG
Thomas, Fay (1923–24)	T		Townsend, Ken (1918–20)	RG
Thomas, John (1963–65)	RE		Traynham, Jerry (1958–60)	LHB
Thomas, Kelly (1981–82)	OT		Treier, Jack (1958–60)	C
Thomas, Kevin (2005–06)	CB		Truher, James (1928–29)	E
Thomas, Lloyd (1926–28)	HB		Tsagalakis, Sam (1952–54)	PK
Thomas, Max (1926–27)	FB		Tucker, Mark (1987–90)	OG
Thomas, Ronald D. (1940–42)	RG		Tucker, Sam (1893)	LE-RH
Thomas, Terrell (2004–06)	CB		Tufs, Ray (1904)	
Thomassin, John (1937–39)	LT		Tuiasosopo, Titus (1990–92)	OG
Thompson, A.P. (1893–95, 1997)	QB		Tuliau, Brian (1987–90)	ILB
Thompson, Dale (2004–06)	TE		Turner, Joe (1980–81)	CB
Thompson, Ed (1904)	C		Turner, Patrick (2005–06)	WR
Thompson, Field (1924–26)	HB		Tyiska, Ryan (1994–97)	LB
Thompson, Gordon (1923)	G		Tyler, Jerome (1982–85)	S

Typton, Cyril (1919)

U

Udeze, Kenechi (2001–03)   DE-DT
Uhl, Jason (1990–91, 1993) NT-DG
Underwood, Walt (1975–77)   DT
Upton, Mickey (1965)   RHB
Urquhart, Daniel (2003)   LB
Ussery, Charles (1980–81)   DT

V

Vaca, Vic (1983)   ILB
Van Blarcom, Troy (2005–06)   PK
Van Doren, Bob (1950–52)   RT
Van Dyke, Vinny (1976–77)   DT
Van Horne, Keith (1977–80)   OT
Van Raaphorst, Mike (1997–2000)
   QB
Van Vliet, George (1958–60)   LE
Vanderboom, Nick (2003–06)
   TE-QB
Vandermade, Lenny (2000–03)
   OG-C
Vasicek, Vic (1945)   LG
Vella, Chris (1971–72)   TE
Vella, John (1969–71)   OT
Vellone, Jim (1964–65)   LT
Verry, D. Norman (1941–43)   LG
Viltz, Theo (1964–65)   S
Volsan, Anthony (1994–97)   CB
Von Aspe, Wolfgang (1994)   TB
Von Mohr, Frank (1921)   G
Voyne, Don (1957)   LE

W

Wachholtz, Kyle (1992–95)   QB
Waddell, Don (1945)   RT

Wagner, Lowell (1941–42)   FB
Walker, Brad (2004–06)   WR
Walker, Glen (1975–76)   P-PK
Walker, Jim (1964–65)   LB-G
Walker, John (2002–05)   CB-S-WR
Walker, Tommy (1947)   PK
Wall, Fred Willard (1944)   RG
Wall, John (2000)   PK
Wallace, Henry (1998–2000)   LB
Wallace, Kenneth (1907–10)   LE
Wallace, Larry (1989–92)   FL-SE
Walshe, Joe (1985, 1987–88)
   DG-NG-OG
Walters, Shawn (1993–96)   RB
Walton (1917)
Warburton, Irvine [Cotton]
   (1932–34)   QB
Ward, Herb (1978–79)   CB
Ward, John (1927–29)   T
Wardlow, Jason (2001)   DE
Ware, Scott (2004–05)   S
Ware, Timmie (1982–84)   FL
Washington, Al (1985)   FL-SE
Washington, Chauncey (2003,
   2006)   TB
Washington, Dave (1960)   RE
Washington, Delon (1994–97)
   RB-TB
Washington, Marlon (1987–89)   SE
Washmera, Ray (1971–73)   FB
Watkins, Travis (2002–04)   OG
Watts, Elbert (1985)   CB
Wayahn, Elmer (1918, 1922–23) FB
Weaver, Charlie (1969–70)   DE
Webb, David (1989–92)   DT-OLB
Webb, James (1932–34)   RHB
Webb, John (1904)   RT

Webb, Lee (2001–04)	FB-LB		Wilder, Glenn (1959)	RE
Weber, Scott (1971)	DE		Wilensky, Joe (1934–36)	LG
Weber, Tom (1952–53)	LT		Wilkie (1916)	
Webster, Steven (1985–88)	TB		Wilkins, John (1959–60)	LT
Weddle, L.V. (1924)			Willer, Don (1940–42)	LT
Weeks, Chuck (1951–52)	RT		Willhoite, Elmer (1951–52)	RG
Wehba, Ray (1936–38)	LE		Williams, Aaron (1996–99)	DT-DE
Weiss, Benjamin (1916–17)	RG		Williams, Brian (1991–94)	OLB-ILB
Welch, Harry (1951–52)	LHB		Williams, Britt (1959–61)	RG
Welch, Matt (1998–99)	OT-TE		Williams, Carl A. (1897–1901)	RT
Wellman, Gary (1987–90)	FL		Williams, Charles A. (1935–37)	RE
Wells, Harry III (1964)	RG		Williams, Don (1926–28)	QB
Welsh, Lou (1950–52)	C-LB		Williams, Eric (1975–76)	ILB
Werner, P. [Moose] (1915)	E		Williams, Hal (1941)	LE
West, Patrick (1944)	FB		Williams, Homer (1964)	FB
West, Troy (1981–82)	S-CB		Williams, John (1949–51)	HB
Westcott, Clem (1925)	C		Williams, Kevin (1977–80)	WR
Westcott, Jack (1925)	T		Williams, Kyle (2003–06)	OT-OG
Westover, Charles (1905)			Williams, Marv (1981, 1983)	S
Westphal, Dick (1954)	LT		Williams, Michael (1986–89)	OLB
Wheatley, Pop (1902–03)	FB		Williams, Mike (2002–03)	WR
Wheeler, Harold (1926)	HB		Williams, Rod (1982–83)	CB
Whitcomb, Ed (1919)	FB		Williams, Thomas (2004–05)	LB-FB
White, Charles (1976–79)	TB		Williamson, Frank (1931–33)	G
White, Jack (1904)	LHB		Williamson, Jack (1932–34)	
White, Kenneth (1921)	E		Williamson, Stanley (1929–31)	C
White, LenDale (2003–05)	TB		Willig, Matt (1988–91)	DG-DT
White, Lonnie (1985–86)	FL		Willingham, Charles R. (1929)	FB
White, Oliver (1926)	G		Willis, Jack (1957)	LH
White, Timmy (1980–82)	WR		Willison, Gary (1985–86)	DT
Whitehead, Duane (1943–46)	FB		Willott, Laird (1954–56)	RG
Whitlaw, Ben (1892)			Willumson, Don (1945)	RE
Whittier, Julian (1929)	G		Wilson, Alan (1990–91)	ILB-OLB
Wilbur, Robert (1934)	G		Wilson, Ben (1961–62)	FB
Wilcox, Paul (1919)	RE		Wilson, Charles (1902–03)	LE
Wilcox, Ralph O. (1928–30)	E		Wilson, W. (1916)	C
Wilcox, Thomas (1927–29)	FB		Wilson, Zach (1999–2002)	OG-OT

Winans, Jeff (1972)   DT
Winfield, John Irving (1928–30)   G
Wing, Paul (1934–35)   FB
Winslow, Robert E. (1937–39)   RE
Winslow, Troy (1965–66)   QB
Wirching, Carl (1909)   RE
Woidneck, Greg (2006)   P
Wolf, Joe (1942–43)   C
Wood, Richard (1972–74)   ILB
Wood, Willie (1957–59)   QB
Woodert, Andre (2003, 2005)   TB-S
Woods, John (1920)   LG
Woods, LaVale (1994–97)RB-FB-TB
Woods, Quincy (1997)   QB
Woods, Ray (1940–42)   QB
Woodward, James L. (1918–21) QB
Woolen, Thomas G. (1907)   LT
Work, Telford (1916)
Worsley, Harry (1924–25)
Wotkyns, Haskell Robert [Inky]
   (1932–34)   FB
Wren, Jim (1996–97)   P
Wright, Eric (2004)   CB
Wright, Foster C. (1895–97)   QB

Wright, Manuel (2003–04)   DT
Wright, Shareece (2006)   CB
Wyatt, Justin (2002–05)   CB-WR

Y
Yary, Ron (1965–67)   OT-DT
Yary, Wayne (1969–70)   OG
Yocum, Sam (1925–26)
Youel, Curtis (1931–33)   C
Young, Adrian (1965–67)   LB
Young, Charles (1970–72)   TE
Young, J.E. (1889, 1992)   HB
Young, John (1968–69)   S
Youngworth, Pat (1889)   C

Z
Zachik, Don (1959–60)   PK
Zado, Pierre (1998)   S
Zampese, Ernie (1955–56)   LHB
Ziegler, John (1916)
Zilka, John (2005)   WR
Zimmerman, Dan (1949, 1951)   E